Restoration Therapy

Restoration Therapy

Understanding and Guiding Healing in Marriage and Family Therapy

Terry D. Hargrave and Franz Pfitzer

Routledge
Taylor & Francis Group
New York   London

Routledge
Taylor & Francis Group
711 Third Avenue
New York, NY 10017

Routledge
Taylor & Francis Group
27 Church Road
Hove, East Sussex BN3 2FA

© 2011 by Taylor and Francis Group, LLC
Routledge is an imprint of Taylor & Francis Group, an Informa business

Printed in the United States of America on acid-free paper
10 9 8 7 6 5 4 3 2 1

International Standard Book Number: 978-0-415-87625-4 (Hardback) 978-0-415-87626-1 (Paperback)

Library of Congress Cataloging-in-Publication Data

Hargrave, Terry D.
   Restoration therapy : understanding and guiding healing in marriage and family therapy / authored by Terry D. Hargrave and Franz Pfitzer.
      p. cm.
   Includes bibliographical references and index.
   ISBN 978-0-415-87625-4 (hardback : alk. paper) -- ISBN 978-0-415-87626-1 (pbk. : alk. paper)
   1. Family psychotherapy. I. Pfitzer, Franz. II. Title.

RC488.5.H357 2011
616.89'156--dc22   2010049069

Visit the Taylor & Francis Web site at
http://www.taylorandfrancis.com

and the Routledge Web site at
http://www.routledgementalhealth.com

To my wife and partner, Sharon. Everything good in my life is connected to you. To my children, Halley Anne and Peter. Helping you grow up has restored much love and trustworthiness with me.

Terry Hargrave

To my wife, Evelyn Seidel-Pfitzer, and our children, Martin, Lara, Anna, and Lukas. Your love and trust have made me change and grow.

Franz Pfitzer

CONTENTS

SECTION III   Utilizing the Restoration Therapy Model

PREFACE

We started work on this particular book with much contemplation and self-inventory. We both come from a background of identifying ourselves as contextual family therapists in the tradition of Ivan Boszormenyi-Nagy (Boszormenyi-Nagy & Krasner, 1986). We both have been personally helped by this approach and have used it successfully in our therapeutic work through the years. Because we believed the concepts of justice and trustworthiness to be so profound and useful in relational processes, we have seen much of our efforts in the field of psychotherapy help the approach become more well known and better understood. In writing this book, we had to look at ourselves carefully and evaluate if we were actually ready to leave this contextual tradition.

In the end, we have found that we can neither totally leave our contextual roots nor exclusively identify ourselves as contextual therapists any longer. Much of what those familiar with the contextual approach will find in this volume will look familiar as we do incorporate the concepts of trustworthiness, justice, entitlement, destructive entitlement, and multidirected partiality. Of these things that we have spoken about, written about, and taught over the years, we still believe in earnest and have much gratitude to our history in the contextual approach. But, we have also felt the need to speak more freely about the advances in our thinking concerning the importance of love and its ability to have an impact on individual identity. We have become convinced that trustworthiness has not only a relational resource that can promote giving but also an essential nature that shapes the individual perspective on the ideas of safety in relationship. Mainly, we have become convinced that these two elements of love and trustworthiness are sufficient and necessary as the twin pillars of relationship and the organizing principle around which we can understand not only individual and relational health but also dysfunction. Thus, while we see ourselves emerging from the contextual tradition, we now organize our thoughts and therapy around what we call restoration therapy.

In addition to organizing our thoughts around these essential elements, we have felt the freedom to start expanding our views of what makes for good interventions in efforts to restore love and trustworthiness to individuals and relationships. We have been using interventions for years that have been directed at helping the individual and family achieve better insights into past damage and use this knowledge to formulate new experiences that can heal. But more recently, taking note of the literature on the brain and more specifically on how individuals make and sustain change, we have been working to develop interventions that focus on skills that sustain the insights and gains that clients make in the therapy room. Like many others in the field, we have learned that if we want the client or patient to maintain the insights and motivations made in the therapy room we must help them practice in a repetitive and skillful way that will bring mindfulness into play. In short, we have learned that change means that we must also work to change the brain. Insight is good and necessary, but we have found it to be insufficient to maintain change. As a result, readers of this book will find not only interventions that are familiar (e.g., understanding, working up and working down, and the work of forgiveness) but also identification of cyclical processes in what we call pain-and-peace cycles and change using a method we call the four steps. Restoration therapy is about combining the interventions of both insight and skills for a powerful therapeutic "one-two punch" to produce change.

In Section I, "Understanding Pain, Coping, and Assessment," we unfold the organizing elements of love and trustworthiness in understanding and assessing human behavior. In Chapter 1, "Love and Trust: The Theory of Relationship," we seek to explain clearly why we see love and trustworthiness as the essential elements in human existence and relationship and why these elements are essential in formation of individual identity and sense of safety in interaction. In Chapter 2, "Coping With Pain: Understanding Behavior and Self-Reactivity," we give a perspective on understanding how human beings use power when they are confronted in relationships with love and trustworthiness or the lack thereof. In this section, we share our new insights and understandings regarding the effects of human agency as well as what we have learned concerning the reactivity of humans through blaming others, shaming self, controlling behaviors, and escape/chaos behaviors. Finally, in Chapter 3, "The Process of Pattern," we try to give a clear picture of how these forces or self-reactivity form the basis for individual systemic processes that confuse identity and make safety in relationships difficult. As well, we seek to give a better understanding of how individuals interact in systemic relationships that tend to reinforce and even provoke the violations of love and trustworthiness that they feel. We feel that Section I gives a good understanding of the restoration therapy framework and the ability to assess individuals and relationships properly.

In Section II, "The Therapeutic Work in Restoration Therapy," our focus is to give a sense of the characteristics that make this type of work unique as well as the essential elements and interventions that become the restoration therapist's tools. Chapter 4, "Becoming a Wise Therapist," provides a sense of the important characteristics that we believe essential in this type of work. We not only focus on the psychotherapist becoming wise in terms of interpreting material from the client or patient but also give our ideas of where the psychotherapist should focus his or her attention during the process of therapy. In Chapter 6, "The Techniques of Working With Love and Trustworthiness," we clearly spell out the insight-based interventions that we use in the restoration therapy model. Readers of our work *The New Contextual Therapy* (2003), will recognize some of these therapeutic modalities of understanding, working up and working down, and right script but wrong players, to name a few. We have expanded these interventions to include demonstrations as well as new and important clinical work on understanding how to intervene to produce different beliefs concerning the truths about identity and safety in relationships. Chapter 6, "Consolidating Change in the Brain," represents some of our most important new work in this modality as we have applied what we have learned from the emerging research on the brain and how individuals change themselves as well as their actions in relationships. It is indeed an exciting chapter to us as it represents significant application of how clients can use insights in a cognitive way to practice both in and out of the therapy room.

In Section III, "Utilizing the Restoration Therapy Model," we give some solid therapeutic examples of the model at work. Although the entire book is laced with clinical examples, in these final chapters we provide certain aspects of therapy fuller and clearer explanation and demonstration. Chapter 7, "Restoration Therapy and Couples," introduces a systematic and clear illustration of how to produce and consolidate change with couples in conflict. We feel like the work in this chapter represents a clear and desirable advance in couple's work as it produces hopeful change in a short time frame. In Chapter 8, "Using Forgiveness in Restoration," we close the book with some of the work that is closest to our therapeutic hearts. We demonstrate the work of forgiveness using the restoration model through four cases that apply the stations of insight, understanding, giving the opportunity for compensation, and overt forgiving.

There is no work, such as the clinical work represented in this book, that takes place in a vacuum. Particularly, we are grateful to the psychotherapists at Amarillo Family Institute in Texas who have worked these ideas out in practice with many clients and patients over several years. We also are indebted to the psychotherapists and owners of the Hideaway Experience, Amarillo, Texas, who have lent their expertise and given the opportunity to courageously apply new techniques and theory to couple therapy. We have deep gratitude for the psychotherapists and doctors at clinics in both North America and Europe who have utilized these ideas and challenged us to become clearer and better at our trade and theory. Finally, we are thankful to the many clients and patients who have endeavored to travel this therapeutic road with us. It is never easy to enter psychotherapy—much less change—but these individuals have courageously pursued both and have helped us also grow in the process.

Finally, to our wives and families, we cannot express enough of our heartfelt gratitude, admiration, and love. You all are our living laboratories of how to perfect and live out the miracle of love and trustworthiness.

Section I

Understanding Pain, Coping, and Assessment

1

Love and Trustworthiness
The Theory of Relationships

> I am alone. I don't mean that I don't have anyone to take care of me, and that I am not in a relationship with anyone, even though that fact of my life is painfully true. I mean that I am truly alone. Lost. I don't even know myself. Every time I am alone and I have that dead space of having to face who I am and the things that I am doing with my life, I slam the door shut because to go there means that I step into a black hole of pain, loneliness, and total confusion. It feels so empty and dark that I run away. I run to anything that will make me forget for just a few short hours that that kind of dark emptiness is there. And who do I run to? No one, really. No one can comfort me because they don't know the real me and the dark loneliness that I hide. I don't have anyone, but mainly I'm alone because I don't even have myself. That is about as painful as life can get.

Painful, indeed: Life without being known is painful enough but is even more painful without ever knowing at all. The fact is that the woman who made this statement was in her early 40s, had run through myriad symptoms and failed relationships, and was saying that relationships are essential for healthy human functioning. It is not just relationships for the sake of our healthy bonding, learning, or attachment, but it is the model of relationships that helps us even to know ourselves and provides us with meaning. Apart from human relationships, we are destined not even to have a relationship with ourselves.

3

There is a fabric to human relationships. It is a beautiful mosaic of colors and textures that weaves its lines and shapes into our lives and into the history of our generations of humanity. Each person and life is unique in pattern, shape, and symmetry and tells a vast story of struggle, connection, pain, and promise. But, even with the variation of individual perspectives and family history, there are common threads that tie us together and make us related. Just as unique and special as all humans are in genetic variation, there is a common sequence or code in the DNA of our species. In the fabric of human relationships, the stories, histories, and personalities are so different and numerous that it defies record, but the thread and the stitches are made the same from person to person, generation to generation. The common elements that tie all human relationships together are love and trustworthiness.

These two elements of love and trustworthiness, we maintain, are not only the common elements that make up human relationships but also are essential to human existence. They are the food and water of the human soul that feed individual identity and provide a context for intimacy with others. Without identity and intimacy, normal development is impossible, and individuality is threatened. Over the past few decades, there have been two particular sources in the literature that took special note of these elements. The attachment literature (i.e., Bowlby, 1988; Johnson, 2004) is replete with emphasis on how love and relationships can be responsible for individual functioning, styles, and personalities. In addition, the contextual family therapy literature (i.e., Boszormenyi-Nagy & Krasner, 1986; Hargrave & Pfitzer, 2003) is robust in terms of clinical material concerning the importance of trustworthiness. Although both theories at points make reference to love and trustworthiness together, the clear emphasis of the attachment literature is on loving relationships, and the emphasis of the contextual approach is more on trustworthiness.

This book, therefore, is about how these two stitches of human interaction form the very fabric of who we are and how we behave in the world. It is our intent to show how these two elements fit with much of what we know about human development, interaction, and process and then point toward how therapists can use this framework to properly assess, support, and intervene to help people along the path to better outcomes. Restoration therapy is a new way of utilizing many old ways of what we know about human beings and their relationships. It is our hope that you will find the theoretical foundations of restoration therapy simple to follow, with assessments that are fluid and helpful to patients and techniques that are

4

useful and produce change in behavior. But, the essential element of restoration therapy is to *restore* the elements of human existence that most often cause individual and relational brokenness. Restoration therapy is about restoring love and trustworthiness to the human condition.

THE USEFULNESS OF THEORY

Several years ago, a friend of mine (T.D.H.) who was a specialist in the solution-focused model wanted to learn more about family-of-origin therapy, and I wanted to learn more about more about the solution-focused approach. To facilitate learning, we did cotherapy for a few cases to see the approaches in action and to stimulate each other's ideas concerning integration of the two different models. To evaluate the work better, we had one of our colleagues who was familiar with both approaches observe the sessions and interview the patients after the therapy.

It was clear to all of us exactly what was done at all times in the process. When the solution-focused therapist was interacting, issues such as focusing on exceptions to the problems, scaling, and miracle questions were abundantly clear. When I was working from a family-of-origin perspective, techniques such as exploring painful past and history issues, crediting, and partiality were apparent. The therapy, while successful, felt like a mishmash of techniques to us as therapists as we struggled to work together and incorporate each other's ideas instead of competing. But, when the observing therapist interviewed the patients who were involved with the therapy, none of the clients could tell that the therapists were doing anything different. In other words, the perception of the client was that we knew where we were headed, we were working together, and there was no distinction that we were coming from different theoretical orientations. Although this was certainly not a scientific study of any kind, it is indeed informative concerning how we hold the importance of theory and our own particular cadre of techniques.

So, if clients perhaps cannot tell the difference in what we do or how we work, is theory really that important? We think so. We do not think that it is so essential in that one approach is much more efficacious than others. Indeed, we believe that most of the sound theoretical psychotherapeutic approaches through the years have shown more or less the same levels of effectiveness. We would agree with Friedman (2007) that the drive to generate or "prove" outcomes is related to anxiety in the psychotherapy field and does little in the end to prove one approach over another or be helpful to clients. We also do not think that theory in itself is important in terms of what is helpful per se to any particular patient. We feel that the elements of the therapeutic relationship, the therapist's confidence and clarity in the process, and the dealing with specific therapeutic opportunities are what most often make a difference in therapy. We think that theory is important because it is important for the psychotherapist in the room to organize and make sense of what he or she is hearing, to formulate and assess, to consider different targets or desirable outcomes of the therapy, and eventually to intervene effectively.

It is a tall order for any psychotherapist coming from any therapeutic perspective to do well with cases. The psychotherapist must at one time (a) keep connected to the content, communication, and interaction that are going on in the room; (b) hypothesize, assess, and make sense of what is going on in the room; and (c) figure out how to intervene so the client or patient is helped in a way that is meaningful. To do these things at one time can easily be overwhelming, as one psychotherapist intern expressed:

> There is just so much when I step into a room with clients. I am concerned about how I'm being perceived and how to be empathetic and ask the right questions. I hear about these impossible situations that I know the client is looking for some kind of help. I want to listen, connect, and understand, but I also want to really make sense to myself of what is going on so I can be helpful to the client. Many times, I sit there, and the further we go in therapy, the more I feel overwhelmed and confused myself. I have all these random ideas about different approaches and techniques going around in my head, and I just hope that one will eventually make sense to me so I will have some direction. I often don't know how to think and certainly don't know what I am doing. My feelings are most often a metaphor for how the client feels, and I can tell you, it does not feel good.

We would maintain that theory is necessary and good for just this reason: It is good in helping the psychotherapist organize his or her thoughts, providing a clear method of direction and assessment, providing targets and outcomes that are achievable, and giving some indication of the types of interventions available that make a difference with clients. Theory is not directly so important to patients, and we sincerely do not believe that one theory is that much more outstanding than another. Theory only affects the client in terms of how well the therapist is able to use the theory to become helpful, connected, and practical. Theory, therefore, is for the *therapist*. As Hargrave and Anderson (1992) explain, good theoretical discipline keeps psychotherapists from becoming "technique junkies" who simply chase one technique to the next, hoping that something will eventually help the patient. To produce techniques and interventions that are effective, we believe that a therapist must be well grounded to make sense of and assess accurately the client's needs and status. The therapist must then be able to accurately determine directions, hypothesize about goals and interventions, and skillfully acknowledge the possible outcomes. Only after this accurate assessment and determination of outcomes do we believe that the psychotherapist is ready to use a technique or intervention. What we are saying is that good theory drives all three frameworks. A conductor has a musical score that gives a context for interpreting the myriad notes played by the orchestra. The score, then, allows the conductor to assess where problems exist, determine action, and then make interventions or corrections. Without the score, the conductor's work is harder and may be impossible. Such is the work of the psychotherapist without good theory (Hargrave & Pfitzer, 2003).

What follows in these pages about restoration therapy is designed to help the therapist organize his or her thoughts to accurately assess, to determine directions and outcomes that will help individuals or families, and then find techniques that are consistent with the framework. We are not saying that this theory is sufficient to replace other theories or, in and of itself, is better than other theories. Restoration therapy is simply a framework that we have found helpful for psychotherapists and, by extension, helpful for patients and families in need.

There is one more note concerning theory. We have noted before that the drive to prove outcomes in therapy has had some negative effects on the field of psychotherapy (Hargrave & Pfitzer, 2003). While we are in total agreement that psychotherapy needs to strive for empirically sound approaches with scientifically proven outcomes, we believe it is foolish for governments or agencies to insist on certain specific protocols, structures, time limits, and techniques in the therapeutic process. While much of psychotherapy is and can be scientific, we believe that it is essential to acknowledge psychotherapy as an experiential art form as therapists endeavor to help individuals and families. Much of the therapeutic relationship and what makes therapy work is not quantifiable. Perhaps, even the most important parts of what makes therapy helpful are not quantifiable. Currently, we are most concerned that therapists retain their artistic, experiential, and qualitative presence in the therapy room. This is essentially our goal in restoration therapy.

DEEP AND UNDERLYING STRUCTURE OF HUMAN RELATING AND BEING

We would propose that to understand human relating and being, one must clearly understand the components or structure that exists in relationships and individuality. While we agree with a constructivist mentality in that truth is constructed within a social or relational context, we would see that these constructs are formed in remarkably consistent ways that are developmentally linked. For instance, all young children formulate and construct different histories around bounding or attachment related to the attention and nurturing given by caregivers. However, the fact that all children construct these ideas and formations around the conditions of bonding and attachment is consistent.

This is similar to the ideas of language developed by Chomsky (1972) from a nativist position. From this position, there is an underlying structure and mechanism that humans possess in which they are enabled to access language along a developmental sequence. If an infant is spoken to and is unhindered developmentally from this nativist theory, the infant will respond by learning the language spoken. Different languages may be spoken to different children, but children learn language in roughly the same sequences, and the focus of language is primarily on object and action. Therefore, while children may speak different languages, the mechanism and structure that exist in humans that allow them to access language remain consistent despite cultural or ethnic variations.

Hargrave and Metcalf (2000) posit the idea that human beings possess a similar structure that allows them to make meaning about who they are and how they are to behave in relationships. They may develop different ideas about identity, concept, worth, security, and predictability in relationships, but just as all languages have words and meanings, all humans develop ideas about who they are and how they are to behave in a relationship. It is as if human beings come into the world with a structure of two spools with no thread. These two spools are taught meaning and behavior around the constructs of love and trustworthiness. As they experience the love and trustworthiness—or the lack thereof—from relationships, the threads of meaning are wound around the spools that serve as the basis for constructing the eventual individual identity and the beliefs about how to behave in relationships (Hargrave & Metcalf, 2000).

The difference in this concept and the narrative therapy perspective is that the truly constructivist model would reject the notion that there is any deep structure to human beings, and that looking for this deep structure tends to produce "thin" explanations of human existence and interaction contrary to the poststructural view (Hoffman, 2002). We would clarify, however, that the narrative therapy perspective tends to be consistent in pointing out that the narrative is formulated around meaning and behavior (White & Epston, 1990). The way that narrative therapy directs questions into the landscape of the narrative focuses on the actions, behaviors, or exceptions to behaviors as well as the meaning, significance, or identity of the individual (Meidonis & Bry, 1995). So, within this context, even a poststructuralist view of reality consistently focuses on the perspective of identity and behavior. While we appreciate the effort and, if you will, the warning of the narrative perspective that too much structure tends to produce thin explanations of human behavior that are easily labeled and that the focus should instead be on the multilayered "thick" influences of beliefs and behaviors (White, 1997), the fact that there is a consistent focus on both meaning and behavior indicates that there is indeed a structure that is common in human existence. Our stories may be different, but we all have stories that entail meaning and behavior.

Likewise, Keeney and Ross (1985) proposed that all human communication and interaction could be qualified in terms of either *semantics* or *politics*. Semantics clearly deals with the meanings and conclusions drawn from a particular communication, while politics indicates more of a form of dealing organization, control, or regulation of communication. In other words, communication can be broken down into the understanding of meaning and behavior. Keeney and Ross (1985) go further in clarifying that semantics and politics mutually form and shape one another in the context of human communication. We form beliefs, ideas, and meanings from our experience of organization or behavior, and those beliefs and meanings form the basis for our interactions and future behaviors. Certainly, we agree with this interactive component. The conclusions and ideas that we form about ourselves as well as what we believe to be the nature of relationships direct a huge aspect of how we choose to behave in the context of a relationship (Hargrave & Pfitzer, 2003).

Individuals are deeply influenced by the behavior or politics that they receive in their most essential relationships. These relationships form the meanings around who they come to believe they are and how they will in turn function in their own behaviors as they interact with relationships. There is, we believe, an essential relational imperative along the lines of what Buber (1958) suggests in the "I-and-Thou" nature of a relationship. We cannot know who we are apart from the context of relating; therefore, this formation of identity, individuality, meaning, and personality finds its root and outcome in relationships. We would say that different therapeutic perspectives are remarkably consistent in pointing out that meaning and behavior exist in the structure of communication and interaction. We would further state that behavior and meaning mutually inform and shape one another as people gain meaning from interactions and meaning modifies behavior. Finally, we would put forth clearly that the elements of love and trustworthiness, particularly in the context of family relationships, are the most powerful forces in communication and behavior, which in turn shape individual behavior and meaning.

THE IMPORTANCE OF LOVE

So, how does the formation of identity and behavior take place within the context of the personality and interactions of the individual? It is as if human beings step onto the stage of life after birth and have two big questions that must be answered. The first question is, "Who am I?" This is the first spool that awaits the thread of answer from the love of others and will be the place where the individual draws the perspective of individual identity. The second question is, "Am I safe?" Here, we have the second spool that must have the thread of care and nurturing to determine the meaning around the trustworthiness of the new situation into which the child is born. Both of these questions are formulated around meanings that are founded on the behaviors of love and trustworthiness of caregivers. But, as the child grows, these meanings about identity and safety quickly form the basis of behavior for the individual, and he or she will in turn love and act in trustworthy ways in other relationships.

What, then, is this love that is necessary from caregivers and forms the basis of identity in human beings? Certainly, at birth a child is vulnerable and in many ways is totally dependent on the caregiver and environment to provide care. Even though cognitive structures in the child are underdeveloped, lower brain functions and emotions are active in the child (Broderick & Blewitt, 2006). This element of bonding and caregiver attention has blossomed into the field of attachment theory, and it is thought to be a critical aspect of the child establishing an emotional link with caregivers, the formation of a style for future relating, (Ainsworth & Bowlby, 1991), and desiring or rejecting human contact through touching, listening, talking, or looking (Pipp & Harmon, 1987). Attachment with caregivers is thought to be critical for the child to develop a sense of self and desire for eventual socialization (Pipp, Easterbrooks, & Harmon, 1992). More recent studies have also suggested that this attachment can be shaped and modified through not only caregiver relationships but also significant chosen relationships, such as with marital partners (Crowell, Treboux, & Waters, 2002; Johnson, 2004). The point is that these contacts through stable attachments are held by this theory to be essential for formation of healthy individuality. In contrast, the person who is unattached or insecurely attached may display rejecting behavior of human attention or be emotionally insecure when left by him- or herself (Lieberman, Weston, & Pawl, 1991).

We would agree that these early attachments are essential and point out that most of this early bonding and attachment takes place before the child is verbal; it most likely has a huge impact on the identity and relational development of the child. For example, children who do not receive adequate or regular feedings are prone to developing anxiety (Valenzuela, 1990). Emotional cuddling and physical contact are important in high-risk infants developing physically, cognitively, and socially (Pelaez-Nogueras et al., 1996). In addition, emotional tension in relationships and individuals to whom the child is exposed are shown to have a direct negative impact on children (Davies & Cummings, 1998). As a whole, it is clear that the relationships to which we are exposed when we are young and even older have a dynamic affect on the shaping of our identities, tendencies, and eventual behavior.

There is little doubt, therefore, that the attentiveness, nurturing, and emotional stability of the caregiver are important in forming essential meaning, security, and an identity element for a young child. But more specifically, it is important to point out how the caregiver is to go about *loving* the child that is essential for identity formation. Although love is difficult to define, we would agree with Tillich (1954) that love moves past just simple emotion or sentiment to have action orientations that are indeed measurable. Hargrave (2000) suggests that a definition of love

11

would include the ideas of giving adoration and acknowledgment, engaging in active companionship and intimacy, and sacrificing for the good of the beloved. We believe that these ideas form an essential basis for loving. These aspects of love can easily be conceptualized into different types of love that are demonstrated through different types of actions. For instance, a type of love that encompasses elements of friendship, commitment, respect, acceptance, and understanding can be described as a companionate love (Bradbury & Karney, 2010). Another type of love that focuses on the strong infatuation, desire for physical and emotional intimacy, idealization, and preoccupation can be described as romantic or passionate love (Bradbury & Karney, 2010). Finally, love can be conceptualized in the concept of giving and sacrifice by which the one who feels love gives up what he or she needs or wants for the good of the one loved (Hargrave, 2000). This kind of love can be described as altruistic love (Saxton, 1993).

Companionate Love

Hargrave's (2000) three aspects of love, then, are absolutely crucial for the formation of identity and the sense of self of the individual. Although there would be developmentally appropriate periods when each type of love may be needed more, each type is essential in helping the individual answer the question, "Who am I?" We usually think of companionate love as associated with commitment and friendship. When a person experiences this type of love, the intimate exchange communicates that the lover enjoys being around the loved, and there is mutuality in the connection. When we receive this type of love, we know that when the hard issues of life come there will be someone there who will give us care, support, and assistance (Hargrave & Pfitzer, 2003). For those of us who have deep friendships that have existed for years, we know that even if we do not see a dear friend for a long period of time, the friend still cares for us deeply and is connected to us. Likewise, when we are reunited with the dear friend, we easily go back to the spontaneity and intimacy that we had when we were around each other on a regular basis. Once you have experienced this type of deep companionate love with another person, it could be argued that it is impossible ever to be alone again. As the accidents, threats, bad health, financial ruin, or disasters of life occur, we know that our companions will be there for us at least in thought and emotion if not physically. Also, as we experience the joys, triumphs, achievements, passages, and developments on the positive side of life, these companions are equally present.

In the formation of our sense of self and identity, this companionate love tells us that *we are not alone* (Hargrave & Pfitzer, 2003). Of course, if this type of love is lacking for any reason, then indeed we feel outcast from intimacy and feel very much as though there is something that is defective about our beings and nature. We most often associate this type of love with friends we make throughout our lives, but of course it is essential that we also receive this type of love from our families of origin and our caregivers. While friends can communicate much about our worthiness in becoming our companions, our families and original caregivers are the first to give us this essential sense of belonging. This type of love is important to the child who is developing as it communicates that he or she is a desirable object of intimacy, an essential part who belongs to the family group; no matter what happens in life, he or she will not be alone (Hargrave, 2000).

Romantic or Passionate Love

Many think of romantic and passionate love as only associated with sexual or mating relationships. Although this type of love can predominate at the beginning of romantic or erotic types of relationships, it also is an essential element of formation in the sense of self. This type of love often carries with it the elements of excitement, fascination, passion, and even obsession. In other words, you cannot get enough of a person for which you have erotic or romantic love. It is as if the love longs for gratification in terms of time, emotion, and interaction with the beloved, and no other person or object will meet or can meet that particular longing. It is easy to see how this love meets a criterion for lovers, but it is also in effect for a caregiver: when a caregiver holds a child and is fascinated with his or her makeup; when the caregiver sees the child, in spite of limitations, as flawless or perfect; when the caregiver focuses attention on the child and is amazed at the child's gifts, talents, or abilities. Although the caregiver does not have sexual attraction concerning the child, the emotional elements of excitement, passion, and focus are all present. When we are the subject of this type of romantic or passionate love (whether from a partner or a caregiver), we cannot help but feel that we are the only special water that can quench the thirst of the person who loves us. When we are the

13

object of this type of love, we will likely feel like we are one of a kind, *precious and unique* (Hargrave, 2000).

Altruistic Love

Altruistic love is the third way that we are loved and carries the implication of sacrifice for the good of the beloved. Research and clinical outcomes have pointed to the positive effects of sacrifice in marital relationships (i.e., Hargrave, 2000; Stanley, Whitton, Low, Clements, & Markman, 2006; van Lange et al., 1997), but it is also essential in the formation of identity in the family of origin and caregiving relationships. There is significant confusion with altruistic love in our humanistic age; we want to equate the concept with *unconditional positive regard* (Rogers, 1961). Although we would certainly support the idea of acceptance as an important aspect of love, it does not get to the heart of the idea of this sacrifice in the framework of altruistic love (Hargrave & Pfitzer, 2003).

True sacrificial love means that the one who loves puts his or her needs aside to meet the needs and wants of the beloved. For instance, if two people are starving to death and they gain some meager amount of food, if one eats all the food, that person will survive; if the other eats all the food, the other will survive. If the two people split the food, they both will die of starvation. Altruistic love would compel one person to give the food to the other person, knowing that the sacrifice would mean personal demise (Hargrave & Pfitzer, 2003). Certainly, in such a dramatic situation we can understand this element of altruism, but it is also apparent in the smaller and less-dramatic sacrifices that those in families make for one another. Examples occur when a parent works more to provide an opportunity or a lesson for a child; when a parent forgoes new clothing so the child can have new clothes instead; when a person gives money or time to another when the person needs the time or money him- or herself, and there is no real hope of the recipient ever being able to pay the person back. Although less dramatic, these examples are just as applicable in demonstrating sacrificial aspects of altruistic love. The amount of altruistic love is not so much measured in the depth of the sacrifice as in the willingness to sacrifice. The giver of the altruistic love does not love to be repaid by recognition or future giving but willingly gives because he or she believes the beloved to be worth it. Such altruistic love truly communicates worthiness to the recipient (Hargrave, 2000).

These are the elements of love that we find essential for the individual to form a healthy self-concept and identify. Through companionship and intimacy, we are loved in such a way that assures us that we are not alone. Romantic and passionate love teaches us that our personhoods are indeed precious and unique. Finally, altruistic and sacrificial love gives our identity the boost of worthiness. By being loved, we learn that we are one of a kind and special, that we are thought of as desirable, as an object of intimacy, and as highly prized in the eyes of our lovers. Of course, no human love is perfect, and when there is an absence of any or all of these types of love, the individual is left to doubt who he or she is in the need for healthy self-esteem. Absence of love may leave us with the idea that we are plain and unremarkable, that we are not desirable or capable of intimacy, and that we are flawed. In short, when we are not loved we are likely to think of ourselves as unacceptable. When we have this deep sense of being flawed and unacceptable, we are likely to feel deep emotional pain as we deal with the nagging questions of why we were not loved or unlovable (Hargrave & Pfitzer, 2003). In the next chapter, we explore the responses to this type of emotional pain as a consequence of lack of love.

THE IMPORTANCE OF TRUSTWORTHINESS

The formation of self-concept through love is an essential emotional dynamic, but it is only one of the twin pillars of relationships. Love is a great thing, but left on its own, it is insufficient for the individual to draw the necessary meaning or semantic from life. Trustworthiness is the other essential element; in many ways, it not only equals the importance of love but also has more impact in the course of relationships (Hargrave & Pfitzer, 2003).

It is fascinating to us that examination of trustworthiness and the psychological impact of this important element has been lacking or little recognized in clinical work. To be sure, the attachment literature, while focused on the importance of love, has included dynamics of trustworthiness (Johnson, 2004). The problem is, however, that much of the importance of trustworthiness in this theory has been lost by including it as an aspect of love. Therefore, the clearest representation and recognition of the essential element of trustworthiness has come from contextual family therapy and the contribution of Ivan Boszormenyi-Nagy (i.e., Boszormenyi-Nagy, Grunebaum, & Ulrich, 1991; Boszormenyi-Nagy & Krasner, 1986;

15

Boszormenyi-Nagy & Ulrich, 1981). Contextual family therapy recognized early that trust is an essential relational resource formed primarily in the dimension of relational ethics (Boszormenyi-Nagy & Krasner, 1986). This dimension of relational ethics is best described in the balance of relationships between what an individual is obligated to give to perpetuate the relationship and what he or she is entitled to receive or take from the giving of others in the relationship (Hargrave, 1994a). It is in this oscillating balance of give-and-take between what an individual gives to the relationship and what he or she takes from another that trustworthiness has the opportunity to grow in the relationship (Van Heusden & Van Den Eerenbeemt, 1987). When an individual experiences trustworthiness in the relationship and indeed trusts an individual, he or she can relax and be calm and confident in the trust that the other will continue to provide what the individual is entitled to receive. The relationship becomes free of coercion, manipulation, and withdrawal to get what the relational partners want because there is simply trust that the partner will continue giving. Trustworthiness, therefore, supplies the essential relational resource that allows individuals to give to one another freely (Boszormenyi-Nagy & Krasner, 1986). If this trustworthiness does not exist in the relationship, partners are left to try to get what they are entitled to justly through *destructive entitlement*. This destructive entitlement is self-justifying action on the part of a relational partner and may include threats, manipulation, withdrawal, or the coercion of innocent partners in other relationships to gain what the partner feels he or she rightly deserves from a relationship (Boszormenyi-Nagy & Krasner, 1986). Boszormenyi-Nagy and Spark (1984) demonstrated clinically how lack of trustworthiness and resulting destructive entitlements can manifest in a wide array of misguided loyalties, hurtful actions, and psychopathology.

We are indeed indebted to the contribution of contextual family therapy in focusing attention on this important intergenerational dynamic of trustworthiness. We feel that the dimension of relational ethics and the importance of trustworthiness is the most important contribution of contextual family therapy to the field of psychology, and it certainly has been dynamic in our clinical work. In an effort to expand the understanding of how trustworthiness works and is created in relationships, we have extended the premise of trustworthiness and the essential meanings and semantics individuals look for when they are considering trustworthiness.

Trustworthiness primarily addresses the issue of safety in a relationship. As stated, on birth the child asks, "Am I safe in the context of this relationship?" This question about safety and trustworthiness is essential not only to the philosophical underpinnings of relating (Buber, 1958) but also in the foundation of how the individual will interact in relationships during his or her lifetime (Erikson, 1963). We believe that there are at least three essential elements that are important for the individual to be able to answer this question of safety and trustworthiness. First, we believe there must be a sense of predictability through responsible and reliable giving for the individual to gain this sense of safety in a relationship. Through this sense of predictability when a caregiver not only supplies what the individual needs but also supplies it in a consistent fashion, the individual develops a sense that the relationship is *stable*. Second, like many contextual family therapists, we believe that there must be a sense of justice or balance in the relational give-and-take. As pointed out, when there is this balance or justice between give and take, the individual is able not only to be fulfilled in this drive for safety but also to find that he or she can engage in the relationship and give to others. This balance or justice gives the individual a deep sense of *security* or *hopefulness*. Finally, we believe that there must be a sense of openness in the relationship for trustworthiness and safety to be achieved. Openness in a relationship allows the individual to confirm that what he or she believes to be true about the relationship is indeed true. What one sees from another in the relationship can be counted on as tied to the honesty and as consistent with the value of what the relationship means. In other words, what one sees is what one actually gets. When this kind of openness and vulnerability exist in the relationship, there are no surprises or angst about misrepresentation or dishonesty. The individual who experiences this type of openness develops a sense of *sincerity* or *truthfulness* in the working of relationships.

Predictability

Chaos or unpredictability destroys a sense of consistency, responsibility, and reliability. When a child comes into a family as an infant, he or she is totally dependent on the caregivers to feed, nurture, and provide an environment conducive to growth. If the caregiver provides the stability some of the time and sometimes does not, the child will experience the caregiver as unpredictable, and the environment will be chaotic (Erikson, 1963). Within this chaotic context, the child will quickly learn that the caregiver and environment are unpredictable, unstable, and untrustworthy; the result will be that the child will learn to rely on him- or herself or will

17

drift into a hopeless inability to stabilize. If, however, the caregiver and environment are stable and predictable, the child will come to rely on the order and consistency and look forward to the interaction. The child will learn to trust the caregiver because, in essence, the child has learned that he or she can depend on the consistency instead of coping with inconsistency. In short, this element of trustworthiness makes the child dependent on the reliable giving of another.

ꞌ   If this sounds threatening because of the old language of *codependency*, then we need to explain further. We would agree with the contextual family therapists that the need for relationship is innate (Boszormenyi-Nagy & Krasner, 1986). We cannot form identity, knowledge of self, and even our personalities or talents without the context of another. We do not reflect ourselves; rather, we see ourselves and learn about ourselves within the context and reflection of relationships. Relationships, as discussed, demand that the individual give to the other and, as a result of the giving, is entitled to receive or take something from the other's giving (Hargrave & Anderson, 1992). Because of these two facts, it is not so much that humans are codependent as they are interdependent. Relationships demand that we depend on the other to provide the giving of that which we need, while the other is dependent on us to give that which he or she needs. This ability to depend on another for what only he or she can provide us is far from unhealthy. It is in fact a healthy expression of allowing the desire for a relationship when there is a consistency on which we can rely. Yes, this fact does make us interdependent, but it also allows us to trust and move toward the exchange of love and intimacy. In turn, the predictability and trust allows us to move into the relationship at deeper and deeper levels of interaction. In essence, we are not fearful or unsafe in our giving to another because past interactions tell us that we will have a stable context for giving. Predictability teaches us *stability*, which in turn contributes to our sense of safety and reduces our fear.

Two important aspects of predictability are responsibility and reliability (Hargrave, 2000). The primary idea of responsibility is that the individual knows or acknowledges the actions and behaviors associated with giving that belong to the individual. People most naturally tend to identify with what they need and want from relationships without gravitating to the idea of what they are responsible to give to those relationships. If it is a marital relationship, for instance, people most often identify with emotional vulnerability, the physical help, and the physical and emotional nurturing expected of the spouse. If the individual is responsible, however, he or she is just as aware of how he or she needs to be emotionally vulnerable, assisting and helping the spouse and nurturing the partner. Responsibility ensures focus for relational partners to acknowledge the things that need to be given for the good of the relationship (Hargrave & Pfitzer, 2003).

Of course, when a relational partner is irresponsible, the question is begged: Who will be responsible for the giving that the other in the relationship needs? Most often, people who are in relationships with irresponsible partners will become isolated because of hopelessness that the partners will meet needs or they will become overresponsible in trying to meet their own needs. Just like a child who tries to fulfill the responsibility for care and nurturing that belongs to an irresponsible parent, the individual may try to meet his or her own needs. The problem is that a child is ill equipped to nurture in adult ways and cannot receive the nurturing for him- or herself any more than any partner can get from him- or herself the nurturing and emotion that rightly should come from the other (Hargrave & Pfitzer, 2003). One cannot receive from him- or herself the giving that must come from the other. Responsibility rightly assigns the giving to both relational parties to provide what the other needs or deserves. Responsibility essentially means that one takes the obligations to give that rightly belong to him or her and then actually gives (Hargrave & Pfitzer, 2003). The focus of responsibility then builds predictability.

As good and as necessary as responsibility is in the building of predictability, it is insufficient to build trustworthiness. It is also important that an individual be responsible in a way that is *reliable*. In other words, taking responsibility only becomes important in this context when the giving is executed repeatedly. Intention to take responsibility that does not actually manifest itself in giving and doing is of no consequence in relating and thus destroys predictability and consistency (Hargrave, 2000). Reliability is the discipline to make the responsibility find meaning in action. When unreliable, predictability and therefore trustworthiness are impossible (Hargrave & Pfitzer, 2003).

Human beings, however, are imperfect and will never be totally reliable. Even in the best relationships and with the best intentions, relational partners cannot be totally predictable. How much unreliability can partners tolerate before predictability and trustworthiness are affected? This is a hard percentage to ascertain, but clinically we see relational partners need a consistency rate of around 85% to 90%. Predictability does not mean perfection, but it does require overwhelming evidence that the giving and relationship will be consistent. Short of this reliability, relational partners are forced into a position of questioning safety and trustworthiness (Hargrave, 2000).

Justice or Balance

Justice and balance are the essential aspects of the dimension of relational ethics we pointed out in contextual family therapy. We believe that this concept is best illustrated in relationships by demonstrating the relational ledger that exists in different types of relationships and how in turn justice and balance are achieved.

The easiest type of relationship to ascertain the essence of this concept is one between relational equals, such as the one that exists between spouses. Since all relationships demand balance, there should be an equality of the obligation (give) that one spouse owes to his or her partner and the merit (take) that the spouse should receive from the partner's giving. This can be easily illustrated by a bookkeeping account ledger such as the one found in Figure 1.1. The left side of the ledger notes the merit or the take that a spouse would be expected to receive from the other. In this case, the spouse merits and should take respect, care, and intimacy. The right side of the ledger reflects what this spouse should expect to give in terms of obligation to the relationship. As is the case with all symmetrical relationships, we expect to see a balance of the same things that the spouse is merited to receive with the obligations that he or she is expected to give. In the cases of spousal relationships, balance actually means that what is received on one side of the ledger is balanced out with similar or the same obligations on the other (Hargrave, 2000).

The type of relationship that is illustrated in Figure 1.1 is called a *horizontal relationship* in contextual family therapy (Boszormenyi-Nagy & Krasner, 1986). The distinguishing feature of these types of relationships

Merit or Take (What Individuals Are Entitled to Receive)	Obligations or Give (What Individuals Are Obligated to Give)
1. Respect	1. Respect
2. Care	2. Care
3. Intimacy	3. Intimacy

FIGURE 1.1   A balanced spousal ledger.

is the symmetrical give-and-take because the relationship is between individuals of equal stature such as spouses, friends, or siblings (Hargrave & Anderson, 1992). It is important to realize that even though the example provides a partial list of what spouses give-and-take, the ledger may be different in terms of specifics. For instance, in a traditional type of marriage, a husband may be more responsible to provide income by working for the family, while a wife may be responsible to give more care and nurturing to the household. But, even in this example in which the specific contributions of give and the merited accrual of take are not the same, the expectation in a horizontal relationship would be that the give-and-take be balanced (Hargrave & Anderson, 1992). If the individuals in the relationship feel that the give-and-take is indeed balanced, then they will feel the relationship is fair, and there is a justice to the give-and-take. When this balance persists over a longer period, the spouses experience that each exhibits trustworthiness. This trustworthiness increasingly accrues to the relationship as the balance between give-and-take is maintained (Hargrave, 2000). In turn, the trustworthiness that is built by balance and justice in the relationship enables the individual spouses to give freely to the other (Boszormenyi-Nagy & Ulrich, 1981). They are not fearful of being cheated out of their just entitlement because the spouse has proven trustworthy that he or she will provide what is needed. Without this fear and with the confidence of safety the justice has provided, the individual spouse is free to concentrate on his or her giving to the relationship (Hargrave, 2000).

If there is, however, an imbalance in the relational ledger, it quickly creates injustice and deterioration in trustworthiness. For example, Figure 1.2 is an example of a ledger in which an individual gives what is required of the spousal relationship but does not receive his or her merited entitlement. When this type of injustice is experienced, the individual will feel angry, resentful, and used. What will he or she likely do as a

Merit or Take (What Individuals Are Entitled to Receive)	Obligations or Give (What Individuals Are Obligated to Give)
Nothing is Received Likely Results in Anger and Resentment	1. Respect 2. Care 3. Intimacy

FIGURE 1.2   An imbalanced spousal ledger.

Merit or Take (What Individuals Are Entitled to Receive)	Obligations or Give (What Individuals Are Obligated to Give)
1. Respect 2. Care 3. Intimacy	Nothing is Given Likely Results in Guilt

FIGURE 1.3   Another example of a balanced spousal ledger.

result? As mentioned, the individual will likely be driven to destructive entitlement as he or she threatens, manipulates, or withdraws in hope of getting the partner to give (Hargrave & Anderson, 1992). Trustworthiness will be destroyed by the imbalance, and the angry, resentful partner will likely stop giving and take retaliatory actions toward the partner.

On the other hand, if the individual receives respect, care, and intimacy from the spouse but gives nothing in return, he or she will likely not feel anger but guilt as he or she unjustly benefits from the giving spouse. This ledger is illustrated in Figure 1.3. What would be the likely outcome of feeling such guilt? As is in the example of Figure 1.2, a lack of relational balance or justice usually perpetuates destructive entitlement in the form of threats, manipulation, or withdrawal. It would not be hard to imagine that a husband who does nothing in the relationship with his wife but benefits from her respect, care, and intimacy might be driven by guilt to abuse her emotionally or physically. He might also manipulate her by trying to make her believe that she is unreasonable to expect him to do anything for the good of the relationship and that giving is all her responsibility. He might also feel the sting of guilt to the point at which he gives up trying and leaves the relationship. None of these results is unlikely whether the actions are driven by anger by giving too much and not receiving or driven by guilt by not giving and overbenefiting at the expense of the partner. Guilt or anger, not giving or not receiving at all tend to produce destructive entitlement and to destroy trustworthiness (Hargrave, 2000).

It is important to remember that the balance of give-and-take in horizontal relationships does not need to be exact at any given moment. Spouses will interact appropriately in relationships, and there are times when one partner gives more to the relationship than he or she receives and times when one receives more than he or she gives. As long as these times oscillate appropriately between partners so that both give and receive in a

Merit or Take (What Individuals Are Entitled to Receive)	Obligations or Give (What Individuals Are Obligated to Give)
1. Physical Provision 2. Protection 3. Nurturing 4. Love 5. Discipline	The Child is Responsible to Give Nothing

FIGURE 1.4   A balanced parent/child ledger.

balanced way over a period, trustworthiness can be achieved. Like when a high-wire artist making his or her way across the tightrope, balance will be shifted back and forth many times to keep the overall balance. In the same way, there are times when one gives more and times when one receives more. The primary point is for the relationship to maintain the long-term balance (Hargrave & Pfitzer, 2003).

Horizontal relationships or relationships between equals are not the only kind of relationship. The other type is relationships between successive generations, for which the giving in the relationship is distinctly asymmetrical (Boszormenyi-Nagy & Krasner, 1986). In these relationships, typically between parents and children, parents are expected to give to children without compensation of receiving entitlement (Hargrave, 1994a). Figure 1.4 shows that an infant is entitled to receive and a parent obligated to give things like physical provision, protection, nurturing, love, and discipline. The child, however, carries no such obligation to provide care for the parent in an equal way as in a horizontal relationship. The child is the one who benefits from the giving from the parent and not the other way around. In many of the seminars that provide, we often ask, "Is this balanced?" The answer is usually an unqualified "no." But, when we go on to ask the question, "Is it fair?" the answer is usually "yes."

To understand how something this imbalanced can also be fair, justified, and trustworthy, is one of the secrets to understanding the dimension of relational ethics and the intergenerational transmission of behaviors. Many would say that it is fair because the child did not ask to be born into the world; therefore, parental responsibility comes into play. In other words, the child cannot care for him- or herself and is dependent on the parent. We point out, however, that the parent may be no more equipped to care for the infant than the infant is able to care for him- or herself

(Hargrave, 1994a). Others would say it is fair because it is only a matter of timing; when the parent is old, the then-adult child will balance the relational ledger by taking care of the parent. We point out also that even if the adult child cares for the older parent in similar ways that a parent would care for a child by feeding, changing, and bathing, the child can never provide for the parent what a parent provides for the child. Only a parent or original caregiver is responsible for the love and trustworthiness that shapes identity and future behavior in relationships (Hargrave, 2001). It is simply that a child can never provide the essential elements or thread that goes around the spools of identity and safety in relationships.

So, then, why is the imbalance fair? It is fair because the child receives this nurturing at great cost to the parent and has no obligation to give it back to the parent but instead holds the merit for future use. When the child grows into a parent him- or herself, then it will be his or her turn to give the provision, protection, nurturing, love, and discipline to the *next* generation. It is a relational balance that oscillates from one generation to the next. The parent was once a child and the recipient of care and nurturing that he or she did not have to return until it was the turn of the next generation to have the care and nurturing. The balance is not between a person and another person as in horizontal relationships; it is balanced between generations in these vertical relationships (Hargrave & Pfitzer, 2003). This is how trustworthiness is perpetuated between generations— through the justice and balance of giving to the next generation.

Of course, the question then begs to be asked: "What happens if a child does not receive this type of giving from a parent?" This is also an essential dynamic to understanding human behavior from a contextual family therapy perspective. What most often happens is that the parent of the child expects the child to fulfill certain aspects of what the parent owes the child back to the parent instead. Figure 1.5 is an example; the parent may supply some type of physical provision and some form of

Merit or Take (What Individuals Are Entitled to Receive)	Obligations or Give (What Individuals Are Obligated to Give)
1. Physical Provision	1. Parent Requires the Child to Nurture
2. Protection	2. Parent Requires the Child to Love
3. Discipline	

FIGURE 1.5 An imbalanced parent/child ledger.

24

discipline but instead expects the child to supply nurturing, stabilization, and love for the parent. This is not unusual for parents who are emotionally unsure of themselves, insecure, or uncertain of other relationships. The child, because he or she is a child, will try to perform these adult duties because he or she desperately wants to please the parent to receive the emotional connection that the relationship can provide. However, at least two unfortunate things happen. First, the child is not an adult and therefore is unable to provide the emotional love and nurturing the parent seeks. Instead of being pleased with the child's effort, the parent will likely be displeased with the child, blame the child, withdraw, or manipulate. This may even drift toward the parent becoming physically violent or more abusive of the child (Hargrave & Anderson, 1992).

The second unfortunate consequence of this action is the likely intergenerational consequences of such action. The child is deserving of the emotional love and nurturing of the parent, and because of the innate sense of justice, the child comes to know that he or she has been cheated of such entitlement. As we have seen, imbalance in the relational ledger produces destructive entitlement, likely manifested in threats, manipulation, and withdrawal; the child will not forget or stop feeling this wrong and imbalance. He or she, likely when older, will seek the just entitlement from another source. The most likely sources the child will seek this compensation of love and nurture from are innocent parties, such as his or her future children or spouse (Boszormenyi-Nagy & Krasner, 1986). Instead of the ledger being a revolving slate of trustworthiness as we have seen when the parent takes care of the child, we have a deteriorating legacy as each successive parental generation expects the innocent child to compensate for love and nurturing not received. In turn, when the parent denies these elements from the child, it does not satisfy the longings of the parent because of the immaturity of the child and sets the stage for the child to be cheated and to make the same type of errors with the coming generation (Boszormenyi-Nagy & Spark, 1984). This is a serious cycling downward of the intergenerational trustworthiness and makes the coming generation more likely to commit destructive entitlement against the coming generation. In many ways, this is the most profound type of injury or injustice that can be dealt in family relationships (Hargrave & Pfitzer, 2003). In short, the innocent victim, the child of the destructively entitled and unjust parent, grows into a destructively entitled parent with the next generation. The deterioration and the "beat" of imbalance and distrust continue.

25

Although lack of justice can produce such destructive actions and imbalance for generations, it is important to remember that balance and justice through the generational lineage can produce tremendous justice and trustworthiness. As generations live in balance and trustworthiness with one another, they give faithfully to one another. From this sense of justice and the child receiving what he or she needs and is justly entitled, the child learns a sense of *security*. We believe that this contextual meaning of trustworthiness as found in justice is the most important concept in what much of the attachment literature calls *secure attachment* (i.e., Ainsworth & Bowlby, 1991; Johnson, 2004). It is not only that the parent is present and responsive to the child, but also that the parent is supplying what the child justly needs and not the parent interacting with the child simply to get what the parent wants or needs. When parents justly provide the entitlement to the child, the child not only is attached to the parent but also is given a sense of security in the relationship. This security is then the major factor in the child achieving a sense of competency to be able to engage and give in other relationships in the future. This competency that he or she will receive what is needed in a relationship builds a sense of *hopefulness* that he or she can supply what others will need. Justice or balance in relationships begets *security and hopefulness*.

Openness

We are prone to so much "search and discovery" in our society that it is sometimes discouraging. It seems that we have politicians, entertainers, or sport professionals we look up to and respect not only for their skills but also for their personal lives only to have an unsavory aspect of their lives discovered. When these disappointing things are brought to light and we learn about the "real" person who we regarded highly or as a hero, it leaves us jaded and questioning everything and everyone. We might ask, "Is there really anyone who is worthy or who really projects him- or herself to be?" It is a good question because it is reflective of the faith that we hold not only in human beings in general but also in our relationships specifically.

We believe that the question needs to be broken down into two parts to obtain the essential impact of openness on the question of trustworthiness. The first part of the question relates to the idea of whether anyone is perfect. Of course, when we state the question in this way, we realize that people are just people—no matter how talented, skilled, or dynamic they appear—they are flawed human beings who make mistakes and have inherent shortcomings. This makes the second part of the question—is the person who he or she projects—all the more important when we try to evaluate whether we really know and understand him or her. A person is only being who he or she projects when including the fact that he or she is not perfect, has flaws, and makes mistakes. In other words, a person is only being human and worthy of respect and admiration when open about flaws and imperfections so he or she can deal with them honestly.

Openness is essential for us to be able to trust in relationships because it allows us to deal constructively with these elements of imperfection. If I know that I am imperfect, am unreliable in the way I perform my responsibilities, or irresponsible toward justice in relationships, then deep down I know that everyone copes with the same problem. When one is open about these flaws, the person is openly acknowledging the areas of deficiency; this makes it much more likely that the person will use the openness as an opportunity to correct shortcomings and to grow. Openness alone about flaws without addressing the shortcoming is unfortunate in relationships because it demands that the other relational partner simply adjust to the shortcoming and live as if a problem cannot be corrected or is actually no problem. While we agree that acceptance in relationships is important (Jacobson & Christensen, 1998), we do feel that untrustworthy and unloving behavior in relationships is unacceptable. If one is disorganized and the other organized, one liberal and one conservative, or personalities are very different, these are legitimate areas of difference that carry little or no moral impact on the status of love and trustworthiness and therefore are opportunities for acceptance. But, even in these somewhat benign areas, extremes and polarization in the areas of difference will eventually show irresponsible, untrustworthy, and unloving actions. Openness is not about saying, "This is the way I am, and to be in a relationship with me means that you take me as I am." Rather, it means, "This is what I see in myself, and I believe that I can be better." When openness points toward growth, our imperfections and flaws and those of our relational partners actually pull us together more closely in an intimate bond.

Of course, openness includes not only information about flaws or shortcomings but also provides an opportunity to demonstrate vulnerability about thoughts and emotions. Vulnerability of any kind in relationships serves as an invitation for intimacy in that it is an act of giving.

When a person shares what he or she thinks about a certain subject, the person invites a relational partner to do the same. When a person says how he or she feels about a relational partner, that person invites the partner to do the same. When there is this openness and honesty, it binds the relationship together at a deeper level because of the mutual giving in the relationship. Our thoughts and emotions, in many ways, are the things that are the deepest and most important to us. When we give those to relationships openly and vulnerably, we are giving the deepest part of ourselves.

Lack of honesty destroys this openness and results in a deterioration of trustworthiness. Essentially, there are two ways in which people are not open. The first relates to misrepresentation or lying. When one is intentionally dishonest in a relationship, the discovery is especially painful on the part of the relational other for two reasons. It is painful initially because the person, thoughts, feelings, and reality that were known turned out to be false. This leaves the relational partner wondering if anything in the relational giving was real or was true. Another way the lying is painful to the receiving partner is that the actions, vulnerability, and openness that he or she gave in response to the lying means that he or she was openly giving of him- or herself when nothing was given in return. In short, the vulnerability of the truthful one in the relationship feels exposed and a bit foolish for giving at such a deep level when nothing was given in return. Giving, in this instance, was not mutual; therefore, the relational partner believed in a false intimacy.

The second way that one can destroy openness and trustworthiness in the relationship is simply to be distant or secretive. While a case can be made for this lack of openness as less toxic than misrepresentation or lying, it nonetheless can destroy trustworthiness. The lack of vulnerability that we mentioned is still present, so there is no giving, no intimacy, and no opportunity for relational growth. Distance and secretive behavior simply result in relationships coming to an intimacy standstill at which there is little interaction or relationship, and partners drift further and further apart from one another into their own individuality. Partners may respond in predictable ways with one another and may even respond in like fashion toward one another that is balanced or just, but if there is no intimacy or vulnerability between the two of them, they will not experience safety or trustworthiness with one another and certainly will not have intimacy together. Openness produces vulnerability, which in turn produces mutual giving, which in turn produces *honesty and intimacy*.

LOVE, TRUSTWORTHINESS, AND PRIMARY EMOTIONS

We have stated that love and trustworthiness are the essential constructs that human beings need for healthy individual identity and a sense of safety in interacting in relationship. We have also stated that we believe that these two pillars of relationship are *innate* in human beings. In other words, all humans come into the world looking for these conditions. We believe that this formulation fits well with the findings of neuroscience and the evolving brain structure during development.

The limbic system or midbrain activity is heavily involved with the processing of emotion and memories (Aggleton, 1992). When looking at the context and creation of primary or the most basic emotions, it only makes sense to look in this area of the brain. Emotional responses such as attachment to caregivers, memories that are foundational to who we are and our most important relationships, making sense and meaning of other's actions, as well as the sensation of our own emotions are all most directly related to this limbic region (Siegel, 2007). It is clear that verbalization of emotions, interpretations of actions, decisions, organization, planning, and more complex motor reactions are affected and processed in the covering or the cortex of the brain, but this cortex is not very developed or active at birth (Siegel, 2007). It is important, then, to realize that the most basic forms of emotion, attachment, sensation, and memories of caregivers are produced in the more elemental limbic system of the brain and are separate and apart from initial cognitive processing found in the more advanced, thinking part of the brain in the cortex (LeDoux, 1996).

We feel that, based on this knowledge of the brain, it is reasonable to suggest that these meanings concerning identity formations around love and safety formations around trustworthiness are not higher-brain functions but instead are more basic and innate processes found in the limbic system. When infants and children are exposed to loving and trustworthy caregivers, the basic emotions related to love and trustworthiness are stimulated. In terms of identity, the child will feel loved with the accompanying identity of uniqueness, worthiness, and existing as closely attached or not alone. In addition, the child will feel safe with the accompanying sense that the environment and relationships are stable, secure, and intimate. In short, the emotions of the child will be in a state of rest or a sense of peace. There will be no sense of threat or fear that assaults the brain, and the child will have the ability to develop a consistent sense of identity and safety (Olds, 1958).

But, of course, the infant or child will not always be exposed to a perfectly loving and trustworthy environment in even the best of situations; at worst, the child may experience hate and abusive actions from caregivers. The research is clear that these types of assaults greatly stimulate and activate the limbic system, particularly the area known as the amygdala (LeDoux, 1996). The amygdala is particularly prone to emotional reactions of fear and anger, which in turn are closely linked with the reactions of *fight and flight* (LeDoux, 1996). In other words, when the infant or child does not receive the love and trustworthiness he or she seeks, it results in stress or distress for the infant, which in turn produces emotional reactions that demand response through fight or flight.

When these ideas are taken together, we believe a powerful suggestion forms that there are primary emotions. In our reasoning, these most primary emotions are related to being loved and being safe. When individuals feel this love and trustworthiness, they respond emotionally with a sense of calm and peacefulness. In other words, when they know who they are and have a sense of safety, they are in a relaxed state and are free to respond in the context of the relationship. When, however, there is a lack of love or safety, the limbic system is activated, and there is stimulation of emotional pain that begs reaction to cope by using either the power to fight for oneself or anxiety to flee and get away from the threat.

Although this kind of primary emotion makes sense for an infant or young child, it is no less true in terms of individuals as they develop and grow into adults. As adults relate well with one another, there is a resonance and peaceful stimulation in midbrain activity (LeDoux, 2002). The cortex allows the processing, verbalization, and organization of these primary emotions, but the primary emotions in the limbic system are still activated. While the primary emotions of feeling unloved or unsafe are not able to be verbalized in infancy or early childhood, they are nonetheless apparent as the child is unattached, fails to thrive, or is in constant distress. Whether expressed verbally or not, primary emotions exist and are a result of this midbrain activity. In adulthood, individuals express the primary emotion related to feeling unloved using various terms: unloved, unworthy, insignificant, alone, worthless, devalued, defective, inadequate, rejected, unacceptable, hopeless, unwanted, abandoned, unappreciated, discouraged, disrespected, and others. In addition, adults express the primary emotion of feeling unsafe in relationships using a variety of words and phrases, for example, unsafe, insecure, unsure, used, guilty, fearful, powerless, out of control, controlled, vulnerable, disconnected, unknown, betrayed, invalidated, and unable to measure up to expectations. We believe that these types of words and phrases as well as similar ones are related to the primary emotions of the individual and originate in the midbrain.

2

Coping With Pain
Understanding Behavior and Self-Reactivity

INTRODUCTION

The following story of a 26-year-old male relates his struggle to retain focus on improving his life:

> You think you have something under control and that you can actually make something of your life like getting a good job or going back to get an education. There are moments when I get the idea that I can make something good like this happen in my life, and then, wham, you get hit with something that sends you over the edge. For me, it is the least little insult. The moment that someone does not appreciate or recognize me. They short me on change at the store or are not appreciative enough when I do something for them. With a teacher, it is the least little look that communicates to me that they don't think I can get it. With women, it is any time they start to expect something more of me that I didn't promise in the first place. Whatever it is, when the switch is thrown on, I am in an automatic rage. I yell, scream, threaten, and yes, have even gotten violent. When that switch is thrown, I am gone, and I have no control over myself. I become someone different. It is automatic. I don't know when and where it is going to happen, but when it does, I am over the edge, and my anger will get me in trouble more often than not.

When primary emotion is violated, as discussed in Chapter 1, the brain is thrown into distress or pain as the individual is not sure of who he or she is or whether he or she is safe in relationships. In other words,

33

the individual's identity and safety are threatened. As a result, he or she will be thrown into a fight-or-flight response to cope with the distress. Like any fight-or-flight response, the reaction has its basis in trying to regain a sense of stability or safety or to remove the threat. These actions, while seemingly extreme (like the anger and rage reactions of the young man in the introductory), are not so unreasonable when put into the context of the primary emotions and distress. The actions and reactions that we may find to be unfounded and unreasonable are actually predictable and understandable if we see the behavior within the context of the primary emotions.

This chapter focuses on taking the information learned from the primary emotions resulting from love and trustworthiness and beginning to understand the predictable ways in which people cope with such emotions. In the restoration therapy model, we believe that if the psychotherapist can accurately understand the emotions as they relate to this love and trust and then make sense of the coping behaviors of the individual, then the psychotherapist is in a position to clearly assess the distressed individual and draw direction in terms of goal setting and intervention.

POWER, ACTIONS, AND AGENCY

Power can prove to be a strange thing. In systemic therapies, most see power as any action or behavior that carries communication to a situation or relationship (Haley, 1987). Seen in this light, power can accurately be described as the politics or actions that accompany the meaning or semantics in human experience that we discussed in Chapter 1. In other words, human beings come equipped to do two basic things in the context of relationships: They make meaning about themselves and decide how to behave or act in relationships. Power, then, is the behavior and action in relationships and represents the other essential "spool" in the human existence. Agency is the extension or use of power in a beneficial or safe manner.

As discussed, power (or actions/politics) and meaning (semantics) are almost always mutually informing. Just as nouns and verbs inform one another about what something is and what something does, power communicates and influences the meaning that we draw or interpret from situations, and the meanings that we draw influence the power we exert in our actions. For instance, if someone steals something from you or abuses you, you draw meanings from the actions that you are unloved by that person and unsafe in the relationship. When this meaning is made, then you make the decision to use your power to act in certain ways in the relationship that are consistent with the meaning. You may use your power to retaliate against the person, negotiate protection, or withdraw. These actions of power on your part in turn communicate meaning to the other person that has stolen or abused you and further informs the meaning you draw about yourself and your safety. We agree with Bandura (1989) that this influence of power or action affects those around us, the situation, or relationship and affects us in an emergent interactive fashion. In simple terms, our actions and use of power affect others, our relationships, and ourselves.

The exercise of power by and large informs at least four aspects of our actions. First, our use of power determines how much *control* we will exert in any given situation. Human beings, in any situation or relationship, have the capability of moving actions and interactions in dynamic, forceful, and even dominating ways or of being static, avoidant, and passive. Whether or not an individual exercises control in interactions or relationships, the behavior has a dramatic affect on the perceived sense of the ability to provide for one's own safety. While one cannot guarantee that relationships or situations are safe, the amount of control and power an individual is willing to exert will make a tremendous difference in a person's perception of safety. This control can be exerted by force of action, repetition, intimidation, pressure, strength or desirability of personality, or even threat.

Second, our use of power greatly influences the *structure* or *hierarchy* that is put in place in a relationship or situation. This concept of structure or hierarchy is, of course, closely related to control. As a person exerts control, he or she is likely to be perceived as the one who is most able to make rules or practices concerning the relationship, to shape the beliefs of those interacting in the relationship, and to influence the rigidity or permeability of boundaries in the relationship (Minuchin & Fishman, 1981). But, while structure and hierarchy are put in place or even maintained by control, the organization exerts power on relationships by maintaining practices over a period of time.

For instance, if parents regularly give direction and advice, provide protection, and make rules for children, the children learn that the structure or hierarchy of the parents in charge and more powerful can be counted on from day to day. As such, the children would adjust to the structure and would resist challenging the hierarchy. In this way, the structure, hierarchy, and actions associated with both produce a powerful influence in constructing beliefs or "the way things are" in the family (Keeney & Ross, 1985). On the other hand, if parents give no direction, advice, protection, or rules to the children, the children likely see the structures, hierarchy, and boundaries in the system as weak. As a result, the structure of the family would likely exert little force or influence on how the children behave or react from one day to the next. Like control, structure and hierarchy in relationships inform individuals about the ability and reliability of safety.

Third, our use of power says much about the way we perceive our abilities, strengths, and talents. This element of power is greatly shaped by the meanings that we make concerning our sense of self. If we perceive ourselves as having abilities, strengths, and talents that are unique, needed, and worthy, then the self-efficacy literature confirms that we will see ourselves as more powerful (Bandura, 1989). Simply stated, as we believe in ourselves we possess the power to become more efficacious or indeed more powerful in relationships and situations.

Finally, our use of power is dynamic in the process of authority that governs our individual lives. In other words, who does the individual give the authority to in shaping the meaning and direction of his or her identity? If the individual sees others or the structure as authoritative in ability to direct his or her identity or actions, then he or she will likely react in a dependent fashion in these relationships. If, however, the individual believes the power of this authority resides with him or her, then the individual will likely behave much more independently in making choices. Of course, control, structure, ability, and authority are all different aspects of power or action and thus are overlapping constructs. However, it is interesting to us that dividing the constructs in this manner allows us again to see how power can influence the actions that one takes in relationships through control and structure as well as the meaning or conclusions one draws about self through abilities and authority. In other words, individuals have power not only to shape the actions they take in relationships (control and structure) but also to shape their own meanings about self (ability and authority).

Of course, not all use of power is equal in terms of its positive or negative effects on individual identities or relationships. It is essential that we draw this distinction to understand how the concept of power can be used most beneficially. The first concept that we draw attention to in the use of power is that of human agency. Human agency (Bandura,

1989) carries with it the idea that humans use their actions and power to produce outcomes that are positive and effective to produce not only rewards for themselves but also what is good for others and future posterity. Our belief is that human agency is a good way to describe what takes place when one is active and positive in shaping his or her identity and the identity of others and focuses actions on having balanced or justified give-and-take relationships with others as well as stable and intimate connections.

The way that this agency works from a contextual point of view is that when the individual gives love to relationships and behaves in a trustworthy manner, he or she experiences a sense of positive and correct relational standing. In short, the individual feels good about him- or herself because he or she is doing the most useful thing that can be done in relationships. It is what we call a "rhythm of rightness" in relationships (Hargrave, 2005). When a person uses his or her agency to govern power, then most of those with whom he or she is in a relationship will respond positively and will give back appropriate love and trust. This mutual giving of love and trustworthiness then creates the positive spiral effect in building increasing mutual giving (Boszormenyi-Nagy et al., 1991). As the individual practices agency toward being loving and trustworthy, the individual gains a sense of entitlement and a "right self" in terms of his or her meanings. In addition, he or she creates the most good, positive, and useful results possible for those in a relationship with him or her and, indeed, for the lineage that will follow. Finally, when he or she uses power for agency, the individual is likely to receive this type of loving and trustworthy giving from others, which enhances the individual's sense of self and his or her trustworthiness in safety.

A few years ago, one of our colleagues, Sandra Perkins, was disturbed by the fact that as therapists we spent much of our time focusing on what went wrong with people in the areas of love and trustworthiness and not focusing on their strengths that came from human agency. We immediately recognized this as true because no matter how damaged or destructive an individual is, he or she is a product of some love and trustworthiness simply by the testimony that he or she survived (Hargrave, 1994a). This led us to recognize that when an individual comes from a perspective that is loving and trustworthy, his or her brain is not thrown into stress or distress but is in a state of peace, as discussed in this chapter. As a result of this emotional soundness, he or she is able to act or use power toward human agency. As seen in Figure 2.1, the individual is not forced into reacting but can choose to act in ways that are good for him or her as a person and are good for others in the relationship. As a result of this agency toward love and trustworthiness, the person can love others and nurture their self-identities as well as love and provide him- or herself with self-value. Further, the individual can be involved in relationships in a balanced manner of giving while receiving from the other and being responsibly and intimately connected with the other in the relationship. We believe that the focus of giving illustrated in Figure 2.1 is the pathway and direction of use of power for human agency. It not only does the individual good but also does well by the prospect for current and future relationships. Power, then, becomes a method of agency to produce love and trustworthiness for self and humanity (Tillich, 1954).

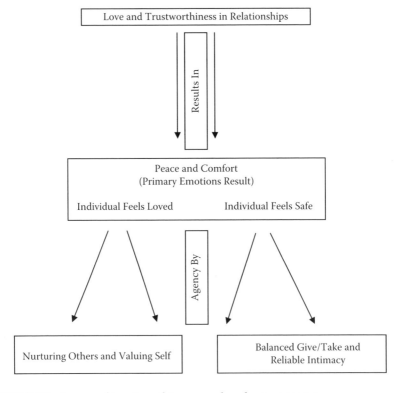

FIGURE 2.1 Love and trustworthiness produce human agency.

REACTIVITY AND DESTRUCTIVE COPING

Of course, most of the people who come to psychotherapy have not had an extensive background of loving and trustworthy relationships but rather have had violations of the same. Some of these violations were severe and traumatic, while others were less severe but still damaging to the identity of self and the security and safety in relationships. In these situations, the stress and pain of the primary emotions come into play in a dynamic way. It is as if the individual from this damaged situation says, "Why was I not loved? How do I live in a world that is not safe?" It is in these situations that the individual does not learn to act with human agency but instead turns to self-reactivity. *Self-reactivity* is a term we use to mean that the individual is prompted to have to cope with the unloving and untrustworthy situations by compensating, albeit destructively, for what is lacking in the sense of identity and safety. This concept is close to the idea of *destructive entitlement* we discussed in Chapter 1 (Boszormenyi-Nagy & Krasner, 1986). The difference here is that the destructive action that the individual takes in response to the unloving and untrustworthy relationship or situation is directed not only into the relationship but also at him- or herself. We suggest here that self-reactivity is the broader term for the individual having to cope with the destructive unloving and untrustworthy forces as they affect both personal identity and chosen actions in relating. Destructive entitlement is the more specific term that suggests self-justifying behavior that is formulated to achieve or take what an individual feels is rightly deserved (Hargrave & Pfitzer, 2003). Both concepts are useful in understanding power and action when there is damage passed to individuals in relationships.

What makes the individual so susceptible to use power in destructive ways in response to destructive actions done to him or her? After all, would it not make sense for a person who has been abused in childhood—who knew the pain and effects of abuse—to resist abusing others and instead use power for agency? Although it does make sense in a reasonable fashion, it is important to point out that these processes that involve love and trustworthiness are not reasonable. As seen in Chapter 1, the part of the brain that reacts to these factors is not the rational, thinking brain that is located in the cortex but the emotional and relational limbic system in the midbrain. The first reason that we react based on these emotions is that the emotion does not take place in a part of the brain where reason can be applied. When people feel emotion from violations, they react in automatic ways of fight and flight to cope or preserve the self (LeDoux, 1996). These power responses are not most thought out but rather are a result of the self-reactivity as the individual is left to try to figure out the emotional pain in a way that keeps some sense of self and some sense of safety. These power actions that come from self-reactivity are almost always destructive.

The second reason that people are prone to use this self-reactivity is because much of the formation of this reactivity occurred when nothing else could be done. When a child is young or an infant, there are simply few or no ways that the child can apply reason to the complex sequences of giving love and trustworthiness to create identity and change the environment to get more love and trustworthiness. The child is not cognitively capable of agency or physically able to do the actions necessary to provide care, protection, and stability. In other words, the young child simply has no choice but to utilize power toward self-reactivity because it is the only thing possible. The infant reacts to the unloving or untrustworthy environment by either crying and protest (fight) or passivity and detachment (flight). As the child grows, he or she may utilize more coping strategies designed to achieve a sense of meaning or protection, but these are still only directed at preservation and self-reactivity. The child simply feels the primary emotion of pain and violation and uses a coping strategy to survive. We believe that as a child performs these strategies, he or she finds which strategies work well. As the child increasingly uses the self-reactivity and the coping strategies, the behavior becomes more ingrained or automatic for child (Hargrave & Pfitzer, 2003). Self-reactivity and coping with pain become a familiar way of life for the child as he or she grows into adulthood. Destructive coping strategies, therefore, are not so much thought out as much as they are simply a power reaction to cope with the lack of identity or safety (Hargrave & Pfitzer, 2003).

While we believe that no person survives a background that is totally devoid of love and trustworthiness, neither do we believe that any individual has come from a situation in which there was perfect love and trustworthiness. All humans, therefore, deal with this issue of using power for the purpose of self-reactivity and survival. It simply is a matter of children coping with pain from the fight-and-flight response from the midbrain. Obviously, however, some individuals experience much more damage, problems, and violations from others, and the self-reactivity is more severe; at the same time, the potential resources coming from love and trustworthiness are rarer. But, in either case, as the child grows through childhood and adolescence, even though cognition is increasingly engaged, the individual does not lose his or her primary reactions to violations and his or her preferred methods of coping and self-reactivity (Hargrave & Pfitzer, 2003).

It is then important for us to understand how an individual copes with this pain using his or her power for self-reactivity. Hargrave and Sells (1997) set forth the initial framework adapted and shown in Figure 2.2. In this figure, we see that as individuals experience the violations of love or trustworthiness, they feel the pain or distress of lack of identity or lack of safety. In response to this primary emotional distress, the individual reacts or copes by extreme fight-or-flight responses. In response to lack of love and loss of identity, the individual may go to one extreme of blame/rage during which he or she expresses aggressive and angry behavior. The individual may also go to the other extreme of coping by

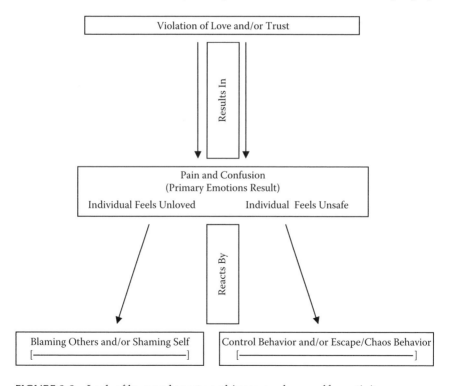

FIGURE 2.2 Lack of love and trustworthiness produces self-reactivity.

41

integrating a deep sense of shame about his or her identity. In response to lack of trustworthiness or safety, the individual may feel compelled to take on control of every situation to the point of being nondependent on others. At the other extreme in this response to lack of trustworthiness or safety, the individual may conclude that safety is impossible and therefore seek to escape the pain of relationships through irresponsible or anesthetizing behaviors.

We feel that these behaviors that flow from self-reactivity form the basis for a multitude of dysfunctional, destructive, and maladaptive behaviors not only for the individual but also for the individual's relationships. It is wise, therefore, for us to examine these reactive coping behaviors in more detail to gain increased understanding not only of how to accurately assess the damage of love and trust but also to gain insight into the assessment of how the individual is damaging to him- or herself and others.

EXPLORING DESTRUCTIVE BEHAVIOR

Clinically, it is important for us to understand that most of our clients actually hate the behavior in which they engage because of reactivity. It is hard for even the stiffest denial to miss the disturbance or destruction that one causes by a raging or violent behavior, long-term negativity or depression, overcontrolling or anxious behavior, and addictive or irresponsible reactions, as for instance, this statement from a man who sexually abused his daughter:

> I really can't believe I would do that to my daughter. I would look at her knowing that I was ruining her life. I would know that the problems she was having in school were caused by me. I knew that the fears and clingy behavior were all because of me. But, I would continue to abuse her. I honestly can't tell you why I would continue to this day. I do know that I thought I was a sick and awful man. I still think I must be to have done such things to my daughter. I hate myself for what I did. I hated myself then while I was doing it.

Clients do not choose this reactivity as much as they adapt to the reactivity and make it a part of their normal day in and day out coping style. It is practiced to the point that the brain becomes comfortable with the reactions. We become familiar even with the behavior that we hate to the point of practice. It is not an easy thing for us to change and is certainly not an easy thing for our clients to change. Therefore, to accurately access our clients, we must always go back to the pain and confusion that they feel over the lack of love and mistrust. If we take this position of compassion, not only will we understand more but also we will actually be more accurate in the evaluation of our clients as human beings.

A Closer Look at Reactivity and Lack of Love

If we look at the violation of love more closely and what people feel concerning their lack of identity, we can concentrate on only the left side of the bottom of Figure 2.2. In Figure 2.3, we can explore violations of love more completely. We list some of the specific words that people use to describe this primary emotion of pain and confusion over identity when a violation of love occurs.

Blaming Others

When an individual feels this type of pain, he or she will choose the extreme behavior of blaming others for the pain felt, shaming self, or both in a cyclical pattern of moving to both extremes. People who are self-reactive with blame feel that they are deeply entitled to be loved and act on the violation in an accusatory fashion. We can imagine that when they feel this lack of identity, they ask themselves, "Why was I not loved?" The driving force of the fight reaction indicates that they were not loved because the others in relationship with them were evil, incompetent, self-focused, or simply ignorant to what they were supposed to provide. In response to the lack of identity, blamers tend to demand or demean others to try to secure the identity and proper sense of self. Simply stated, they are never satisfied with the way they feel and punish others for not being able to make them feel differently. For instance, in the following comments, a woman blames her husband for the feelings she has of being alone, unwanted, and devalued:

> You are a freak. A statue that has no feelings and can't respond to anything I need. You say you care for me, well then you should show me. You don't speak to me, you don't do the things I ask you to do, and you hardly ever want to be with me. Even when we make love, you can barely answer the call, and it never is satisfying to me. You are a pathetic excuse for a husband, and I don't think you will ever be able to make me happy.

Imagine the husband listening to this woman berate him for his behavior and shortcomings. Not only has he suffered an extreme attack

43

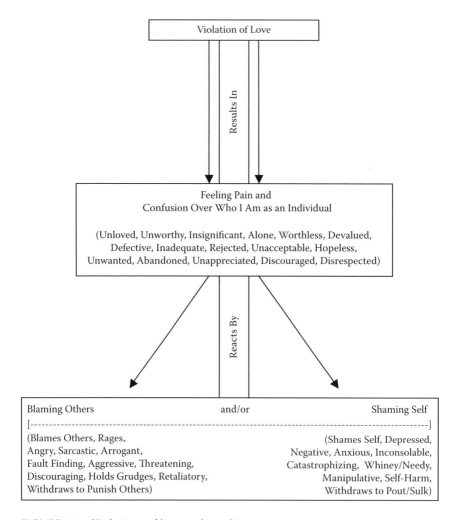

FIGURE 2.3 Violations of love and resulting reactivity.

by his wife on his own identity, but also he most likely will want to do nothing more than get away from her and stay away. We examine these types of cyclical patterns of relational partners in the next chapter, but for now, let us just focus on the words of this woman. Although it is understandable that she wants something from her husband that she is not getting, the extreme blaming behavior makes it highly unlikely that she will receive it. In addition, the blaming of the husband does absolutely nothing to make her feel any more of a sense of identity but instead leads her to believe that she is indeed an angry, aggressive woman who can become out of control quickly.

Individuals who are self-reactive in blaming others often have arrogant attitudes that appear to be narcissistic. When we see this attitude, we most often recognize it as an attack on the other in the relationship to prop up the wounded identity the individual feels. In other words, if the blamer can make the relational other into nothing, then the blamer will feel like something. This kind of arrogance only produces a pseudoidentity as the blamer can only make him- or herself better by putting down others. In the following story, a 52-year-old man talks about his job:

> I'm really the only one in the whole system who knows what is going on and how things should work. Everyone else—and I mean everyone—is simply a pinhead that doesn't know the first thing about the operation. If it were not for me, I don't see how the operation could continue. I've come to just regard the people I work with as junk—you know, sort of an artist who works with this salvage material to make sculptures. I make these crappy people look good, but I still know that they are nothing but crap.

It is as if this particular blamer feels that people fail miserably at all endeavors and are inadequate not only in their work but also as objects worthy of his connection. He does not like people for who they are or what they do. Although he covered for himself by acting as if he was the only person who did things correctly or, as he implied, the only one who was not "crap," his reflection on the state of other humans likely points to the fact that he lacked self-identity and handled this by blaming others so he would feel okay. Of course, this action not only denied him essential human connection that might make it possible for him to experience love, but the arrogance or false sense of self that he projected did nothing to make him deal with who he is in reality. Like the demanding and demeaning woman in the preceding example, the man did not make himself feel better, and his behavior was not likely to be effective in any kind of relationship.

But, by far the most destructive form of blaming is aggressive and threatening behaviors that often spill into retaliation, punishment, rage, and violence. When the individual is stimulated with a sense of violation at this level, destructive entitlement seems to take over to a dangerous level, and the person feels that he or she has the right and necessity to *make* others in relationships behave as he or she wishes. When individuals are to this point in rage because of reactivity, there is almost total focus on doing emotional damage to the other through demanding, demeaning, and arrogant behavior. These types of blamers are seen as particularly heinous in our society; legal systems, relational members, and even the therapeutic community often want to punish them. We would point out, however, at the root of this type of destructive behavior is the same type of damage in sense of self and violation of love that the blamer perpetrates. The following is the story of a 28-year-old man who was responsible for physically abusing his wife:

> I feel like everything I do or feel is right on the edge of falling apart—like a house of cards waiting to fall. I know that my wife is okay and a fine person, but I feel such tension all the time. I feel like it is her job to make me feel better or at the very least, stay out of my way so I don't have to deal with more tension. The least little thing, from a small request like taking out the trash to something bigger like complaining about something, just causes me to snap. At that point, my focus is not to get things better but only to hurt her. I hurt her with my words, my violence, and my fists. Sometimes when I look at it when I am calm, I think if I hurt I am going to make her hurt.

Like any kind of blaming, the process guarantees that nothing will get better. In this most aggressive form of rage, threats, and violence, severe violation is perpetuated to the individuals in a relationship. Even if others love this blaming individual, they can never trust the relationship and are constantly in tension as they try to control the situation so that the blamer does not fly into the rage. This, unfortunately, ensures that the blamer will be alone and further complicates the feeling that he or she is not loved. But, equally damaging is the blamer's behavior with regard to his or her identity. It is a sad thing to know about yourself that you are capable and guilty of damaging innocent people, and it takes the most persistent denial not to hate oneself for this action.

Shaming Self

People who shame themselves are dealing with the same violation of love and the same type of primary emotions over confusion of identity as are blamers. The primary difference is that when they ask the question, "Why was I not loved?" they come up with a different answer. Instead of blaming someone else and believing that it is the relational other's responsibility to make him or her feel differently, instead the person draws the conclusion that the reason for lack of love is that he or she *is unlovable*. In other words, the person believes that original caregivers or others in important relationships are correct in treating the individual as unlovable because there is nothing about him or her that is unique, worthy, or desirable for companionship and intimacy. As a result, the individual that shames him- or herself often hates him or herself and engages in self-loathing. For instance, a young adolescent woman explained what it was like to look at herself in the mirror:

> I really can't stand to even look at myself. First, there is everything about the way I look, from my face to my physical features. I do not have one attractive thing except my eyes. But, every time I look into my eyes, I see what is on the inside. I see this pitiful excuse of a human being that no one cares for and no one loves. They are exactly right about me. I hate what is on the outside of me and what is on the inside of me.

It is not difficult to understand that when one feels this way about the sense of self, negativity and depression are usually present. There is a sense on the shamer's part that he or she is beyond reach, and nothing about him or her is changeable. These shamers often feel that they are innately flawed, and the world would be better off without them. As a result, they are often inconsolable about their identities. Twenty well-meaning and trustworthy people could form a line and each in sequence tell the shamer about a heart-felt appreciation of or quality in the shamer, and the shamer would reject every comment. You see, as long as the shamer holds tenaciously to the belief that he or she is unlovable, he or she refuses to accept any kind of love from someone else.

People who feel shame are usually also pessimistic, negative, and hopeless about relationships. The characteristic forms a double bind in relationships (Madanes, 1981); the shamer wants someone to love him or her, but he or she refuses to believe the relational other when there is relational engagement. For instance, a 51-year-old female could not move out of her shame even when others engaged her at a positive level:

47

> People will tell me something positive about myself, but I never believe them. I know who I am. I know that there is nothing special about me. If they got to know me more, the real me, they would not want to be around me. Anyone who ever spent any significant time with me has ended up leaving me. I am the common denominator with all those past relationships, so it has to be me. I would like not to be lonely, but I don't see any realistic hope that it will ever happen.

This reflects one of the central characteristics of shamers that plays out in this double bind: They wish that someone would make them an object of desire and love them. As a result, they tend to act *relationally needy* and have little confidence in their ability to contribute to others but make it clear that they want others to contribute to them. However, when others do take the initiative and try to invest in the shamer, the shamer often experiences the effort as unbelievable and unreliable because it does not fit with his or her identity. As a result, the relationship often does not make any appreciable difference in the negativity and hope-lessness of the shamer, and the relational other often feels discouraged and disheartened by the lack of loving exchange in the relationship, so they often leave. Both the blamer and the shamer feel the lack of identity and love; therefore, any relationship is dominated by the blamer's and shamer's reactivity to the violation. In short, the relationship is all about them and their pain. As a result, relational others are reluctant to stay in a relationship with this kind of reactivity and manipulation.

As we can see, people who are locked into the reactivity of sham-ing themselves are extraordinarily prone to depression, negativity, and hopelessness. At the extreme, this type of reactivity can lead to self-harm. Self-harm can take many behavioral forms, but here we are concerned specifically about the self-harm that flows from the desire to bring injury to the self because of self-loathing or self-hatred. One may isolate from relationships because he or she desires to be in con-trol of vulnerability, but the shamer is likely to be isolated because he or she believes no one can find anything useful or desirable about him or her. One may drink or do drugs to ease emotional pain and escape reality, but the shamer usually does these types of activities to excess with the express purpose of doing injury to him- or herself. Extreme withdrawal, self-mutilation, suicidal ideation, and suicide attempts can all be reflective of this type of self-harm that flows from the shamer's self-hatred. A 39-year-old male expressed this hatred of self stemming from his suicide attempt:

The attempt was not a cry for help or even an expression of hopelessness. For me, it was way beyond just those things. It was a desire to punish myself. It was an effort to make myself experience as much pain as I felt I was worthless. I tried to find the worst way of ending my life that would fit how despicable I felt I was.

Of course, this extreme of shame is dangerous; as a result, the psychotherapist must always exercise care in dealing with a person in such pain. Shamers are not "feeling sorry for themselves" any more than blamers are evil human beings. They are not weak or pitiful; they are, in fact, human beings who are hurting from a severe violation who have carried reactivity and power to cope to a destructive extreme.

A Closer Look at Reactivity and Lack of Trustworthiness

In a similar way, when we look at the violations of trustworthiness more closely and what people are feeling as a result of lack of safety in relationships, we concentrate on only the right side of the middle and bottom of Figure 2.2. In Figure 2.4, we explore these violations of trustworthiness more completely. Notice again that we list some of the specific words that people use to describe this primary emotion of pain and confusion over being safe in relationships when violations of trustworthiness in relationships occur.

Control Behaviors

In taking a look at reactivity due to these types of violations, it is again important to remember that the individual is not choosing these reactions per se but rather is adapting to the natural reactions from the repetition of fight-or-flight responses. In the same way that attachment issues set the stage for interactions in future relationships (Johnson, 2004), we believe that most of these coping behaviors and use of power in reactivity do not come from the individual personality but rather the need to achieve identity and safety. When speaking about lack of or violations in the areas of trustworthiness, it is as if the individual is asking, "What must I do now that I know that relationships are not safe?" Driven by a "fight" response to the stress and pain caused by this realization, the controller moves to make sure that he or she depends on no one. One of the hallmarks of those who depend on control behaviors to achieve safety is in fact that they make themselves *invulnerable* to others and do not depend on anyone in relationships. Take, for instance, the following

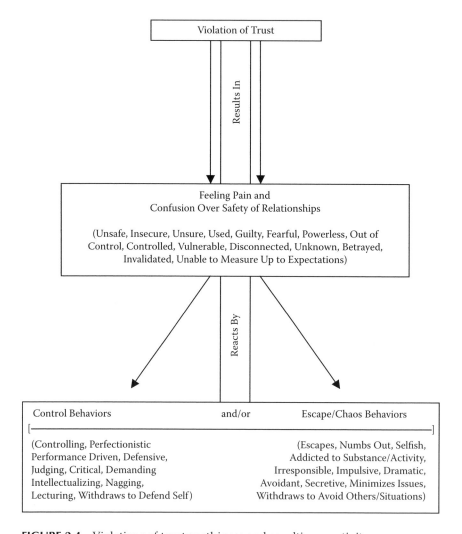

FIGURE 2.4 Violations of trustworthiness and resulting reactivity.

statement by a 26-year-old single female graduate student as evidence for this characteristic:

> If there is one thing that I have learned in my life is that you can depend on no one but yourself. Sure, I would like to have a family and get married one day, but I will make sure that I depend on no one. When my parents divorced, I learned that no matter what people say about being there and standing beside you, it is basically not true. You are on your own, and you better learn quickly to adjust to the fact that depending on people will only bring you heartache and disappointment.

When a person decides to engage in this type of control behavior, it is as if he or she is saying that relationships and the dependency and intimacy that they require are too risky and will likely only result in pain. As a result, the controller only depends on him- or herself and rarely engages in any behavior that would make him or her dependent on another or open and transparent with another individual. Any type of relationships the controller engages in is usually guarded, with the controller dictating the ways that things will be accomplished in terms of tasks and the level of intimacy that will be achieved. Being invulnerable and not depending on relationships often leads these controllers to be overresponsible and perfectionistic in their lives. Controllers are often given positive feedback for these behaviors, especially in the spheres of school and work. This makes sense particularly in the light that controllers not only do not allow themselves to become vulnerable in relationships but also make themselves invulnerable in any area that may pose a threat, such as finances or evaluation. Controllers are most often responsible in paying bills and keeping themselves financially protected. They have a knack for finding out exactly what is expected of them in performance situations and then exceeding those standards to protect themselves from any negative feedback. As they are reinforced positively for these behaviors, they lean and depend increasingly on being in control as a way of life and safety.

While society as a whole may give controllers positive feedback, those who must work in close proximity or be in a relationship with this type of reactivity often find it intolerable. The invulnerability and perfectionism that the controller uses to protect him- or herself from lack of safety also often turn to attitudes and behaviors that are judgmental, critical, demanding, and nagging. This only stands to reason as the person who uses control behaviors does so to protect from a perceived lack of safety. The way that he or she protects him- or herself is to do things alone and at a standard that exceeds perceived threat levels. It makes sense, then, that another individual could seldom perform a task well enough to match the standards of the controller because of the way the controller sees him- or herself as the only one worthy of dependence. As a result, the person who works with or is in a relationship with the controller is under constant scrutiny and evaluation because he or she is a potential safety threat for the controller. Such was the case with a 39-year-old married male without children:

> I don't want to depend on anyone because it just causes too much anxiety that eventually overwhelms me. If my wife pays the bills, I have to worry if she paid them correctly, got the amounts right, and protected our financial information. If I have to give anything to anyone at work, I'm always concerned if they are performing the job right or doing to my standard. As a result, I'm always checking, and invariably, I find mistakes or at least things that I would prefer be done differently. I know that people and my wife perceive me as someone who cannot be pleased and is a micromanager, and maybe that is true. I just know that I can't deal with the anxiety of not knowing exactly what is being done. I really don't know if I could ever tolerate being a father because I know that kids are bound to make mistakes. I just hate opening myself up to that possibility.

As in this illustration, it is important to remember that the controller is simply trying to achieve a sense of security and safety. He or she has judged any relationship as a threat to the ability to maintain that type of security; therefore, he or she is in a constant state of reassuring him- or herself by the amount of control over the situation. As we have seen before, control is generally a positive attribute in human agency and the positive use of power because it attests to an individual's ability to interact and change situations. What is different in this type of control behavior as a result of self-reactivity is that it uses power to become, in essence, all powerful in any given situation. It is the use of power without any interaction and dependence; instead, control is only sought for one's own safety at the expense of the control, power, and efficacy of others. Control and power are good things when used so the individual can be active, organized, and assertive but become harmful when that same control is taken from another individual. In most cases, controllers responding to self-reactivity will absolutely demand that things be done their way and up to their standards. If things are not done to their standards, they often react by withdrawal from the relationship. This characteristic is seen in the following statement by a 25-year-old student:

I never like to work on a group project with anyone. It is just less work for me if I do everyone's work myself. I prefer it that way because I don't want to open myself up to their mistakes or have to check on them. That is the way I am in relationships also. If you don't like the way I do things, then don't let the door hit you on the way out of my life because I'm not changing. I do it this way because it is the only way I am comfortable.

Another way that people who protect themselves from perceived lack of safety in relationships through control behaviors is to be performance driven. Typical of this type of performance-driven behavior is the wish by someone to absolutely ensure that that there is no perceived vulnerability in terms of safety. If, for example, the controller determines that he or she could be safe by having a financial savings account of $10,000, he or she would likely work to achieve the goal. But, after the goal was achieved, he or she would discover that the financial vulnerability still existed. He or she would feel driven perhaps to double the amount of money to $20,000. Of course, no matter how much money the controller saved, he or she would still feel vulnerable and then have expectations about how he or she should handle or invest the money. In other words, each step of performance with the money sets the stage for a more complicated and higher performance level. Controllers often find this performance double bind with finances, achievement, education, status, and career, just to name a few areas of struggle. At each new rung of performance achievement, the controller finds that there is no more a sense of safety than at the previous rung. But, instead of going back or assuming that the pursuit of performance is futile, the controller will often press on to a higher performance level, hoping that the next rung will provide the sense of security, safety, and lack of anxiety that is sought.

Often, people who are performance driven not only are seeking safety but also are driven because of the lack of identity that accompanies shaming oneself. In this dynamic, the individual believes that he or she may be able to achieve some type of identity by performing to a level that brings some type of recognition. For instance, the following is the story of a 55-year-old mother of two adolescent children who is a classic performance-driven controller:

I always feel terrible about myself. I keep thinking that if I can just remake myself, then I will feel better. First, it was being married. If I could just get married, then I could be assured that I was loveable. Then, it was mothering. If I could just love and nurture my boys well enough, then my life would mean something. Then, it was education. If I could just get my degree, then I would be okay. Then, it was getting a master's degree. Now, it is about a job. I've spent my life trying to perform my way out of feeling bad about myself.

As illustrated by this woman's story, performance-driven behavior does not satisfy the drive for identity any more than the drive for achievement satisfies the need for safety. The controller eventually learns that the performance or achievement never stands on its own in a cumulative manner and never achieves peace. In essence, when an individual tries to control his or her sense of safety or identity through performance, the individual is only as good as his or her last performance or achievement. Because the control behavior comes from anxiety about the lack of safety and security, the behavior in and of itself cannot and does not satisfy. Relationships and circumstances are not totally safe, and the controller can never make them so by his or her performance or achievement. Human agency and proper use of control and power are not intended to provide total safety or guaranteed results; rather, they are to provide an environment that is predictable in which the individual may give and take from another and he or she can be open and vulnerable in an intimate way. In short, it is not so much about the results to be achieved as the way the individuals work through the process with another.

Controllers often look domineering, unfeeling, and unsympathetic. Although they often look anxious, they also may intellectualize interactions to the point at which it appears that they are untouched by emotion. In our experience, this type of intellectualization is often simply a result of protecting oneself from the vulnerability of intimate expression or openness. In other words, intellectualization is often a way for the controller to hide from intimacy and keep his or her sense of self secretive. But, whether the control behavior manifests itself as invulnerability, judgmental or critical behavior, performance-driven behavior, or intellectualization, the controller is simply trying to cope with deep primary feelings related to pain. These individuals look tough and protected, but in reality they have the same types of vulnerabilities, pain, insecurities, powerlessness, disconnection, invalidation, and sense of failure that all have who suffer from violations of trustworthiness.

Escape/Chaos Behaviors

Controllers answer the question, "What must I do now that I know that relationships are not safe?" by basically saying that they will make it safe for themselves by depending on no one. People who engage in escape/chaos behaviors come to a different conclusion that is primarily driven by a flight response in the brain. Their conclusion is that there is no successful way that they can make the relationship or situation safe for themselves, so they either seek an escape from the situation or relationship or consent to the powerlessness of failing to try to succeed or be intimate. It is as if the person who engages in escape/chaos behaviors proclaims, "There is no way that I can have any effect on this situation, and it will produce pain for me, so the best that I can do is avoid or numb the pain." As a result, the main feature of the escaper/chaos producer is one of disconnection from the relationship or situation. The thought of having the abilities, talents, or gifts to be able to engage in a situation or relationship seems impossible or distant. In short, these types of people simply give up and do not try. This not only robs the person of any chance for identity but also makes intimacy in relationships almost impossible. For instance, a 16-year-old male described how he reacted when people were talking to him about his academic performance:

> As soon as anyone starts talking—Mom, Dad, the teacher, or whoever—it is like by the end of the first sentence all their words turn to nothing. I am tuned out and only listening for the next time to say yes or no so I can stop the conversation. All I want to do is get away because I know that I won't be able to please whoever is talking.

Of course, with this type of disconnection, you find that the person who engages in escape/chaos behaviors produces a tremendous amount of irresponsibility. This characteristic, more than any other, makes this reactive choice unmanageable and chaotic. It is not that the person lacks strengths, gifts, or talents; simply, the person is convinced that he or she cannot succeed in making the relationship safe or successful and therefore does not try or tries little. People in relationships with escaper/chaos producers—including therapists—get frustrated in these situations and tend to write the person off as uncaring, uncooperative, lazy, unmanageable, and hopeless. As a result of these kinds of responses and their own disconnection, people who resort to escape/chaos behaviors in the face of lack of safety rarely achieve any type of safety in relationships or even intimacy at any significant level.

Escapers/chaos producers, because they do not deal with the pain directly, also have a tendency to escape or anesthetize the emotional pain that they feel. At the low end of coping, this may result in a person seeking relief from the discomfort by engaging in escape behaviors such as sleeping, shopping, or eating too much, to list a few examples. At more serious levels of escape, the person may depend on a substance like alcohol or a drug or behavior like gambling or viewing pornography to escape the painful primary emotions. At the most serious levels, the escaper/chaos producer may be into full-blown addictive behavior, uncontrollable impulsive behavior, or disassociation. Addictive behavior may show up in any of the coping reactivity previously seen, but people with escape/chaos behaviors are particularly prone to use substances or behaviors that can easily lead to addiction. A 63-year-old woman with five adult children recounted her life of escape/chaos:

> I never can remember having one situation that I thought I could stand up to on my own. My whole life was difficult—painful. It just became easier to take the edge off that pain by drinking a little or taking something. Pretty soon, anything that was a problem was a cause to drink or drug more. It could be something big like losing a job or something small like one of my kids having trouble at school. One day you wake up and realize that the alcohol or drug has you—instead of you using it to stay in control, it is controlling you. All the time you wasted now just adds up to realizing that you are going to waste even more of your life.

People who tend toward this coping and reactivity usually have characteristics of impulsivity and secretiveness. Escapers/chaos producers often report that they are not aware of the reasons they do things or the reasoning behind the choices that they make. This is consistent with the idea that they are reacting because of the natural flight reaction of the brain in an effort to protect. They do not analyze situations in terms of consequences or long-term effect because the analysis itself produces pain, anxiety, and lack of safety. Therefore, they often make decisions that reflect impulsivity. Such was the case of a 59-year-old male who made the decision to drink after a session with the therapist:

> I just don't want to think about those types of things. I don't want to think about my past or talk about my problems. Whenever we talk about serious things, all I can really think about is how much I want to get drunk.

Indeed, just after the session the client did get drunk and only told the therapist in the next session. The same lack of reflection on consequences or long-term effects that drives impulsivity in escapers/chaos producers is the thing that also drives the secrecy. It is not that the person knows nothing about him- or herself or chooses not to share with anyone, it is primarily that the person does not engage in reflection long enough to gain a sense of understanding. Most report that the reflection on who they are or what they do produces triggers to the primary emotions that are so powerful that they immediately move to some type of escape or chaos behavior. A controller will typically be secretive or not open in relationships because it is a chosen way to defend him- or herself. An escaper/chaos producer, on the other hand, will likely be secretive because he or she wants to avoid the feelings and relationship altogether because of the potential for pain.

It is hard for people who do not cope in this manner to understand the reactive behavior because it appears to be so self-destructive. We would be careful to point out, however, that the escaper/chaos producer is no less destructive in relationships than the controller. While it may be true that the consequences that the escaper/chaos producer inflicts are socially more unacceptable, both types of self-reactivity produce people who are not intimate, imbalanced in the natural give-and-take in relationships, and not open with others. Both are driven by pain and lack of emotional safety and security. Controllers simply are more demanding and organized in the way that they require others to adjust to their coping behaviors; escapers/chaos producers have few expectations but tend to produce big messes that require the time and effort from others to compensate for the irresponsibility.

Withdrawal Is Common but Different

From a contextual framework, common reactions to violations or imbalances are threats, manipulation, and withdrawal (i.e., Boszormenyi-Nagy et al., 1991; Boszormenyi-Nagy & Krasner, 1986). We feel that threats usually reflect blaming others or controlling behavior, while manipulation is more representative of shaming the self or escape/chaos behaviors (Hargrave & Pfitzer, 2003). However, one of the behaviors common to all four self-reactive styles is withdrawal. Most psychotherapists would assume that withdrawal is always associated with protection of oneself, but we find that this idea is much too broad to encompass the variations in behaviors that we find in the different types of self-reactivity.

The intent of withdrawal is different from one coping style to the next. For instance, when we clinically find withdrawal by a person in a self-reactive style of blaming others, we most often find it is with the intent of punishing others. In other words, the withdrawal itself is part of the aggressive, threatening, or retaliatory style the individual uses to cope with his or her pain. Such was the case of this 69-year-old man; he was describing his withdrawal:

> My children want me to be more involved with them and their children. Well, all I have to say is that the phone lines go both ways. I don't need them as much as they need me. I don't need to talk with them, and I am just fine without them. They will get the idea sooner or later that if they want me to be involved, they are going to have to contact me more regularly. I can wait them out just fine until they get it.

Individuals who shame themselves because of self-reactivity, on the other hand, usually do not withdraw to punish but rather to pout or sulk in their own emotional unhappiness. It is as if the shamer desires someone or some situation to know how badly he or she hurts, and if discovered, then the someone will make efforts to reassure or make the shamer feel better. Shamers usually do not want someone to take some form of punishment, but they do want someone to take the responsibility to try to make them feel better about themselves. People who are in relationships with individuals who shame themselves usually report that when the shamer withdraws, it looks manipulative, pitiful, and weak.

In terms of controlling behaviors, withdrawal is usually done with the effort to defend oneself. Controllers are trying to cope with the pain of lack of safety by managing their vulnerability in such a way that their risks are minimized and they have the most power possible in their situations. In many cases when the controller feels that he or she cannot manage such a risk or cannot maintain power, the controller will withdraw to protect him- or herself. This is reflective of the following statement from a 58-year-old man speaking about his wife:

> She is going to say what she is going to say no matter what. I simply just let her go on, and in the end, I will do what I want anyway. There is no use arguing with her over any detail because she is not going to change me, and I doubt if I'm going to change her. I'm there, but I'm not listening.

The last style of self-reactivity is escape/chaos behavior. In the other reactive styles, the withdrawal not only may be literal but also may be representative of emotional withdrawal, such as silence or ignoring behavior. In escape/chaos behavior, the withdrawal is almost always physical because the intent is to avoid the relationship or the situation. Escapers simply want to avoid the situation or relationship as an extension of their desire to escape the pain or intensity of the situation. Intimacy, responsibility, connection, and openness are all impossible if the individual is not present, and escapers use withdrawal to keep the pain of emotional involvement at a minimum.

Fight, Flight, or Both

It is essential for the psychotherapist who is seeking to understand and assess a patient accurately to understand that it is not uncommon for patients to have experienced violations of both love and trustworthiness. In addition, it is also common for patients to have cyclical behaviors of both fight and flight responses in different situations. For example, it is common for people who feel a lack of identity to cope in a reactive way of shaming themselves and then blaming others. We call this phenomenon *turnstiling* (Hargrave & Pfitzer, 2003) because the process continues in a patterned way in which the patient will blame others vigorously and then turn to themselves, shame themselves, and not hold others to any responsibility. This cyclical pattern is usually predictable and goes back and forth at the extremes (Hargrave & Pfitzer, 2003). This turnstiling behavior is evident in the story of a 30-year-old father of one child:

> I don't know how I feel since it is so erratic. There are times that I can't believe the things that I do with my anger, and I am absolutely convinced that I am no damn good. Then, something happens like my child disrespects me or something unfair happens on the job, and I am so angry I could burst. I yell and scream and threaten. Frankly, I make an ass of myself. Then, I am right back into the remorse and regret over who I am and what I have done. I don't know whether I am angry, raging, ashamed, or guilty.

When we think about this man's story, it is important that we see that he indeed was coping in a reactive way with both blame and shame. He turnstiles his behavior quickly from shaming himself and all the guilt and negativity that it brings to his identity to blaming others with condemning, threatening, and aggressive behavior. He will be convinced that he *feels* angry, guilty, or shameful. In the restoration model, however, we would see that these things that he defines as confusion over what he feels are not the basis of feeling. Rather, the anger, guilt, and shame are what he does in response to the threat of not being clear about his identity (not being loved) and not feeling safe (not being in a trustworthy situation). Pay careful attention to his story: He stated that the things that touched him off into such behavior were his child expressing disrespect or something unfair occurring on his job. Disrespect from his child likely hits the chord that he is not loved and throws his identity into distress, while unfairness on the job makes him feel that he is threatened or unsafe. In short, his primary feelings are that he is unloved and unsafe, which he then plays out by mobilizing self-reactivity, which is sequentially both blaming of others and shaming of self. What the man thinks he feels is actually tied up more with how he is reacting and behaving in using power.

It is not surprising that the man was confused about what he felt because many therapists would also report this same confusion. In actuality, however, the restoration framework helps us easily locate the primary emotion that the man felt as well as make sense of his sequence of coping and self-reactivity to feeling unloved and unsafe. Of course, an individual may simply tend to cope and react by either shaming self or blaming others, but this type of turnstiling by doing both is common. On the other axis of responding to violations of trustworthiness by controlling behavior or escape/chaos behavior, turnstiling also may occur but seems to be less common. When it does occur, individuals usually report that they feel a sense that they will "pull themselves together" followed by a sense of discouragement and disempowerment. Such was the case of a 35-year-old woman who struggled with her lack of direction in life:

> There are times where I really pull it together and get on track for my life. I start hanging out with the right kind of people, enroll in a class to complete my education, start exercising and eating right; I'll even continue with these things sometimes for months at a time. Then, something will happen that will close down my heart with discouragement. I will feel that no matter what I do or what I have done, I am just kidding myself, and that life will not allow me to succeed. I will see the whole task of getting my stuff together as too big, and so I will let everything go. I isolate and hide from people, drink too much, and shut down. I will just numb myself out for weeks and sometimes months, then I will pull it all together again for another try. When I am disciplined, I am great, but when I am not, I ruin my life. At this point, I have accomplished only half of what I should have.

As psychotherapists, most of us would likely affirm that this woman spends a good portion of her life functioning in a healthy and responsible manner. However, from a restoration therapy standpoint, we would likely assess this woman as having a turnstiling behavior between control and escape/chaos. When she is being responsible and enrolling in school, it is likely not because she feels safe and is working toward using her power to secure agency for herself or others; rather, it is likely that she is reacting out of fear that life is unsafe, and the only way that she can protect herself is to perform well and become more competent. She, in fact, tries to make herself invulnerable to relationships instead of using her power to advance and participate in intimacy. When she gets discouraged or overwhelmed, it is that she has judged her coping of controlling behaviors as inadequate to deal with the difficulty of life. She then swings to the other extreme of coping and reactivity with the flight behavior of escape/chaos. The restoration therapist will see that neither her control nor escape/chaos is a particularly healthy coping mechanism, and both reactions come from self-reactivity. To accurately understand this woman's behavior, the psychotherapist must understand the primary emotion that this woman feels in terms of life and relationships not being safe and trustworthy. Tracking and assessing this emotion allow the therapist not to be misguided by seeing controlling behaviors as functional and "good" while the escape/chaos behaviors are dysfunctional and "bad."

We have mentioned that love and trustworthiness always have a mutually informing capability. In other words, what I feel about myself and my identity informs how I perceive relationships, and the interactions I gain from relationships inform me about my identity. It makes sense, then, that as a result of this interaction, I may mix and match the coping and reactivity behaviors in response to feelings of lack of love or trustworthiness. A person who suffers from questions of identity or safety may cope by using just one of the behaviors or any combination of two or three or all four behaviors. For instance, it is not uncommon for a person who copes with lack of love by shaming him- or herself to try to perform well enough into identity. In fact, he or she would be coping initially using a shame response followed by a controlling behavior. Even though the violation with this individual may have originated from a feeling of being unloved, the individual sought to cope by turning to a controlling behavior to manage future relationships in the hope that it would suffice for the feeling of being loved or prove the individual lovable. In working from the restoration perspective, it is essential that the psychotherapist accurately assess not only the primary coping mechanism or reactivity of the patient but also all secondary or systemic coping mechanisms that person uses to gain complete therapeutic understanding.

61

A CAUTION AND FINAL WORD ON ASSESSMENT

Boszormenyi-Nagy and Krasner (1986) detailed contextual therapy as a multidimensional approach to therapy that includes facts, individual psychology, systemic interactions, and relational ethics. In making assessments concerning patients, it is always important to keep in mind that individuals and systems carry this characteristic of multidimensionality. There are, in other words, genetic, cultural, socioeconomic, societal, and historical factors that affect individuals and relationships. We believe that the psychotherapist cannot ignore these different dimensions in favor of only looking at violations of love and trustworthiness. We believe that there are genetic and possibly chemical influences on identity, safety, and subsequent behaviors. We also believe that individuals are deeply influenced by the systems around them in social networks and culture. As we have stated in other places, we see that subjective influences on individuals through their own psychology and family relational ethics greatly affect the more objectifiable influences in individuals through their factual makeups and systemic interactions and vice versa (Hargrave & Pfitzer, 2003). These dimensions and mutual influences must be given due consideration in therapy, and there are ample examples in the literature of how to assess these different aspects or dimensions.

We believe, however, that the restoration framework is a way to accurately identify, understand, and assess the pain and stress that an individual experiences in terms of the most basic of human needs: love and trustworthiness. We are not making a case that precludes a psychotherapist from doing a complete assessment of the patient's health, influences, and background but rather making a case for accurately understanding the dynamic influences of love and trustworthiness on the client. While it may be true that we hold these elements as most essential in the assessment of the patient, we also believe that it is essential to give attention to these multidimensional influences.

3

The Process of Pattern

INTRODUCTION

If you go to any local gymnasium, you will no doubt find a variety of people engaged in a process at distinctly different stages. You may observe any activity you wish—weight lifting, cardioaerobic activity, yoga, running, or some type of competitive sport—and if you watch long enough, you will observe beginners, intermediates, and experts at the process. Even though they are engaged in the same or a similar activity, if you observe beginners as opposed to experts, you will see a different process. Beginners will be slower, less efficient, and generally less fluid in their routines, while the experts will work quickly, have no wasted activity, and look sharp in their exercises or activities.

It is not that beginners have no talent for physical activity and experts are particularly endowed with the same; the bulk of the separation in the performance is based on learning and practice. *Learning* is a broad term that describes a relatively enduring form of change in knowledge or behavior based on experience (Hockenbury & Hockenbury, 2000). As we have seen, when an action or what is learned is practiced repeatedly, it is processed into the brain in such a way that the behavior and action are automatic or effortless (Siegel, 2007). The reason that an expert at any gym activity is an expert is because he or she has learned and practiced the activity until it has become automatic.

The same is true when we start talking about the activities associated with the core feelings of identity and safety. We posit that these ideas of meaning are much like the process we go through while learning and practicing at the gym. Our brains use a series of neuronal firings to produce thoughts, experiences, and images. An image, for instance, does not exist in our mind in reality; rather, a series of neuronal firings produces a sequence by which we can think about and even experience the image with our five senses as if we actually do have an image in our mind (Siegel, 2007). Our brain, as it experiences new behaviors, images, and experiences, moves those images into our long-term memories. As our brain accumulates more images and experiences, it classifies each image and experience of learning into familiar categories and classifications so that these can be quickly accessed by us in the future for our own understanding and reaction (Kosslyn, 2005). As a result, the way that we have learned to think about ourselves and the trustworthiness and safety of relationships becomes a practiced and automatic response. If we think of ourselves as unloved and unsafe in relationships, we most readily recall those images to mind from our experiences whenever we encounter a new stimulus that would indicate an unloving or untrustworthy environment. Further, once we have those images that affect our identities and safety, the pain and stress produce a reactivity or coping that we practice repeatedly. Soon in our lives if we come from a history of violations of love or trustworthiness, we become practiced experts in calling to mind not only the images of being unloved and unsafe but also how to perform the self-reactivity of blame, shame, control, and escape/chaos.

We believe that this imagery, experience, practice, and automatic reaction happen at an individual level, but we also believe that this process and pattern take place at a relational or systemic level. In other words, we find ourselves in relationships—by design or by chance—that tend to develop the same learning patterns, images, and experiences that produce practiced and automatic responses in the relationships. Our goal in this chapter is not only to delineate some of those common process patterns that happen individually but also to detail some of the emotional processes behind some of the more well-known process patterns found in relationships.

INDIVIDUAL PROCESS

Whether the individual is in the framework of being in a loving and trustworthy situation that produces a power response of agency or an unloving and untrustworthy relationship that produces a power response of self-

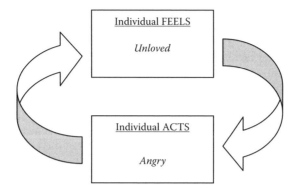

FIGURE 3.1 The destructive cyclical process of individual feeling and behavior.

reactivity, the common component to each is that the individual *feels* something with regard to identity and safety and then *acts* with some intention. As seen in Figure 3.1, an individual might feel unloved, insignificant, and alone. If that individual were a blamer in the framework found in Figure 2.2, he or she might be angry, sarcastic, retaliatory, and threatening.

We can see from Figure 3.1 how the very thing that the individual does to cope with primary feelings of pain reinforces the likelihood of that type of feeling recurring. For instance, in this example, the more this individual acts in a manner that is angry, sarcastic, and threatening, the more likely it will be not only that he or she will get information from relationships that is negative but also that the behavior will confirm to the person that he or she is indeed unloved, insignificant, and alone. It is not just feedback from others; the action from the individual is self-reciprocating (Balswick, King, & Reimer, 2005) and reinforces the feeling with which he or she is trying to cope.

This same phenomenon is true when we speak of human agency and the individual feels a sense of love, trustworthiness, and resulting peace and comfort as found in Figure 2.1. For instance, Figure 3.2 illustrates what happens when an individual feels a sense that he or she is loved, valued, and accepted. When this individual feels these things, he or she is free to act in ways that are consistent with agency and are nurturing, loving, and accepting in relationships. The more the individual acts in nurturing, loving, and accepting ways in his or her relationships, the more he or she will gain reinforcement through personal behavior and that of others that he or she is loved, valued, and accepted. The first systemic lesson that the

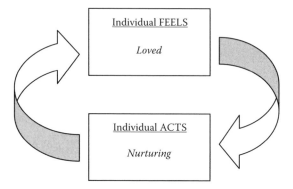

FIGURE 3.2 The constructive cyclical process of individual feeling and behavior.

restoration therapist learns in dealing with the individual who is in either severe pain or peace is that the way the individual acts reinforces the very feeling that prompts the behavior.

As stated in Chapter 2, there are individuals who feel a violation in love or trustworthiness and move to singular reactivity or coping. It is common, however, for the individual to have more complex reactivity involving any combination of blaming, shaming, control, or escape/chaos. It is essential to remember that the meanings that an individual derives from lack of safety and lack of love also mutually inform one another. For instance, if the individual feels that he or she is loved, nurtured, significant, and valued, then those beliefs enhance the likelihood that the person is loved, nurtured, significant, and valued and affect the person's feelings of confidence, power, and success in relationships. In other words, if he or she feels loved, then he or she will likely feel much safer in relationships and vice versa. These derived meanings in these two areas of identity and safety are determining factors in the individual's self-efficacy (Bandura, 1997).

The same is true for those who have a weak sense of identity and feel unloved, unwanted, insignificant, and devalued. The individual who associates these meanings with him- or herself will likely question whether he or she is capable of meeting relational expectations and feel powerless, unsafe, and disconnected. The violation in one area of love or trustworthiness is capable of triggering the feeling or question of meaning or safety in the other (Hargrave & Pfitzer, 2003). As a result, we see individuals who have a primary violation that is identifiable in either love or trustworthiness having self-reactivity or coping in all four areas. As such, the therapist must take care not only to understand clearly each individual's past and history of violations of love and trustworthiness, but also to delineate clearly each reactive and coping behavior and its corresponding reinforcement to the primary emotions. With that said, we can point to some common process patterns of coping as a way of illustrating how this delineation can take place.

Shaming Self and Control Behaviors

We see shaming self/control behavior as one of the most common individual patterns of coping and self-reactivity. Usually, the patient has experienced a violation of love that has led him or her to cope using the shame mechanism. The individual would typically shame him- or herself by condemnation of self as having no worth, being unlovable, or being worthless or defective. Further, the person would be somewhat depressed, negative, and inconsolable. These individuals, however, find another reactive mechanism to manage the deep feelings of pain by seeking to control their pain and identity. It is as if the person who experiences the shame says to him- or herself or is given the following message by an important caregiver: "If I perform well enough or am perfect enough, then people will love and accept me, and I can believe I am lovable." As a result, the individuals with this two-step coping reactivity usually drive themselves hard to gain increasing recognition, accomplishments, or perfection.

Although this type of controller usually does not have the full-blown features of judging and being critical of others' performance—a quality that is likely born of their shame—they nevertheless are controlling of their own performance or tasks. The problem with this type of coping by the exercise of control to deal with the feelings of shame is two-fold. First, if worth is based on performance, then the person is only as worthy as his or her last performance. In other words, the person who feels unloved or unwanted does not try to address the real issue but instead tries to cover it or convince him- or herself otherwise by controlling behavior and performance. If the accomplishments or perfection stops, then it means that the person returns to exactly the same primary feelings of pain. The shamer/controller knows this bind well and therefore usually seeks increasing accomplishments or perfection. This invariably leads to the second problem with these individuals trying to deal with their shame through performance or perfection: The drive to do more produces a tremendous amount of fear and anxiety. Besides the anxiety of always having to do more, bigger, and better, most of the individuals who work from this combination of reactivity have a deep fear of being "found out" by others as a fraud. They believe that they are unloved, unworthy, and defective. The accomplishment or effort is unable to commute a change in this sense of identity, and the fear that these individuals feel is very real. They believe that it is only a matter of time before others will discover that they are indeed unlovable and unworthy. This anxiety and fear then begin to drive the primary feelings that relationships are not safe and are untrustworthy. Figure 3.3 shows a possible individual process and pattern of this sequence.

Notice in Figure 3.3 that the behavior and feelings, even though they are more complex, are again self-reciprocating in that the individual tries to cope with the feelings of being unloved using a reactive combination of shaming and controlling feelings and behaviors. Although there might be variations in the types of specific feelings and actions of a person who uses this combination of reactivity and coping, there is an identifiable process and sequence as the individual proceeds from the primary feelings to the specific coping behaviors of self-reactivity. The therapist using

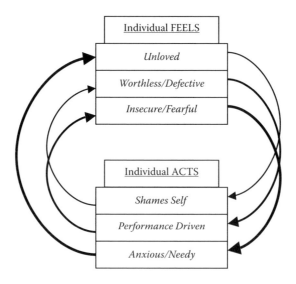

FIGURE 3.3   The process pattern of shames self/control behavior.

the restoration model of therapy will be careful to delineate and understand this sequence to be able to follow the patient's individual process and pattern.

Controlling Behaviors/Blaming Others

Another pattern that we see often in the process of therapy involves individuals who seek to cope with feeling a lack of identity or feeling unsure of relationships by controlling behaviors/blaming others. Figure 3.4 is an illustration of this type of process and pattern. Most individuals we see using this coping framework start out with a deep sense of violation or betrayal in terms of relational trustworthiness. In response to the primary feelings of lack of safety, they move to counter by being controlling and perfectionistic in terms of their attitudes and behaviors. However, these individuals quickly run into relationships or circumstances that are beyond their control or are threatened by the control of others. In response, they often report feeling vulnerable or out of control. Since they find that they have limited power, they often try to control others by being particularly critical and demanding,

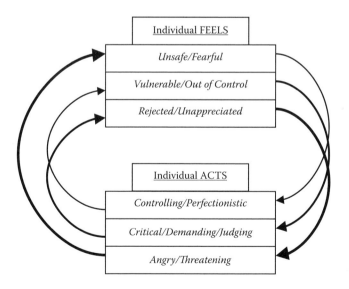

FIGURE 3.4   The process pattern of control behaviors/blaming others.

which can often lead to these individuals also considered judgmental or nagging.

As one can imagine, this demanding and judgmental behavior does not fair well for the individual in relationships or situations such as a job or career. People simply do not respond to the implication that they are somehow lacking and respond even more negatively correction. This often prompts the person who is a controller/blamer to have the primary emotion that deals with lack of love or, as in Figure 3.4, a distinct feeling of being rejected and unappreciated. Many times, controllers/blamers report that they do not understand why people respond to them the way that they do. After all, they reason, they are just expressing their opinions and trying to be helpful. They usually experience these feelings of rejection and unappreciative behavior as an assault to their identities. From there, they often turn to blaming behavior and are often angry, arrogant, fault finding, aggressive, and threatening.

This blaming behavior, however, does nothing to address the primary emotional violation of safety. It does, in fact, reinforce the individual's belief that people and situations are unreliable, threatening, and unsafe. Again, Figure 3.4 is simply one illustration of how this pattern takes shape with an individual; there are variations in the specific feelings and behaviors. However, the common thread to this type of self-reactivity is the controlling behavior and the eventual blaming of others when it is impossible to control every circumstance.

Shaming Self/Escape/Chaos Behavior

A common process and pattern that we see with individuals who tend to have violations of both love and trustworthiness is shaming the self and escape/chaos behavior. Because the process may start with a feeling of being either unloved or unsafe, the sequence of feelings and behaviors becomes somewhat interchangeable. However, this pattern of shaming self/escape/chaos behaviors can often lead to volatile, unstable, and dangerous behavior. Figure 3.5 illustrates what happens to a shamer/escaper who initially feels a sense that he or she is worthless, defective, or unacceptable. As often is the case, the individual integrates these primary feelings and is self-reactive, using shaming behavior exhibited by negativity and depression. These behaviors also stimulate individual feelings of powerlessness and the inability to measure up to any expectations in relationships. Notice that actions that flowed from the self-reactivity to

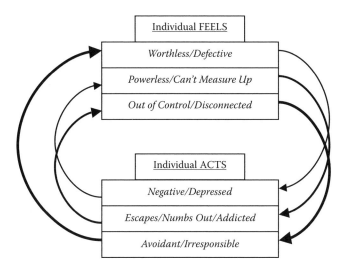

FIGURE 3.5 The process pattern of shaming self/escape/chaos behaviors.

the primary emotions that dealt with identity stimulated feelings of lack of trustworthiness and questions of safety or security in relationships. When the shamer/escaper feels these primary emotions of powerlessness and hopelessness in never being able to meet expectations, it often triggers the irresponsible, chaotic, escape response. In the case of Figure 3.5, the individual may escape the expectations or "life" in general by numbing behavior or perhaps by slipping into some type of addictive behavior (i.e., drinking, taking drugs, viewing pornography, etc.). However, since the shamer/escaper is not dealing with the reality of the issues, he or she tends to be irresponsible in relationships and undependable in situations. This likely stimulates the feelings that he or she is out of control, disconnected, and alone. Instead of confronting the irresponsibility, the shamer/escaper is likely to drift into avoidant or withdrawing behaviors and to be further irresponsible in relationships.

This particular pattern of self-reactivity can become unstable quickly because of two potential issues. First, the person who numbs him- or herself using behaviors or substances becomes extraordinarily vulnerable to addiction to that behavior or substance. Addictions are tenacious problems that consume the individual both physically and emotionally and usually require specialized treatment to calm the addiction before issues of process and pattern can be addressed successfully. Second, since the person is in a pattern of shaming self and escaping, negativity and depression often worsen. Any depression carries with it the possibility of self-harm, but the shamer/escaper engages in a pattern that tends to spiral downward both emotionally and in terms of responsibility. Many shamers/escapers who engage in self-harm not only are seeking an escape but also are convinced in one way or another that they deserve the punishment and pain of self-harm.

Shaming Self/Blaming Others/Controlling Behaviors/Escape/Chaos Behaviors

Certainly, we want to emphasize that it is likely that individuals might have any combination of self-reactivity and coping behaviors, but shaming self, blaming others, controlling behaviors, escape/chaos seem to be the most common and are good examples of how a therapist would go about the process of delineating the individual's feeling and acting as the therapist seeks to understand the process and pattern of the client. There is, however, one more pattern that we feel obliged to mention in some detail. Although the pattern is not as common as the ones described, it is particularly puzzling and difficult for therapists to decipher. This pattern is one in which the individual is involved in all four forms of self-reactivity (blaming, shaming control, and escape/chaos) and is usually found in individuals who have experienced severe violations of love and trustworthiness, like sexual or physical abuse, victimization through criminal acts, intentional harm, or neglect. An example of this process and pattern is found in Figure 3.6.

All individuals who experience violations of love and trustworthiness are in particular levels of pain, but when an individual ends up feeling this type of complicated pain in most of the areas of primary emotions associated with love and trustworthiness and cope using self-reactivity in all four areas, it truly becomes overwhelming emotion (Hargrave, 1994a). Many times, the primary emotions and coping behaviors become indistinguishable from one another, and most of the time the emotion and behaviors seem contradictory and erratic. As a result, individuals who experience this wide range of emotional injury and three or all four of the reactive coping behaviors often are diagnosed with an Axis II personality disorder.

The individuals who experience these types of feelings and behaviors are not labels or diagnosis; they are human beings who usually have experienced a tremendous amount of pain and disturbance from important

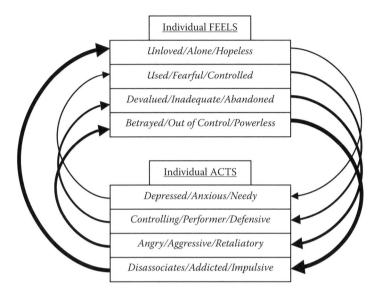

FIGURE 3.6   The process pattern of all four coping behaviors.

relationships, most often associated with primary caregivers. Although we do not rule out the possibilities of organic or genetic causes of personality disturbances, our clinical experiences most often tell us that these types of disorders are usually a result of severe violations of love and trustworthiness. These individuals are in great pain; therefore, therapeutic processes are often slow and difficult as both the therapist and the patient struggle to make sense of violations, reorganize identity and safety issues, and begin formulating plans for stable uses of power.

In the next illustration, a 23-year-old single woman who had been married twice described her life, thereby giving the therapist details of her process and pattern.

> I am overwhelmed with anxiety as I speak with you today. Do you think you can help me, and is there any hope at all for me? I have been to therapy so many times that I cannot count, and always it doesn't help, and the therapist terminates with me. Please tell me that you think I can be helped, and you won't terminate with me.

The woman interacted with the therapist in such a way it indicated extreme anxiety and fearfulness about the process. Although she did not speak directly about her feelings about being unloved, alone, and hopeless, her expressed neediness in the interaction indicated that these were indeed the very things that she felt as she again began therapy. After the therapist offered her some words of reassurance that he would work to make the environment safe enough so that she could tell her story, the woman's emotional tenor changed quickly:

> You had better believe that I have heard that kind of thing before. Every person from my parents, to friends, to husbands, to therapists have told me that they will understand me and stand beside me. I don't see how anyone would ever expect me to trust them again. If you want me to believe you that you are different, you are going to have to prove it with your actions. You want me to trust you with my story and my past, you better just know that you have to earn that trust first.

Notice how the woman obviously felt threatened and unsafe with the therapist's efforts to reassure. Instead of having a calming effect on the woman, she likely felt that the therapist was moving too quickly and might be trying to control her. This caused the woman to shift from the sense that she was unloved to focus on the situation that felt unsafe. This lack of safety in turn likely triggered all the feelings in the past that she had been used and abused by trusting others. From her reactivity, you see her turn to controlling behaviors to dictate aggressively what her expectations were of the therapist and how he would have to prove trustworthiness before she would give him any part of her story. The therapist, who was surprised by the woman's emotional shift and reaction, backed off and told her that she would be in control of what she told the therapist, and that he would not push her to reveal anything. After a discussion back and forth regarding what the therapist would do in terms of listening and giving her space, the woman again quickly shifted her emotional tone and interaction with the therapist:

> Oh well, I guess that is just great for you. I tell you that I need something from you that will show me that you will stand beside me through this work that I have to do, and you give me this "I'm the one in control" bs. I am so sick and tired of therapist talk. Do they train you to say this stuff? Why can't someone just be honest with me and give me some type of response that I can count on? Is that so hard? You will go home to your wife, your kids, and your house after this session, and where will I be? I will be stuck in the same old pain, and you don't really care.

Again, we see the shift of the woman's tone to the threat of her identity. She revealed in this section that she wanted the therapist to provide her with some sense that she was cared for, and when she felt that the therapist did not provide it adequately, she moved into the self-reactivity quadrant of blaming others. She accused the therapist angrily and aggressively not only of not caring about her but also of being insincere in his expression of help. In essence, she put down the therapist and his profession and attacked his identity. The therapist then reflected back to the woman the thoughts and the feelings that he heard her say. The woman continued to speak, but after about 10 minutes her emotional tone started shifting, and she became increasingly distant and quiet.

> This already doesn't feel right [*looks away and stares at the floor*]. I can't believe I already lost it in the first session. Maybe I am crazy [*long pause*]. I don't know how you could ever get to the point where you would believe me. It just all feels hopeless [*long pause*]. I just know I'm going to end up alone.

Here, the woman likely felt the brunt of her lack of control and powerlessness and even mentioned that she could never do anything that would connect with the therapist again. As we look at these pauses, we see them as the woman withdrawing, numbing herself, or possibly disassociating in the session. In this kind of state, what might the woman do? Perhaps she would seek some type of further escape through a substance or behavior or have an impulsive reaction. It is also important to see that the woman predicted her future process and feelings in saying that she would likely end up alone. We see this as a clear indication that she was already contemplating the feelings of being unloved and unwanted again.

One of the things that is amazing about the dialogue of this woman is that it demonstrates how erratic and how quickly emotions and reactivity can shift. Although these feelings were complicated, all were related to the identity and safety issues the woman felt or basic issues of love and trustworthiness. From a restoration therapy model, we see that most of the issues that proceed in individual processes and relationships are related to these two basic issues. We believe that this framework is invaluable to the therapist in understanding and assessing a client or patient.

The restoration therapy model is not opposed to diagnosis as long as the diagnosis of a patient makes sense within the context of love, trustworthiness, and pain. We believe, for instance, that many of the mood disorders originate in the patients' struggle over identity and the self-reactivity of shaming the self. Likewise, we find that many anxiety and eating disorders are related to patients having some questions about safety, trustworthiness, and identity as well as self-reactivity related to controlling behaviors and shaming the self. Threats to safety are also involved, and self-reactivity related to escape/chaos behaviors is often diagnosed in substance-related disorders, dissociative disorders, and impulse control disorders. Personality disorders, psychotic disorders, and many adjustment disorders can have multiple roots in violations of love and trustworthiness as well as self-reactivity or coping coming from one, two, three, or four of the power disturbances detailed in this and previous chapters. Diagnosis, in some cases, can be helpful in multiple forms of treatment for patients and clients as they seek relief from painful emotions and behaviors. Our case here, however, is to point out that assessment is tied not only to diagnosis but also to the understanding of the origins, human beings, and relationships that are connected with the diagnosis.

PROCESS AND PATTERN IN RELATIONSHIPS

There has been much interest in psychology about the unconscious and seeking relationships to fulfill or correct a need, desire, or relationship from the past. Such is the case with psychoanalytic theories and concepts like object relations (i.e., Fairbairn, 1952; Scharff & Scharff, 1987); introjections (Kernberg, 1966); transference (i.e., Bowen, 1978; Freud, 1905); and family myths (Stierlin, 1977). Although there is no doubt that some of these theories are valid in terms of motivations, unconscious urges, and felt obligations, we find much more utility in understanding the basic premise of the restoration model that individuals seek relationships because they are imperative for the way they form identity and a sense of how to interact in safe and trustworthy ways. We believe that, unconscious or not, individuals are dependent on relationships to get a sense of their very being (Hargrave & Pfitzer, 2003).

We do not feel that individuals seek relationships so much because they mimic the behavior of or relationships with their caregivers; rather, we believe that individuals seek all relationships because they need this sense of identity and safety. Human beings are built to seek love (Johnson, 2008) and look for relationships to be trustworthy, balanced, justified, and fulfilling (Hargrave & Pfitzer, 2003). Because all relationships have these characteristics, it is virtually guaranteed that deep and primary relationships will present these issues of identity and safety. Unfulfilled and unmet needs in a relationship with a spouse resembles unfulfilled and unmet needs with a person's primary caregiver not so much because of his or her unconscious as that all relationships in general bring out those needs related to love and trustworthiness. Whenever the relationship is important to an individual, such as a marriage, a deep friendship, or a parenting relationship, the person will be looking for identity and safety, and unmet or unfulfilled issues that have existed in the past will be sensitized in those present relationships.

We are not saying that it is okay for an individual to seek from his or her spouse or child the love and nurturing he or she did not receive from a parent. We are, however, saying that it is normal for those primary emotions surrounding the past to come up in the important relationships of the present. Further, we are saying that the individual is not so much *choosing* relationships that mimic unresolved issues or unprocessed behavior in past relationships (i.e., a man marries a woman just like his mother or ex-wife), but that current relationships simply tend to bring out our unresolved and painful issues. As a result, we can reliably say that the process and pattern that the patient experiences on an individual level will likely be played out also in his or her relationships. Further, the more intense the relationship, we believe the more likely it will be that the process and pattern of the individual will be displayed. In other words, when intensity is up, the way the person has made sense of and coped with identity and safety issues will surface.

With this said, there are common patterns in dyadic relationships that form patterns that have previously been identified in family and systemic therapies. Two types of patterns found in systemic relationships are complimentary and symmetrical relationships (Watzlawick, Bavelas, & Jackson, 1967). In complimentary relationships, the patterns of the partners tend to be at opposite extremes. For example, if one individual is dominant, the other may be submissive. If one is assertive, the other partner may be avoidant. We find that in these types of relationships between relational partners, behavior remains fairly stable because both partners are feeling and doing something different from the other in the relationship. In other words, if one becomes more assertive, the other partner can counter simply by becoming more avoidant, and although frustrating, the relationship stays stable because of the lack of change.

In symmetrical relationships, the pattern of the partners tends to be of the same nature. For instance, if one partner is blaming, the other is also blaming. If one is controlling, the other partner also tends to be controlling. In these relationships, behavior, intensity, and feelings tend to escalate because partners do more of the same behavior.

Complimentary relationships can work together well when the focus of the relationship is constructive, appropriate, and loving and trustworthy. For instance, a parent of a young child may feel loved, fulfilled, and optimistic and therefore parent the child in a manner that is authoritative, instructive, and involved. In return, the young child would likely feel loved, competent, and not alone and would be submissive to the direction of the parent, cooperative with instruction, and intimate/open. Likewise, symmetrical relationships can work well and be positive when the focus of the intensity and escalation are in a loving and trustworthy direction. For instance, imagine lovers interested in showing love to one another and spending quality time with one another. They might reciprocate with increasing numbers of gifts, conversations, and activities that continue to reinforce love and care for one another.

However, in both types of relationships when there is a question of identity and safety in the relationship, complimentary relationships and symmetrical relationships can frustrate and agitate partners, and the relationship itself can reinforce the unloving and untrustworthy behaviors that existed in each partner's past. In short, what one partner does in his or her behavior reinforces the feelings of lack of love and safety, and the other partner's self-reactivity tends to reinforce the lack of love and safety in the first partner. Whether the relationship is complimentary or symmetrical, it is certainly cyclical in terms of producing feelings and behaviors between partners.

These cyclical patterns have been identified in several approaches. For example, integrative behavioral couple therapy has long recognized patterns of mutual coercion (Jacobson & Christensen, 1998) and polarization (Karney & Bradbury, 1995). Emotionally focused couple therapy has identified the central tendency of problems to be maintained by partners consistently responding to attachment injuries by learned behaviors of avoidance or aggression (Johnson, Makinen, & Millikan, 2001). Psychoeducational approaches such as the Practical Application of Intimate Relationship Skills (PAIRS®) tracks the cyclical process in relationships through an emotional "infinity loop" in which a trigger event caused a behavior by a partner that activated emotions, beliefs, and eventual negative behavior in the other partner (DeMaria & Hannah, 2003). In addition, the National Institute of Marriage utilizes a similar cycle that helps partners identify key emotional fears that eventually result in dysfunctional or damaging behaviors directed at the partner, which in turn stimulate fears and behaviors from the partner (Smalley & Paul, 2006).

The restoration therapy model makes use of knowledge of the cyclical process to assist individuals in understanding destructive patterns in relationships (Hargrave, 2010). It is important for the therapist to know not only the process and pattern of the individual but also the process and pattern of the individual in the context of a relationship. In this way, the therapist is assessing not only the intrapsychic process but also the interpsychic or systemic processes. This is essential because we believe that how an individual reacts in relationships is fairly consistent from one setting to the next. We wish to illustrate how these cyclical patterns work within the context of several types of common patterns identified in the literature.

Pursuer/Distancer Pattern

The first illustration of this cyclical pattern in relationships is the *pursuer/distancer* relationship (Guerin, Fay, Burden, & Kautto, 1987). In this pattern, the partners usually have distinct and differing intimacy needs, with the pursuer desiring a close and more emotionally enmeshing relationship, while the distancer values more autonomy and individuality (Hargrave, 2000). In a restoration framework, we might assume that the pursuer in the relationship has difficulty holding a consistent sense of self without having someone to reassure the person of love and affection. As illustrated in Figure 3.7, the individual may initially feel unloved or alone, which may prompt him or her to react or behave toward the partner in such a way that indicates neediness or try to manipulate the partner toward more intimacy. This reactivity, of course, comes from the coping behavior of shaming self.

The distancer in this example would likely feel unsafe as a result of the neediness and manipulation of the pursuer. The distancer might feel that the pursuer will never be satisfied with his or her efforts and actions and might feel somewhat powerless to be able to meet the pursuer's needs. As a result, he or she copes with this pain from escape/chaos behaviors and withdraws to avoid the partner. This action from the distancer leads the pursuer to feel unsafe because he or she cannot control the environment enough to get the intimacy desired. This vulnerability might then cause the pursuer enough pain that he or she would react because of the control behaviors and thereby become critical and

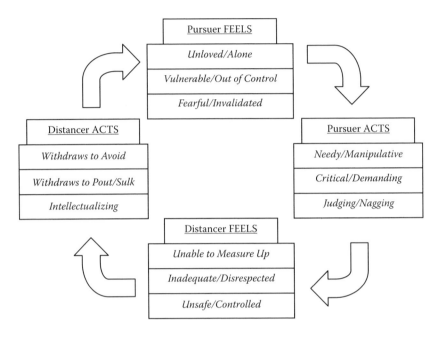

FIGURE 3.7 Process pattern of pursuer/distancer relationship.

demanding of the partner. This further stimulates a cascading negative cycle, which may bring the distancer to the feeling that he or she is inadequate or disrespected. These feelings are associated with the distancer's identity, and in the example, he or she may respond in a shaming self manner and withdraw to pout—hoping that the pursuer would take back the critical and demanding behavior that stimulated the feeling that he or she was not loved.

The reality of withdrawal from a pursuer's perspective, however, is that the partner is actively moving away, and this is likely to cause further threat and pain to the pursuer. As a result, he or she may feel fearful because of the inability to have a relationship with the person he or she desires and will likely feel invalidated by the discrepancy in the give-and-take in the relationship. In short, the relationship will feel not only unloving but also untrustworthy. This might likely stimulate even more reactivity of judging and nagging behavior as the pursuer tries to get the distancer to do as he or she wishes in terms of being close and intimate. The distancer, on the other hand, is likely to feel a further complication of safety as a result of the nagging as he or she begins to tune out the unreasonable and intense behavior. Instead of just giving in to the pursuer or withdrawing, he or she may move to a controlling behavior of intellectualization, by which he or she tells the partner all the things that are unreasonable or wrong about being critical and nagging. This intellectualization, although not withdrawing per se, is a way that leaves the partner emotionally isolated. It also will likely lead to the pursuer feeling small about him- or herself and again result in feelings that he or she is unloved and alone in the relationship.

It is important to remember that this sequence is an example, and there may be many combinations of different feelings and reactivity in the actual pursuer/distancer relationship. Like any complimentary relationship, we see the frustrating nature of the behavior in which the more the pursuer pursues, the more the distancer distances (Guerin et al., 1987). The helpful addition from the restoration model, however, is that there is a set of feelings that both the distancer and the pursuer feel in relation to one another that are interpreted by each as a lack of love or a lack of trustworthiness. Further, the very actions that are taken by each partner because of self-reactivity that are intended to deal or cope with the pain over love and trustworthiness end up violating love and trustworthiness with the partner. In the restoration therapy model, the psychotherapist is seeking to understand not only the pattern of behavior but also the primary emotions and pain that fuel the behavior.

Overfunctioner/Underfunctioner Pattern

In a similar example of a complimentary process and pattern, Figure 3.8 illustrates an overfunctioner/underfunctioner pattern (Guerin et al., 1987). From the restoration therapy perspective, this kind of pattern classically illustrates individuals who are both threatened in terms of safety and trustworthiness and have self-reactivity at the two extremes of control behaviors (overfunctioner) and escape/chaos behaviors (underfunctioner). Many times, this pattern occurs because the relational partners behave in two different ways or have two different personalities. While enlightening, we find that this understanding serves little purpose in promoting change among the partners. For instance, following excerpts are from a 33-year-old husband and wife who are locked into this pattern and only complain about each other's behaviors. These are the comments from the wife:

81

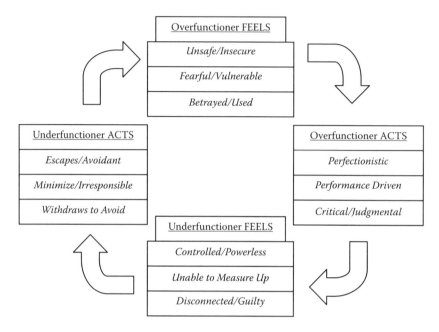

FIGURE 3.8 Process pattern of overfunctioner/underfunctioner relationship.

I know that he must have some reason for not doing what I ask him to do, but at what point do I say that this guy is just incapable of being my partner. He does nothing, and I do everything. It is unfair. If he cared for me just a little, he would do something that I ask him to do. Instead, he is just like pushing string. It may be the way he is, but I'm done.

The husband has a similar focus on the wife's behavior:

I just don't understand why you have to make everything so difficult. Everything has to be done your way, and we always have to be busy. Whenever I do anything, it is redone or critiqued by you. I can say exactly the same thing—that if you cared for me you would stop doing all the time and just be a little of the time. It is not great for me either.

Both partners were cued into the fact that the other person's behavior was driving him or her crazy. The woman (overfunctioner) is perfectionistic, performance driven, and judgmental and critical when the husband does not do things her way or tries to perform. The husband (underfunctioner) is avoidant and irresponsible and withdraws or escapes the interactions with his wife whenever possible. But, when the therapist started discussing the primary emotions behind these behaviors, the overfunctioner and underfunctioner actually began to realize that they had common emotional ground. The woman felt fearful, vulnerable, and taken advantage of in the relationship. In other words, she felt that the relationship was unsafe and untrustworthy. Likewise, the husband felt controlled, powerless, unable to measure up to the wife's expectations, and guilty for being unable to do so. Again, he felt unsafe in the relationship and doubtful that his efforts could ever yield a trustworthy, balanced, and secure outcome. Both partners contributed to an environment that was not safe and practiced behaviors or self-reactivity that indeed confirmed the very feelings they were both wishing to solve or address. When the couple started hearing each other's feelings about the lack of safety in the relationship, the focus shifted their perspective dramatically, as best demonstrated in the following words of the wife:

> I've never really even considered the possibility that we were feeling the same types of things. I knew we were both frustrated, but I guess I really never thought about the fact that neither of us feels safe. We've always talked about how different we are—I guess we're really not as different as we thought. We both want to be safe and in a place we can trust. Maybe if we can keep that in mind, we can move forward a bit.

There indeed is power in shifting the focus of relationships from concentration on reactive coping or behaviors to what the relational partners actually feel. This is true not only for clients participating in therapy but also especially for the psychotherapist. When the psychotherapist only concentrates on reactivity or behavior, he or she misses the primary emotions that fuel behavior and a tremendous opportunity to assess, understand, and eventually intervene. Other complimentary relationships that are similar to the pursuer/distancer and overfunctioner/underfunctioner relationships are the rigid/chaotic pattern (Olson & DeFrain, 1997) and the aggressive/avoidant pattern (Kilmann & Thomas, 1975).

Blamer/Placater Pattern

An additional common pattern seen in relationships is the blamer/placater pattern (Satir, Banmen, Gerber, & Gomori, 1991). Here, the partners are usually feeling pressure or pain in the areas of identity and feeling unloved. The blamer usually is functioning according to self-reactivity

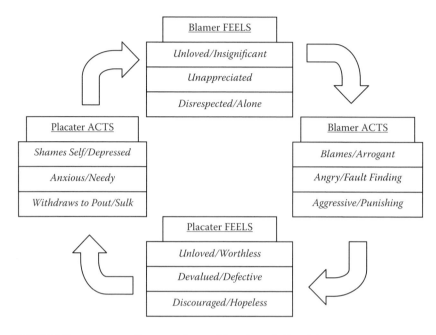

FIGURE 3.9 Process pattern of blamer/placater relationship.

that is blaming others; the placater's reactivity and coping are related to shaming the self. This pattern is illustrated in Figure 3.9.

In Figure 3.9, we see that the blamer and placater both feel primary emotions related to being unloved, with the blamer specifically reporting feeling insignificant, unappreciated, disrespected, and alone, while the placater reports specific feelings of being worthless, defective, discouraged, and hopeless. But, in terms of self-reactivity, the complimentary style occurs: The blamer is arrogant, angry, and aggressive and the placater is depressed, anxious, needy, and withdrawing. As this pattern develops, it almost always comes to be at least emotionally abusive of the placater, and many times develops into physical and sexual violence.

What is most interesting to us from a restoration perspective is the common reaction to this pattern from a therapeutic standpoint. Most psychotherapists take the position of protecting the placater by implementing no violence contracts and safety plans. While we certainly are in favor of such actions to protect the placater (Hargrave, 2000), we often find that there is a threat of punishment for the blamer. It is as if psychotherapists have become so sensitized to violent perpetrators that they often will believe that the perpetrator deserves punishment. There are some excellent programs for violent batterers, but most often attendance in these programs is ordered by the court and comes within the context of punishing the perpetrator. We acknowledge that this is a difficult issue to deal with because we certainly do not advocate violence, but the primary emotion that usually fuels the emotional and physical abuser is the same emotion that is fueling the individual who shames him- or herself and interacts in a relationship as a placater. We find that while psychotherapists have done well in making connection with and therapeutically intervening with placaters and shamers, there has been less adequate empathizing with and intervening with blamers. Again, we point out that both the blamer and the placater are driven by pain concerning issues of identity and love. At the minimum, the restoration model advocates for better understanding, connection, empathy, and intervention with people who are blamers in general and specifically may be perpetrators of emotional or physical violence.

Symmetrical or Escalating Patterns

As mentioned, symmetrical patterns in relationships tend to deteriorate quickly because both relational partners have not only the same type of hurt in their primary emotions but also the same type of self-reactivity. If both partners are blamers, they blame one another intensely, and they both will feel more unloved and alone. As a result, they escalate the blaming behavior, perhaps to a dangerous level of aggression, threats, and retaliation. If both partners are shamers, they tend to feel unloved and unwanted and escalate their reactivity into greater levels of depression, negativity, neediness, and manipulation. In short, it is often difficult to determine who is hurt more in these types of relationships. In a different symmetrical pattern, if both relational partners are involved with escape/chaos behaviors, they may withdraw, isolate, and avoid each other so much that there would functionally be no relationship between the two of them.

In Figure 3.10, we see a symmetrical pattern of interaction between two individuals who are both controllers. Although we could see this pattern in any type of relationship, from marital to work, this relationship is representative of a mother and older adolescent son who came to therapy because of the mother's complaint that the son would not do as he was

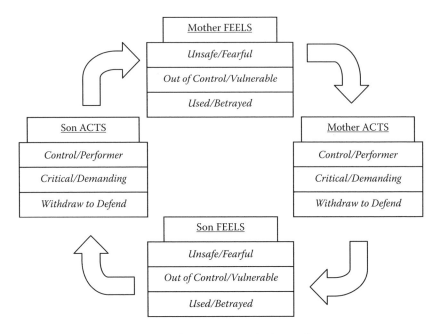

FIGURE 3.10 Process pattern of a symmetrical relationship.

told and cooperate in the family. In the following narrative, observe how the mother and son interact, and each one's behaviors strike the other's heart and emotion with a sense of fear and lack of safety.

Mother: You cannot possibly know how I am afraid for you and concerned about your life. I know that you think that I am some kind of nag, and that I just want you to do things my way, but I am your mother, and I really do have your best interests at heart.

Son: [*Looks at the mother in disbelief.*] You really are serious? You really think that you have any idea who I am and what I really want to do with my life? You are constantly on me about my schoolwork, my friends, my clothes, my room—everything. You have no idea how hard I work at the things that I want to accomplish.

Mother: Your computer? Gaming—now that's a way a life! [*Very sarcastic.*]

Son: You can make fun of that all you want and ignore the fact that I've organized a team, written a program, and have a following. What have you done? I can tell you. You manage a house, nag and complain to me, and drag me to therapy because I don't want the life that you want.

Mother: So, that is what you have to say to me. I work, and I try to give you a stable life and give you a foundation you can build on. What do I get? You attack and criticize me.

Son: [*Raises voice and throws out arms.*] And what is it that you are doing to me? I really feel like I've worked to create something with my friends and my talent, but all you see is that I'm not doing what you want.

After this exchange, both the mother and son sat for an extended time in silence as neither wanted to say the next word. The reality was that they both felt like further conversation would be useless, so they both worked to move into a framework of defending themselves through withdrawal. Symmetrical interactions most often have these types of escalation in which there is a flurry of intense emotion and activity and then a mutual withdrawal. The intensity in these symmetrical relationships can be minor as in the discussion or major, as would be the case with partners who are increasingly aggressive and violent with one another. The same variation can be found in the duration of the withdrawal from one another. The silence and withdrawal may be relatively brief in terms of these controllers, who might reengage in their battle for control within a matter of minutes, or it may be for days or even weeks, as in the case of withdrawers who use the distance to avoid one another. The specifics of the pattern—whether it is control, escape/chaos, blaming, or shaming—will vary, but the characteristics of the symmetrical pattern will tend to produce the same types of results. Both partners will feel a similar violation of love and trust due to the escalating behavior.

FINAL THOUGHTS ON PROCESS AND PATTERN

Human beings are ultimately fascinating. We are, at once, able to interact systemically with ourselves as thoughts about love and trustworthiness inform one another and our emotions and actions. At an even more complicated level of interaction, these ideas of love, trustworthiness, emotions, and actions can systemically interact with the same processes of other individuals, thereby mutually affecting each other. These levels can continue as we look at multiple relationships that occur in the family, our social networks, and societies as a whole. But, no matter the level of complexity, there are consistent interactions of processes that become patterns that we chose individually, relationally, and societally. Love and trustworthiness do not occur in a vacuum; they occur as a result of internal and relational processes and patterns. As the restoration therapist better understands these processes and patterns, he or she will become more empowered to intervene and change those patterns and individuals.

Section II

The Therapeutic Work in Restoration Therapy

4

Becoming a Wise Therapist

INTRODUCTION

Most of us know the story of George Washington and the harsh winter at Valley Forge during the American Revolution. Troop strength had dwindled from an expected vitality of 40,000 ready and able fighting men to around 8,000 who were ill-clothed, underfed, and sick with dysentery and weakness. Washington was a fighting man, and at this early stage of the war as the winter was coming to a close, he felt the particular need somehow to strike a meaningful blow to the strong British army. He thought about striking at New York and then at Philadelphia. But, as Washington surveyed his ragtag band of rebels, he realized that all he could reasonably do was retreat and live to fight another day. It was a discouraging day as Washington and his troops marched out of Valley Forge in the spring of 1778 only to lead a life of defensive maneuvers in the hope that they would one day gain allies, and the army would recover strength. And, it was not a matter of a few days or months before the army recovered enough to be a substantial fighting force able to take on the British. The fact was that Washington's army spent the greater part of five more years fighting a defensive struggle and biding time for a favorable opportunity.

Even though that was a discouraging day and victory seemed not even a remote possibility, most historians agree that this decision not to fight was the strategic decision that led to American independence. In other words, as long as Washington did not lose the army, he would eventually wear down the British, who could not muster enough strength to dominate the countryside because of the tremendous financial and emotional cost. As it turned out, the only way that Washington could win the war was to determine that he had to resist the temptation to try to win on one particular day. Instead, he had to do whatever was necessary to hold on to the army.

As therapists, we know that we have much in common with Washington as we work with patients and clients. They come to us, usually in great emotional pain and sometimes in tremendous messes with relationships. We listen, empathize, suggest, and intervene while they work, reason, and try to think and live differently. But, this is a slow and tiring process that often results in one step forward, two steps back. Patients and clients get sick and tired of the work and efforts that they muster yet are unable to greatly affect change in themselves or their relationships. Continuing this process as psychotherapists, we often must confess that we also get sick and tired of covering the same ground and wonder why it seems so difficult for people to change emotions and behaviors that they clearly know are bad for them or damaging to others. Like Washington, you probably are so sick and tired of being sick and tired that you often want to strike a strategic blow—one way or another—either to get the patient or client to change or to get the person to leave because they are resistant or uncooperative. Basically, you hope for change or want to be out of the misery of the relationship.

All psychotherapists feel this way at times about certain individuals or relationships in their work, and many of our patients and clients have the same feelings. But, there is a lesson that is deeply rooted in this story about Washington. The truth is that many of the therapeutic processes in which we take part do not involve strategic "wins" and "losses" as much as the fact that we keep in play the effort to change, grow, and adapt. This is not "flashy" or even built on dramatic technique; it is in fact communicating that if as a psychotherapist you will keep the opportunity for change and growth in play amidst all the ups and downs of life and the patient's efforts, you likely will find that the patient will indeed make those strategic changes and modifications to his or her process and relationships. But, to do this, you must resist the temptation to "strike a decisive blow, one way or another." You must realize, like Washington, that the only way the individual or relationship will be lost or end is when you try to rush things through because of frustration or mistiming. This does not mean necessarily that all therapy will be long term, but it does likely mean that most of the therapy that you do will not have a clear and glorious victory. It is a process of looking for small gains and the opportunities to make more significant progress, and when that progress comes, finding ways to consolidate the gains and progress made. In short, being a wise therapist often means learning how to hold on instead of winning battles. Learning how to be that kind of therapist is really the topic of this chapter.

WHY DO PEOPLE COME TO THERAPY?

All of us have been trained to ask the patient or client directly about his or her conceptualization of the problem and transcribe the answer as closely as possible into our records. This statement or answer in many ways has come to represent the most important torch in finding our way in the therapeutic process and certainly has become the dominating feature as increasing entities press for outcomes. So, while the answer may be obvious to some, we believe that not considering and giving weight to the reason people seek therapy leads us many times to direct our patients toward the wrong outcomes. In short, therapy becomes muddled because we are working on the wrong issues.

Solving Problems

Many people come to therapy with the expressed wish to solve some type of problem that causes life distress, such as "I want to stop drinking" or "I want to stop being so anxious." We have been around long enough to see the advent of solution-focused therapy (de Shazer, 1985, 1988; O'Hanlon & Weiner-Davis, 1989); the "revolution" in therapy was actually to focus on the problem and those instances or "exceptions" when the problem does not exist. While we are not solution-focused therapists, we certainly have employed the method at times and see the value of asking these questions to try to address solutions that the client seeks and wants. We are reminded of a story we heard from Bill O'Hanlon in one of his workshops that we have mentioned previously (Hargrave & Pfitzer, 2003).

The story is that a man arrives at a major airport and needs transportation to his hotel. He asks someone at the information desk for help. "I need to get to my hotel," he says. The information clerk says, "Of course I can help you, but first tell me where you are from." Confused and a bit annoyed, the man responds that he is from a particular state, but he does not know what that has to do with getting to his hotel. "Be patient," the clerk says and next says, "Now, tell me about your family." Becoming agitated, the man barks, "All I want to know is how to get to my hotel. Will you help me?" The information person looks surprised and says, "All I'm trying to do is find out the best way to assess your needs and the possible solutions. Are you aware of how resistant and angry you are becoming? Maybe you and I should look at this at a deeper level."

O'Hanlon's point is well taken. We would agree that there are times in the therapeutic process when people just need directions and help in finding solutions to the problems that bring them into therapy. But, we would also counter that there are many times when people come to therapy seeking solutions to problems for which they already know the solutions. For instance, the person who comes into therapy and wants to stop drinking knows that the solution for him or her is actually to stop drinking. As well, the person who wants to stop being so anxious actually knows that the solution to the problem is to relax. Indeed, most of the patients and clients that we see have tried the obvious solutions to their problems and have failed miserably. Even if we give solutions and help them with answers, we will likely be revealing answers or solutions that the client has already tried without success. For instance, in a modification of the O'Hanlon story, when the man comes to the information counter to ask for help, the person could respond, "You could take a taxi." The traveler then responds, "I don't feel comfortable with taxi drivers. They may take me in directions that are incorrect or even dangerous." In response, the information person tells him that he could take a bus. The traveler looks crossly and says, "I cannot be expected to ride with people who I do not know." Finally, the information person says, "I suppose that if you can't take a taxi or a bus, you could walk." At this point, the traveler becomes angry and says, "Is that the best solution you have? I cannot walk that far." Given the rejection of solutions, the wise person will look at the traveler and ask, "Tell me where you are from."

Most often, it is not that the patient or client rejects the solutions as much as the person simply has tried to do these things on his or her own and has failed. Excellent therapy, therefore, is not so much suggesting or finding solutions to people's problems because they usually know these solutions and have tried them. Excellent therapy by a wise therapist is much more about finding out why the patient or client cannot have success with the solution to their problem. Most therapists who we see struggling with patients or clients are too focused on the solutions and obvious suggestions that the patient or client already knows. When the client does not respond to a solution or suggestion, the therapist is quick to suggest another solution or a particular technique. When that one does not work, the therapist is on to even more solutions and suggestions. If obvious solutions do not work, it most often is an indication that there is something deeper within the patient or client that is locked in their primary emotions. Often, the patient or client who wants a quick fix to a problem will not immediately want to go to this deeper level of examination, so it is essential that the therapist have the clarity of direction of understanding how identity and safety issues can impact behavior and be able to explain the issues coherently and quickly. The art of therapy is helping people learn how to succeed with the solutions that they already know but cannot do on their own for some reason.

A wise therapist learns from those clients who come to solve problems that they are often trapped somehow between knowing what they should do and being unable to do it. Being unable to unlock those perspectives of the client history and "where they are from" is most often the answer to being able to help the client get unstuck and escape from his or her trap of incongruity.

Changing Someone Else

Many patients or clients come to therapy with the purpose of securing change in someone else. The essence of seeking therapy for this reason is that the individual needs someone to be or behave differently to be okay him- or herself or to be safe in the relationship. Sometimes, we can imagine that this is true and is rooted in solid intentions. For instance, a parent who takes his or her job seriously encounters a behavioral or identity problem with a child that seemingly cannot be solved with the parent's resources, or perhaps a spouse who has dealt with multiple infidelities of his or her partner is unable to handle further indiscretions. In both of these cases, we can well imagine that it is justified or well meaning for a person to seek therapy with the express desire to change another person. But, the fact remains that it is often a strategy that leads nowhere for a therapeutic relationship for several reasons.

First and most obvious, the individual seeking to change another person is most likely missing large issues in his or her own life that govern a large portion of the problem. We have learned for years from systemic therapists that symptomology and problems most times do not belong to one person but are instead inherent in the relationship or system (i.e., Haley, 1987; Madanes, 1984; Minuchin, 1974). In their technique of challenging

95

the symptom, Minuchin and Fishman (1981) make an excellent case for tying interaction together in the context of systemic relationships that makes clear that problems usually belong to more than one individual. We believe that this is most often the case in therapy, and that when an individual comes to therapy to change someone else without seeing him- or herself as an object of change, it is often because of self-reactivity. This reactivity is most times rooted in control behavior or blaming others but can also be rooted in the context of shaming oneself. The point is, however, that therapeutically the issue of changing someone else is often done out of pain or coping and therefore many times will represent actions that are unloving and untrustworthy. Individuals who seek therapy for the purpose of changing someone else almost always are tied in systemically with their own coping and self-reactivity; therefore, they have personal issues that need to be changed or modified. Good and wise therapists will be able to see these issues and be careful to point them out in the systemic interactions, contribution to symptomology, contributions of the person seeking to change someone else and his or her own self-reactivity, and the mutual responsibility that often lies at the heart of deteriorating relationships.

Second, it is not helpful for a person to seek therapy to change someone else because it often is simply a waste of time. We often think of ourselves as good psychotherapists in that we see root causes of pain quickly and have a vast array of techniques and understandings to help move a client or patient along in the ability to change. But, as good as we sometimes think of ourselves as therapists, we openly acknowledge that we are simply not powerful enough to change another human being. Humans alone are responsible for their own insight, understanding, responsibility, and motivations and at least the most responsible for their own personality and outcomes compared to anyone else. Haley (1984) used to state emphatically that if the client did not change, it was because the therapist failed to use the correct intervention that would prompt change. Although we have great respect for the strategic school of therapy and use many of the techniques to increase motivation and behavior change, we would disagree because in our experience the therapist's power to prompt change in another is miniscule when compared to that of the client. An individual cannot be made to change. If it is true that an individual cannot make another change for trained and wise therapists, it is certainly true for those individuals who are not trained. When patients and clients come to therapy with the express purpose of changing someone else, listening too much or giving too much empathy simply perpetuate the idea that the client is correct in his or her thinking. It will lead the client down a road of not giving due consideration to his or her own issues and, worse, wrongly encourage the perspective that complaints will change the other.

Of course, the only hope of changing another is to use the very systemic truths that we discussed in the favor of the client. If the client changes him- or herself, whether in behavior, motivation, or attitude, it systemically affects all who are in relationship with him or her. I cannot guarantee that the person who I wanted to change will change in the exact ways that I wanted, but change on my part necessitates some type of change among the individuals who are systemically connected with me. A wise restoration therapist not only looks to give empathy to clients and patients who come with the expressed purpose of changing someone else but also looks for opportunities to help them change in ways that are not tied to their own self-reactivity and instead are directed toward human agency of love and trustworthiness. This is where the hope of change lies with someone who seeks change in another.

The final reason that we believe that therapy leads nowhere when a patient or client comes to change someone else is because it is sometimes true that it is the other person who actually needs to change. As we have stated clearly, we do not believe that even the most damaging and demeaning human beings are beyond hope of change, but this does not mean that we do not see clearly that there are individuals who commit bizarre, heinous, and dramatic insults to love and trustworthiness in their relationships with others. When an individual comes to therapy who is connected to one of these individuals, it may indeed mean that the client or patient needs to look at his or her own behavior and acknowledge that he or she cannot change the damaging person, but to ask the individual to stay in a relationship that is clearly damaging to him or her seems little justified. Most of these relationships are with violent, victimizing, or highly irresponsible people, but the truth remains that in many of these cases the focus of therapy must be on recovery of the patient or client from such painful violations of love and trustworthiness. As psychotherapists, we unfortunately do not most often have access to the individuals who are these types of victimizers because they refuse to come in or are required to seek help elsewhere. But, even when we do have access, our focus must be on helping the victimizer do the hard work of recovery for him- or herself, just as the victim must do the work of recovery so that both may one day enter the relationship in a different manner. We do not seek to change the victimizer for the sake of the victim first but rather seek to change those patients and clients who come to see us for their own sakes and recoveries so that they can truly engage in relationships that are loving and trustworthy.

Telling Stories

Some patients and clients do not come for therapy for any particular reason connected with change at all, but come rather to get some validation of their stories. We are believers in the power of a story and the validation and clarity that comes from a person's narrative (Hargrave, 1994b). We feel that there is tremendous wisdom, care, love, and trustworthiness expressed in the process of these stories that not only serve to clarify the values and motivation of the patient but also the relationships to which they are connected (Hargrave & Anderson, 1992). Further, we believe that the therapeutic relationship is built, at least to some degree, on the psychotherapist's willingness and ability to hear, reflect on, empathetically connect with, point out wisdom, and handle the patient's story in a trustworthy manner (Boszormenyi-Nagy & Krasner, 1986; Hargrave & Pfitzer, 2003).

In these cases, it seems essential that the wise psychotherapist realize what is going on with the patient or client and be able to focus correctly on the story. Our training, particularly in this day and age of outcomes and insurance, has led many of us to focus and stay directed on problems and issues related to the problems exclusively. While this is understandable, it also leads us many times to forget that the most important thing we do with patients and clients is to establish loving and trustworthy relationships ourselves. In other words, it is the intimacy of the therapeutic relationship that is often the most important thing in determining the results or problem solving. In many cases, the intimacy of the relationship is the most important thing because the client or patient is only looking for that intimacy to have his or her story validated and heard.

How do we validate and hear effectively as wise therapists? First, we must be accurately hear and empathize with the narratives that people bring to us. One of the key aspects of intimacy is the reflection of material back to an individual so that he or she is able to understand him- or herself better (Kieffer, 1977). Second, we must be able to reflect on the story and help point out the strengths, limitations, and wisdom in the history of love and trustworthiness. As discussed, people make meaning along the process of identity and safety, and this element of reflection helps clients and patients clarify those meanings. Finally, we point the story in terms of where it can be validated further. Therapists are important people in the lives of clients and patients, but we are not the most important in terms of relationships. The most important relationships are those that are connected in the intergenerational lineage of the patient and client, and the validated narrative, rich with the triumphs and tragedies of love and trustworthiness, is where those intimate expressions are best used in trustworthy ways. In this way, therapy never becomes just a client or patient paying for the intimacy of the psychotherapist, but there always is a validation point when to learn to tell the story and to take the result to other intimate and closer relationships.

The wise therapist will be able to recognize when patients and clients come with this need for validation. Often, they come after experiencing trauma or grief and need a caring individual to listen. Many times, they come in a phase of life such as middle or old age in which reflection and validation have become much more important. But, no matter why the individual seeks a therapeutic relationship to tell his or her story, it is important that the therapist not automatically move into the position of problem solver or even discoverer; rather, it is essential that the therapist be a patient listener.

Change or Grow

It seems ironic to us that most people who seek psychotherapy do not have an idea of self-change and growth as a primary goal. Perhaps it is mostly societal influence that has caused people to think of happiness as the primary motivator and direction finder in our lives (Hargrave, 2000). Perhaps it is because we are simply focused so much on reactivity that the idea of being in charge of our own change and growth does not easily occur to us. Whatever the reason, however, it seems a rarity that a patient or client comes to psychotherapy with the expressed goal of growing.

As rare as it may be, it is hoped that we can see that the goal of therapy must always include this perspective of change and growth. There is a natural developmental direction of maturity to all of life, and picking up on that developmental perspective and helping people grow up is perhaps the most important element in psychotherapeutic goals (Hargrave, 2000). Our thoughts about ourselves and our individual meanings, our behavioral directions and actions that we take in relationships, as well as the relationships in which we engage all combine to present us with further questions of how much we are loved and how much we will love, how safe are we and how safe we will make others in relationships. Each question and relationship points out a further opportunity for us to learn more about ourselves and to change and grow into our full potential as human beings (Rogers, 1961), thereby benefiting other relationships (Boszormenyi-Nagy & Krasner, 1986).

The truth is, however, that no matter the reason that the patient or client seeks therapy—to solve problems, change others. or tell stories for validation—the wise therapist will recognize that all opportunities point toward this idea of change and growth. When we look at the profession of psychotherapy, change and growth provide the opportunity for the psychotherapist to produce loving and trustworthy relationships. Most of us go into the profession with the unclear goal of "helping" people. But, what were we looking to help them to do? If we analyze this question at any depth, most of us will find that we are vested in helping people to gain more of their potential (growth) or a greater sense of peace (trustworthiness and safety). The wise therapist recognizes that the tools of the trade that we ply along a continuum of time are the elements of love and trustworthiness. We cannot make people change and grow, but we can point out the direction of this change and growth by consistently helping people deal with their own pain regarding love and trustworthiness and helping them consider how they can be more loving and trustworthy to others. All therapy, one way or another, comes down to patients and clients learning how to change and grow or using their own change and growth for the benefit of relationships.

WISE PROCESS IN THERAPY

If we are to be believed that therapy is really about helping the individuals change and grow so they can be better for themselves and their relationships, then it is necessary to talk about those elements or practices that make those therapists the best that they can be at opening up those possibilities to clients and patients. The therapist has to have the capability of getting to the heart of the client and his or her history of love and trustworthiness. The better equipped the therapist is at utilizing these practices to understand the patient, the more successful he or she will be in affecting the status of identity and safety. The subjects discussed next are not exhaustive, but they are directed at what we believe to be the most essential elements of the therapeutic process in becoming a wise restoration therapist.

Multidirected Partiality

Our roots are in the contextual approach and multidirected partiality are identified as the most important therapeutic tool for the contextual therapist (Boszormenyi-Nagy & Krasner, 1986). Partiality is a way by which the psychotherapist can easily form a solid therapeutic relationship with the client because the process initially facilitates careful listening and connection. In addition, multidirected partiality allows the psychotherapist to access the history of love and trustworthiness from multiple directions of past relationships without condemning or judging. This process encourages the patient or client to be transparent or real as the therapist demonstrates trustworthiness.

Multidirected partiality is not so much a therapeutic methodology or intervention strategy as it is an attitude that a contextual therapist carries. In terms of attitude, multidirected partiality means that the psychotherapist is aware and accountable to all people in the relationships who may be potentially affected by interventions. In other words, all human beings connected in the relationships with the individual you are seeing (particularly his or her family) have a story of love and trust that is affected by the psychotherapist's interventions. The psychotherapist is also aware and partial to every person's story of love and trustworthiness who is concerned with difficult relationships. In other words, every person, whether considered a victim, victimizer, or both, is a human being and is equally entitled to the psychotherapist's consideration and respect of his or her humanity as well as recognition of his or her story or side in the intergenerational relational ledger (Boszormenyi-Nagy & Krasner, 1986). As a methodology, multidirected partiality is also a technique of crediting all relational parties for the different concerns, efforts, and impacts of what they have done in relationships or what has been done to them. It is always important to note that multidirected partiality is not the neutrality of impartiality; rather, it is sequential siding with and recognition of family members' efforts (Goldenthal, 1996). In terms of technique, there are a few aspects that are notable, such as empathy, crediting, acknowledgment of efforts, and accountability (Goldenthal, 1996).

Empathy

One of the most powerful healing and connecting aspects of the therapeutic relationship between psychotherapist and patient is empathy. The ability of the psychotherapist to make and express emotional connections with a patient's loss, fear, and pain connects the patient in the relationship and works to promote intimacy, insight, and trustworthiness (Goldenthal, 1996). Empathy is part of the multidirected partiality in that it helps the patient or client know that he or she is listened to and understood and that his or her perspective on love and trustworthiness is taken into due consideration.

Crediting

If a psychotherapist can empathize with a patient or client, then it opens up the possibility of further partiality through crediting. The first aspect of crediting has to do with the psychotherapist acknowledging and accepting the unfairness, violations, and relational insults that the patient has experienced in life (Goldenthal, 1996). It is important to remember here that the psychotherapist is not making proclamations of who is right or wrong in actions in family relationships but rather simply acknowledging that there is a history of painful violations that occurs with every individual. The psychotherapist not only would do this in partiality for the individual patient in the room but also would be willing to do crediting for individuals involved with relationships who are not present. For instance, a psychotherapist may acknowledge the pain caused by a victimizer who is not present to a victim who is present but later in the session also acknowledge that the victimizer who is not present likely has a history of his or her own victimization. The second aspect of crediting is possible if care is taken to ensure the first. This second aspect of crediting is to acknowledge aspects of relationships that were loving and trustworthy that were apart from the harm that was perpetuated (Hargrave, 1994a).

Acknowledgment of Efforts

Each individual who has a history of pain associated with love and trustworthiness seeks to deal with that pain in the most constructive manner possible. As pointed out, this self-reactivity was usually developed in a context and at an age when survival was paramount, and there was little choice but to try to cope. As such, self-reactivity and coping are worthy efforts of acknowledgment because they came in the context of the individual doing the best he or she could under circumstances that were unloving and untrustworthy. The technique of acknowledgment of effort is related to crediting but changes focus. In short, acknowledgment of efforts focuses on the efforts and contributions that the patient has made to relationships. In showing partiality through acknowledgment of efforts, the psychotherapist acknowledges the patient's contributions first and then moves others in the relationships to recognize their efforts (Goldenthal, 1996).

Accountability

Multidirected partiality not only means that the psychotherapist empathizes with, credits, and acknowledges efforts of the individual but also means that the psychotherapist is concerned about the violations of love and trustworthiness that the patient or client commits in relation to others. Even though these actions proceed from the patient's own history of violations and pain, the psychotherapist does not excuse irresponsibility toward love and trustworthiness in any relationship. As a result, the psychotherapist is also partial to those in relationships who are done damage by the client or patient. Accountability holds all relational parities responsible for damage done (Goldenthal, 1996).

Process Versus Content

It is one of the ironies about the psychotherapeutic process that for clients or patients to feel well connected to the psychotherapist, he or she must feel well listened to and empathetically understood. From a restoration therapy perspective, however, the story or content that the client or patient tells is not the most essential element in the psychotherapist's understanding of the client. We believe that much more of the understanding of the client is derived from how he or she interacts in relationships, handles issues stemming from conflict, perceives his or her identity with regard to relationships, interprets the nature and trustworthiness of relationships, and motivates him- or herself toward action in relationships. In other words, we derive much more information from the *process* reporting of the client rather than the *content* reporting of the client. For instance, in the following narrative, a 39-year-old mother interacts with the therapist in an individual session; notice how the therapist uses what the woman says in the way of content to move into the issue of process in the therapeutic relationship:

Therapist: It sounds as if you have been in many situations where you have felt exploited and misunderstood.

Woman: [*Looks very intense and angry.*] You could say that to say the least. I have never been in a situation where anyone cared about me at all. Anything that I have been able to do has always been on my own without any help from anyone else.

Therapist: Who are the people that have tried to help you?

Woman: [*Angry and sarcastic.*] Certainly no one has tried to help me from my family. There have been a few people that have tried to help me a little from my church, but they don't stick around long. They haven't got what it takes to help. And then there are the therapists—people that are paid to help and say they care but only are there for an hour every other week. I think they have caused me as much damage as anyone.

Therapist: So, people that have tried to help have ended up hurting you. In what way have therapists hurt you?

Woman: They pretend to listen and give you a safe place, but they go off line as soon as they are off the clock. Maybe you feel a little connection with them, but then they are on to the next person, and you are left in exactly the same place you were when they come in. They go home to their lives, and I'm stuck in exactly the same place.

Therapist: I see. You feel that therapists in the past connect with you in session, but you don't feel they help you outside of session. You feel hurt because they go on with their own lives, and you have to go on in your painful situation.

Woman: [*Looks doubtful.*] Yes, that's right.

Therapist: Well, certainly I do want to connect with you and help you, but I will have other patients that I see after I see you, and I will go home to my life and you to yours at the end of the day. I wonder if I will be just another therapist that lets you down.

Woman: [*Looks up slowly at the therapist and pauses for a while.*] I don't know. I don't know what would make you any different.

Therapist: I'm not sure that I am any different, especially if I don't know what you are expecting. I do know that I have limits. I do want to help, but I have many people that I have to help during the day and week. What can I do here that will make a difference to you with that kind of limitation?

Woman: [*Long pause; stares at the therapist.*] You can listen to me and then tell me straight some things that I can do that will help my situation. You can remember what I say from one session to the next and care to follow up on what you give me to do. You can think about me every now and then during the week.

Therapist: [*Long pause, then leans forward.*] I think that I can do those things if you will be willing to tell me straight when you are feeling like I disconnect from you and when you are shutting down. We will probably not move forward if I am doing something that makes you angry and blaming and I act like I don't know it.

Woman: [*Looks at the therapist a long while.*] I'm not angry with you, and I can probably level with you.

Here, the woman expresses content about her past therapeutic relationships but is also clearly expressing her anger and disdain for therapists. The therapist in this case had a choice in terms of talking about the past relationships and what made those situations painful and unprofitable for the woman. But, the reality is that if the therapist makes the choice to stick with the content of the stories of the past, he would miss the opportunity to talk about the process he has with the client. Instead of reassuring her that he will be different, he confronted her with the reality that all the issues she brought up applied to him as a therapist. This allowed him to deal overtly with the therapeutic process by confronting the lack of trust she had for him, clearly spelling out some of his limitations, asking her overtly about her expectations for therapy, and asking her for some specific expectations she had for him. As a result, the woman and the therapist had a real and more profitable exchange because they were engaged in a face-to-face process instead of conversation about past relationships dealing with content. In short, there was more chance for connection, clear progress on issues, and more opportunities for change on the part of the patient. A wise restoration therapist tries not to miss these opportunities to make comment and change in the dynamic and process.

Classically, this practice of concentrating on process rather than content brings the therapeutic issue into the room and observing the dynamics first hand. When we are able to comment on, make suggestions about, and change those dynamics in the room, it greatly increases the chances of the patient or client being able to carry that changed dynamic outside the room and apply the change (Madanes, 1984). When a psychotherapist only stays with the content the patient is discussing, at the most he or she can only comment on the process of insight and deal with the cognitions of the patient. When the therapist deals with the process, the patient can be fully engaged cognitively, emotionally, and, at times, kinetically.

105

Of course, these process dynamics can be clear when dealing with the interactions of multiple members in therapy, such as in marital or family therapy (Hargrave & Pfitzer, 2003). When the therapist has more than one member in therapy, he or she can see the dynamics and process unfold as clients interact. However, as the case illustrates, the therapist can also point out these relational dynamics with the way the patient or client interacts with him or her in individual psychotherapy. To make this dynamic and process clear, however, the psychotherapist must be in tune with not only the content of the story but also the dynamic process of what the client is doing to the psychotherapist during the session. We often say that the psychotherapist must be in touch with his or her own "gut" or emotions during the therapeutic process. The psychotherapist must constantly be assessing what the client or patient is doing and how it is making the psychotherapist feel and think. As the psychotherapist evaluates this material, he or she can pick out the dynamics of how the client feels about him- or herself as well as clearly pick up on the self-reactivity of the client. In addition, when the psychotherapist evaluates this dynamic of emotions and thoughts involved with the process or relationship with the client, it clarifies the process and relationship, and the psychotherapist is much less vulnerable to issues of countertransference (Corey, 2008).

Insight and Skills

Therapeutic processes from a variety of schools and models all have a similar purpose in that they all want to help patients and clients and change self-defeating and harmful behavior. But, we can look at some of these therapeutic approaches and recognize that there are ones that at the basis of this desire help the belief that *insight* is the necessary element to help the client change. We would normally think of psychoanalytic therapies (Luborsky, O'Reilly-Landry, & Arlow, 2008); emotionally focused couple therapy (Johnson, 2004); humanistic or client-centered therapy (Rogers, 1951); existential therapies (May & Yalom, 2000); and gestalt therapies (Perls, 1969) as those approaches that focus on bringing about insight to the client or patient to produce help, growth, and change. On the other hand, there are some therapeutic approaches that focus on behavior or *skills* to produce change. In these therapies, the focus is clearly not on the production of insight as much as on learning new behaviors and adopting new practices that solve problems. We would usually think of behavioral therapy (Krumboltz & Thoresen, 1969); cognitive-behavioral therapy (Beck

& Weishaar, 2008; Ellis, 2008); solution-focused therapy (de Shazer, 1985); strategic therapy (Haley, 1987); and Bowen systemic therapy (Bowen, 1978) as approaches that primarily focus on skill building or changing behavior without the focus on insight. Although neither of these lists is exhaustive in terms of identifying all the theories that primarily use insight or skills, the intent here is to draw a line of demarcation so that we can clearly understand how different models approach change and therapy.

There are therapies that identify themselves as integrative or eclectic in terms of this insight and skills. For instance, contextual family therapy is sometimes identified as a theory of theories (Gurman & Kniskern, 1981), and multimodal therapy is clearly associated with technical eclecticism (Lazarus, 2008). While we appreciate the integrative or eclectic nature of these theories, they still clearly depend on either insight or skill building. We feel that contextual family therapy, for instance, is clearly focused more on insight, while multimodal therapy concentrates more on behavioral skills.

The restoration therapy model leans between these two divisions. In our opinion, our therapy leans more toward insight, but we also believe that this model has a strong focus on the practice and development of skills, as discussed in Chapters 5 and 6. We feel that there is tremendous value in the focus on insight with patients and clients: If there is understanding, there is the ability to make cognitive connection with motivation for change and emotional congruence to make the necessary change. We agree with Johnson (2004) that new emotional experiences within the context of this new insight can produce healing, attachment, and resolution of old injuries. In our opinion, insight and therapies that focus on insight do the most good in producing environments in which clients and patients are well understood and well motivated for change.

We also, however, find that many times insight does not lead to any sustained change from the self-defeating beliefs and behaviors of clients. We also agree with the disclosure of Atkinson et al. (2005) that they have been in therapy processes with clients in which significant therapeutic insight was shared. Not only did these therapists report feeling good about the insights they offered, but also the clients and patients believed the insight was helpful. As they reported, the clients often did not change as the result of this insight or particularly find the insight memorable later. Like most therapists we know, we have had this same experience in our therapy with clients and patients. As good and as motivating as we find insight and still believe that it has utility to clients and patients in helping

107

them change, we find that it is insufficient in bringing about long-lasting change. What is needed is the addition of skills that fit with the insight that motivates the client or patient and the practice of those skills to the point at which it makes a prolonged impact on the learning in the brain (Atkinson et al., 2005).

Wise therapy brings both insight and skills to bear in the therapeutic processes. The psychotherapist understands that these two ways of working do not represent a dichotomy but rather an effective "one-two punch" in the ability to bring about change. From a restoration model perspective, insight into issues of identity, safety, and self-reactivity help the patient or client get the cognitive connection and leverage needed to understand not only where he or she feels pain but also where his or her vulnerabilities and reactions take place in an automatic manner. Skills, on the other hand, help the client or patient have a clear behavioral and mental map of what needs to be accomplished to make the changes that are clear due to insight. Further, skills provide the client or patient with the ability to practice change so it becomes habituated. Both skills and insight clearly have advantages in therapy, but the wisest and most beneficial therapy will make use of both to maximize effectiveness and change.

Pain, Change, and Getting Stuck

It is easy for psychotherapists to get lost or stuck in therapy with clients or patients. We often find ourselves not knowing or understanding enough about the backgrounds or pain of the people who we are trying to help; we have feelings of being overwhelmed by either so much of the emotional turmoil that client finds him- or herself in or the multilayered problems that look solvable; or we are frustrated and confused about why our patients and clients have difficulty taking even simple steps away from the beliefs and actions that prove to be so destructive. It is sometimes helpful for us to remember that these indeed are the very things that we find difficult in our own lives. We should be able to relate to the emotional turmoil that causes us pain as well as how difficult problems can be at times. We also should be able to understand clearly how difficult it is to change our own beliefs and behaviors. In general, we find that when we lose touch with our own humanity as psychotherapists, we are apt to lose patience, identification, empathy, and connection with our clients and patients. When we lose this therapeutic connection, we are more vulnerable to frustration, exploitation, countertransference, and manipulation with our clients. When we stay in touch with our own humanity, we stay in touch with our clients' and patients' humanness; we see these people for what they really are—human beings just like us.

There is no doubt that this keeping in touch with our own humanity is key to being a wise and good therapist, but it also points us in the right direction of understanding where we need to go therapeutically when we feel we are getting stuck with a patient or client. We believe that there is a natural weave that clients feel between their thoughts and actions, identity and safety. These play heavily in the context of relationships. Not only do we need a balance of insight and skills to make significant and long-lasting changes in our lives, but also we need to know that we are appreciated and heard. We need someone to understand how our identity has developed and have empathetic connections with our situations and pain. As well, we need to feel like there is someone who will help us learn and do so in a trustworthy, supportive, and noncondemning manner as we go about the process of change. We need these things, and our clients and patients need them as well. When they do not have these conditions, these clients or patients most often signal us by resisting progress or regressing to old patterns.

We most often see this process occur with clients and patients when the therapist has made significant insight and connection with the pain of the individual and is starting to move him or her into work on skill building and behavioral change. Sometimes when this transition takes place, the individual feels threatened that the therapist no longer makes the empathetic connection or entitled that he or she should not have to put forth work without someone first making a change or that suddenly the individual is no longer being heard in terms of previous and past violations of love and trustworthiness. However, we often see that when the psychotherapist encounters this resistance or regression, he or she will continue to press the client for change, trusting that the understanding, empathy, and patience displayed in earlier sessions should make it possible for the patient or client to "press through" a difficult spot with more confidence. Simply stated, the client or patient does not experience the love or trustworthiness of the therapist, and the therapist does not understand why love and trustworthiness are questioned. In not understanding, the therapist then presses the process forward, and both the client and therapist become stuck.

We often repeat to the psychotherapists that we are training that they must be willing to "chase the pain" with clients and patients whenever and however it arises. What we mean by this is that there will be many times in the therapeutic process when the client or patient has long-standing vulnerable feelings of love and trustworthiness triggered, and they are thrown into self-reactivity. While reasoning and commenting on the process is sometimes helpful, we most often find that it is much more helpful to explore the emotional pain that the client is experiencing. Take, for instance, the case of a 58-year-old married woman who was trying to take steps to improve her marriage with her husband. In past sessions, the therapist had made good connections and insights with the woman in her past violations of love and trustworthiness not only in her family of origin but also in the relationship with her husband. During the eighth session, the woman became resistant and hopeless when the therapist made some behavior requests of the woman. In this first part of the dialogue, notice how the therapist pressed the woman to make additional change even though the woman was clearly resistant.

Therapist: I would like you to turn to your husband now and express to him what it is you feel you could do to make the relationship a little better.

Woman: [*Stunned look; hesitant.*] I don't think that I could do that right now.

Therapist: [*Pause.*] I can appreciate why this is hard to do because you have been hurt in your family that you grew up in as well as being hurt in this marriage. [*Pause.*] I do think, however, that there is a time that you have to use the understanding of your past in order to become more responsible for the future. If someone does not take the first step, the relationship will not go anywhere.

Woman: Maybe that is true, but I just don't think that I can always be the one that is responsible for the relationship. I'm tired of trying and tired of always being the one that makes the effort.

Therapist: Clearly I do not want you taking his responsibility for change. All I want you to do is to take responsibility for yourself and tell him the change that you are willing to make.

Woman: [*Angry.*] I can't make anymore changes. If that means that the marriage is over, then I guess you need to start helping us come to grips with that reality.

Here, we see that the therapist was pressing the woman on an issue that she clearly was feeling unable to do. Instead of looking at why the woman was unable to tell her husband some areas where she would be

110

willing to change, the therapist started pressing her harder to do what she was unable to do at the time. We see this as a common trap for therapists. As the psychotherapist presses the woman more, she made an even more extreme statement, suggesting that it was time that she and her husband should divorce.

When we see this type of resistance or regression, the wise therapist must train him- or herself not to press the change but instead chase the pain. In this case, the psychotherapist wisely took a few minutes of silence to regain composure ; the therapist realized that she was pressing the situation and needed to hear the pain that the woman was feeling.

Therapist: [*After a long pause of several minutes.*] I think that I have made an error in not hearing something that you are trying to tell me. In my experience, when I am asking someone to do something that that he or she can't do, it is because he or she feels something deeply. You feel something deeply that I am missing.

Woman: I don't know, it is hard to explain. [*Long pause.*] I just think that my whole life has been one time after another where it falls on me to make something right. I remember as a girl feeling like I was the one who had to make my parents feel better after they had a blow up. I was the one who had to move them along. I was the one who had to be responsible to get them in a better place. I've always felt that I had the same obligation with him.

Therapist: [*Long pause.*] And how did that make you feel about yourself and the situation when you had to take that responsibility as a girl?

Woman: It always made me feel like I was not heard or invisible. My feelings did not matter, and the only thing that was important was that I do the right thing and make it right for everyone else.

Therapist: [*Long pause.*] So, what I was doing was making you responsible for something with your husband, and it felt like you no longer counted, and this situation is not safe.

Woman: [*Long pause.*] Yes.

Therapist: That does make a lot of sense to me now. Is there more that I need to know about how it feels for you because I don't want to press you into those old feelings?

Woman: Actually, that is exactly what I needed to say. I know that you are not trying to press me into an unsafe situation. I just had to express this fear that I was carrying. I think I can say to him the things that I am willing to change.

111

Notice that when the therapist took the time to connect with the woman's pain, the woman again felt understood and connected. The ability to connect with the pain did not make it harder for her to move into a change behavior; rather, it enabled her to be willing to do so. When a psychotherapist runs into resistance, we believe that it is a sure sign that the therapist has not heard enough regarding the client's or patient's pain. This can be true at any time in the therapeutic process but is particularly true when the psychotherapist is beginning to ask the client to proceed into skill building or change.

The weave of good psychotherapy in general and restoration therapy specifically is the ability to move between the ends of an ellipse. At one end, the therapist must have a connection with the client's story and pain and at the other end must be cognizant of the changes and skills the individual needs to be loving and trustworthy him- or herself. Both ends of the ellipse must be consistently explored and understood. Also, the client or patient must be challenged to explore both ends of the ellipse. The psychotherapist will do his or her best work as he or she learns to oscillate between the two extremes with consistent ease and interpret overreaction, resistance, or regression as a signal to move to the other end of the ellipse.

FINAL THOUGHTS ON BEING A WISE THERAPIST

The poet b. f. maiz would often speak to psychotherapists and say, "All good poetry is therapeutic and therefore, all good therapy should be poetic." We think about this often when we think about being a good and wise therapist. Part of the artistic nature of psychotherapy is having the ability to understand clearly the standing of the client or patient and why he or she has come to therapy while having the ability to utilize the array of therapeutic techniques wisely to help the client or patient grow. We can definitely tell you that there is a need to balance these issues and techniques of partiality, process, content, insight, skills, pain identification, and change. However, we cannot tell you exactly where the balance lies in every situation and with every client or patient. It is necessary, therefore, to be constantly aware in the therapeutic process of where the rhythm of therapy lies in making the process poetic. If you find this rhythm, you will find that you will be practicing in a balanced way that is not only wise but also helpful to the individual and family.

5

The Techniques of Working With Love and Trustworthiness

INTRODUCTION

The Earth is an amazing place geologically in terms of plate tectonics, the study of the geological processes of the continents actually moving across the surface of the Earth. Because of the way that the Earth is made with a hot core, a cooler and fluid mantle surrounding the core, and a cool and thin crust, the broken pieces of the crust move in enormous plates along the surface of the Earth. In those places where the plates have run together (i.e., where the Indian subcontinent has run into the rest of Asia), there is potential for tremendous upheaval in the crust or surface that can result in mountain ranges such as the Himalayas. As one plate runs alongside another, there is also potential for increased tension and pressure along the fault lines where the plates meet that inevitably results in sudden quakes and shifts from time to time.

But, perhaps the most volatile areas of all are where these plates either come in contact and one submerges the other or pull apart from one another. These zones not only produce quake activity but also volcanic activity. As plates pull apart, the fissures in the surface of the Earth allow magma from the interior of the Earth to escape in a usual oozing of lava and ash that eventually hardens to make new surface on the crust. At the other extreme, one plate submerges under another, and the pressure and heat from the process cause the rocks and solid plate to return to a molten state, creating the possibility of violent, explosive volcanic activity as pressure and gas build at these points along the surface. In simple terms, we realize that the crust of the Earth, through plate tectonics, is always in the process of losing part of itself on one end and creating more of itself on the other. It is a cyclical process of creating and re-creating on a global scale as gigantic continental plates move slowly but constantly from molten to solid states, appearing and disappearing from the surface.

Human beings are also subject to this constant state of creating and re-creating as we change and grow; we both lose part of ourselves and add new things. Part of the challenge in the therapeutic process is to be able to help people lose those parts of themselves that are damaging, stagnant, and harmful to others as found in the elements of self-reactivity. Also, there is great opportunity to help people move past these old violations and coping to new ways of functioning found in human agency and the perpetuation of love and trustworthiness not only to themselves but also to others. But, psychotherapists must know that these processes of creating and re-creating in individuals and families often produces pressure that is volatile. There may be times of extreme emotion that the psychotherapist must be able to connect with and hold with clarity while the client or patient works through the emotion. There is usually time of relational upheaval as members of the relationship struggle with one another to be able to discuss old violations of love and trustworthiness and create new opportunities for connection that are healthy. And, there are times of struggle as individual clients or patients have to work and practice at integrating new agency behavior into their repertoires of being.

We have come to the conclusion that as psychotherapists we often do not ask our clients or patients to change. In our opinion, there are many therapies that do an adequate job of conceptualizing problems and understanding behaviors that clients and patients bring to therapy. We also believe that many psychotherapists do an adequate job of connecting with, empathizing with, and exhibiting patience with individuals, marriages, and families. But, we often feel that therapeutic practice among psychotherapists is lacking in terms of asking clients to change their behaviors and providing them with clear maps or practice that is needed to change those behaviors. Even when we do provide those clear directions and opportunities to practice new behaviors, we often do not persist with the practice in the therapy room or provide adequate follow-up on requests for change. Instead, we often recycle back into understanding the

114

problem, connecting with emotions, and going in other therapeutic directions that seem more solvable.

We believe that to produce change, the psychotherapist must indeed have the background and theoretical underpinnings to understand as demonstrated in the first section of this book. But, we also believe that the psychotherapist must have an effective cadre of intervention strategies that are able to help individuals and those in relationships make clear changes, and that the psychotherapist should have the courage to ask for and persist with those individuals and those in relationships to produce change. To that end, this and the next chapter are about the therapeutic techniques of restoration therapy designed to reorder or restore issues of love and trustworthiness. In this chapter, we deal with interventions that are directed at self-healing, relational actions designed to produce love and trustworthiness, and issues of legacy and reconciliation in restoring love and trustworthiness. In Chapter 6, we specifically focus on the need for behavioral practice of these types of issues in connection with brain research.

INTERVENTIONS DIRECTED TOWARD SELF-HEALING

It is difficult for us to hear the narratives of people who have been damaged in the past, and although these violations can come from sources such as societal tragedies or disasters, school experiences, mentor disappointments, or even experiences with friends, we find the saddest and most difficult stories come from people's family of origin. These are saddest in that these families had the opportunity to do original programming of a child and to write a beautiful story of love and trustworthiness but instead chose to use the opportunity to deny, neglect, or abuse and left individuals with the deep abiding sense that they were not loved or safe. As we have seen, these violations form not only a damaged sense of identity, but also a damaged self-reactivity and coping style that violates others with destructive entitlement. To illustrate the various techniques that we use in self-healing, we focus on one particular case in which a 40-year-old man sought therapy. He came to therapy because of an ultimatum from his wife that he get help or she would pursue divorcing him. He was normally a passive and quiet man at home who would add little in the way of emotional support or involvement to his wife or his three children but would at intervals explode with anger when he "had enough" of his wife's pressure or expectations. At these outbursts, he would become loud, yell, and say hurtful things to both his wife and the children. He then would withdraw and brood for days and sometimes weeks without saying anything significant. In the following exchange from his first session, the man reveals some of the violations from his past:

Man: Basically, I know that my wife is right in wanting to leave me. I know that there is not much that is good about living with someone like me. I don't even care for myself, so I sure can understand why she has difficulty caring for me. I wouldn't want to be married to me.

Therapist: Help me understand why you would not want to be around yourself.

Man: I am nothing. I've accomplished very little, and I most of the time just want to be left alone. I don't connect well, and I feel empty. When my wife tries to get me involved or complains—which basically is right—I will just snap at times. The only time I'm emotional about anything is when I am angry.

Therapist: Often, I see people that carry much with them from the past that they grew up with that was damaging and hurtful. You were definitely hurt from the family you grew up in.

Man: [*Long pause.*] Yes, I was. My father left my mother when I was 2 years old, and I didn't hear from him again. My mother then married a man who was abusive to me. They had a daughter together and treated her like she was a princess, and I always felt like I didn't belong. I wanted to cry out to my mother that it was unfair and how much this man was hurting me and abusing me, but I never could.

Therapist: [*Long pause.*] You couldn't tell your mother?

Man: I always had this pressure from my mother that was like, "Don't you screw this up for us. This man takes care of us, and we don't have any other choice. Just keep quiet, and things we will be okay." She knew exactly what was going on but would never step in for fear that we would be out on our own.

Therapist: And where did that leave you?

Man: Totally alone. I never remember a time of feeling like I could actually depend on anyone, and that it was my job just to go along and make it okay no matter how I felt.

Therapist: And how did you feel about yourself and your situation?

116

Man: I felt worthless, alone, uncared for, and powerless to do anything about my situation. I still feel that way now.

The depth of this man's pain is obvious as he described the pain of being unloved by a mother who left him to fend for himself and put her safety needs above his. He felt deserted by her as she used the situation to make a stable life for herself and used him by giving him a covert message that it was his job to go along with the unsafe situation as an act of taking care of her. He obviously grew up in a home where he was deserted by his biological father and left by his mother to take care of himself. It is little wonder that the man felt deep primary emotion associated with the violations of being unloved and in relationships that were untrustworthy.

As well as the primary emotions that he felt from the violations of love and trustworthiness—that he was worthless, alone, uncared for, and powerless—he also revealed much about his self-reactivity and coping. We can see from his report that he felt that he was deserving of the ultimatum that his wife gave him and thought that there was little good about him. These are primary indicators that he was active in *shaming self*. He likely felt that his sense of worthlessness was his fault, and that somehow his mother's actions were correct because she and his stepsister were somehow more worthy than he was. This also likely resulted in a neediness that the man felt as he longed for and desired someone to make him feel loved, worthy, special, and important enough to be a companion and stand up for him. He also revealed that he spent much of his time by himself and took little initiative in relationships. This may indicate that he avoided the pain of any type of relationship by sequestering or perhaps numbing himself through *escape/chaos behaviors*. Because he likely felt the pain of relationships and was unable to make them safe, he escaped by chronic withdrawal. Finally, he also indicated that he exploded with anger at times, which is a reliable sign that when his shame and escape reactive coping was played out in the relationship and could not be continued, he resorted to *blaming others*. Although he probably disliked himself for displaying this behavior, he also likely felt self-justified in showing the anger because he had a long history of receiving little from others.

It is always essential to remember that connecting with and understanding the pain that the individual feels is paramount in assessment and setting the framework for intervention. We often do this first by carefully exploring the past situations, feelings, and history of actions as described in the first part of this book. In addition, it is always essential to maintain the position and attitude of multidirected partiality (Boszormenyi-Nagy & Krasner, 1986) as described in Chapter 4. The psychotherapist must always be willing to "chase pain" with the individual as he or she starts the therapeutic process in reorganizing constructions around love and trustworthiness, thereby helping clients and patients rectify the behaviors that add to the intergenerational legacy of violation.

Understanding

Understanding is a therapeutic modality discussed by Hargrave (1994, 2001) that helps an individual come to grips with the violations of love and trustworthiness and to re-form ideas concerning the reasons for those violations. As discussed, when an individual comes from a background of not being loved, he or she will have the question, "Why was I not loved?" which permeates his or her identity. This is particularly true when these violations come from the family of origin, in which there is a clear justified expectation that love should be provided. The individual longs for the comfort of feeling unique, worthy, and not alone.

When individuals feel unloved, the question "Why was I not loved?" becomes a driving force for self-reactivity and coping. The individual may answer the question in terms of believing that the family or people who should have provided the love are simply inadequate, malicious, or intentionally abusive. In these instances, the likely pattern of self-reactivity is to blame others. In essence, the individual believes that these people who were charged with loving him or her were "monsters" or evil because they failed in this most basic of obligations. As a result, the individual consistently reacts to the feelings with a drive of retribution to make the ones who should have provided love pay for their neglect or failure. Of course, this reactivity usually spreads to other relationships and innocent parties as the individual consistently carries the violation and acts with coping and self-reactivity with anyone in a relationship with the individual (Hargrave, 1994a).

The alternative to answer the question "Why was I not loved?" is to spiral downward into reactivity to blame oneself as unlovable. As we have seen, this coping of shaming self spirals the person into negativity, depression, hopelessness, neediness, and often withdrawal. Basically, the individual draws the conclusion that he or she is worthless, faulty, or somehow bad as the individual believes that he or she was unlovable or unworthy of love (Hargrave & Pfitzer, 2003). In both instances of answering the question, however, the individual draws the conclusion that there is something desperately wrong with either him- or herself or his or her caregivers. The intervention of understanding is potentially helpful in this situation.

If the individual believes that the people who should have loved him or her are monsters or evildoers, then there is a bind because monsters or evildoers are only built to do damage and harm. On the other hand, if the individual believes that he or she is unworthy of being loved, then there is little positive behavioral action that the person can take that will ever make him or her lovable. The victim of the lack of love and trustworthiness paints him- or herself into a corner where the belief itself prevents any change. If the victimizer is indeed a monster, then he or she cannot be held accountable because he or she is simply doing what he or she was created to do. Further, the monster can provide no redress of the damaged love and trustworthiness to correct the victim's lost worth (Hargrave, 1994a).

Of course, people are not monsters or evil, and they certainly are lovable by nature. Humans are humans and make mistakes, but we are firm in our assertion that they are respectable, loveable, capable, and *responsible* for their actions. Instead of spinning into a spiral of self-reactivity, by using understanding we seek to confront this basic question with the reality of the humanity of both the victim and the victimizer. In essence, the technique of understanding is about helping the individual who experienced the violation of love and trustworthiness to understand and recognize the limitations, circumstances, and development of the victimizer and to realize that if he or she were placed in a position with the same limitations, circumstances, and development, he or she might make similar mistakes (Hargrave & Pfitzer, 2003). Essentially, it is the victim of the violation putting him- or herself in the footsteps or shoes of the victimizer and understanding that victimizer's history of violations. This potentially has two powerful effects. First, the understanding technique redresses the primary emotion of feeling unloved by making a new cognitive construction of self possible. Victimizers do not have to be monsters, and victims do not have to be unworthy. The bind is released as individuals realize that all involved make mistakes and are potentially victims of violations. But, even with these flaws, they are worthy of being loved and being held responsible as human beings. Second, understanding sets the stage for the individual to understand clearly his or her process and how self-reactivity may have resulted in violating love and trustworthiness with others (Hargrave, 2001).

In the case of the man discussed in this chapter, he was locked into a continual cycle of mostly shaming himself as unlovable and unworthy with an occasional explosion of anger and blame. In the fifth session, the psychotherapist began to tease out the connections of humanity of both the man and his mother:

Therapist: It is always surprising to me that your mother left you on your own to fend for yourself. What do you think was behind that action?

Man: I don't know. [*Long pause.*] I suppose she was just scared to upset the status quo.

Therapist: What made her frightened?

Man: She was always a frightened woman. She still is scared. She grew up in a household where her father was an alcoholic and was really volatile. I think she grew up always trying to avoid a situation where her father would blow up, and her mother was totally ineffective in helping her.

Therapist: So, what did she do to survive?

Man: She laid low. I think that she married my father just to escape the house, figuring that anything would be better than where she was living. I don't really know anything about my father, but I'm sure that it was no bed of roses for her.

Therapist: I'm sure it wasn't. So, what do you think she learned about herself through those experiences?

Man: I'm sure she felt as if she wasn't worth anything. Basically, everything she knew was out of control, so she just stayed out of everyone's way in order to minimize her hurt.

Therapist: And then you came along.

Man: Yeah, I came along. She probably didn't know what to do with me. She probably just felt like I was another potential thing that could get out of control. She laid low with me. It sure didn't do me any good.

Therapist: No, it didn't, and it hurt you because you never were really sure if she loved you and was willing to make sacrifices for you. Instead, she expected you to lay low also and make it easier or more controlled for her.

Man: That's absolutely true. I always felt like if I wasn't worth something to my mother that I really must be worthless. It was more important to her to keep her fragile life together than protect me from her husband.

Therapist: [*Long pause.*] You think your mother's actions were about you being worthless.

Man: [*Long pause.*] Not really. I mean, that is my knee-jerk reaction to feel like I was unloved. But I think deep down my mother loves me. She was so frozen up with her stuff that she sacrificed me and herself. She probably feels worthless most of the time also.

The man demonstrated that he was starting to make some identification with his mother's story and situation. He acknowledged the possibility that his mother's actions were not because he was unworthy, but rather that she was scared and was protecting herself. He further acknowledged identification with her feelings of worthlessness. The therapist then used this as the opportunity to secure the identification to loosen his perception of being unlovable and unworthy:

Therapist: You said that deep down you think that your mother loves you. Tell me more because your mother simply didn't put your interests above hers.

Man: [*Long pause; stares at the ground.*] I say that because I've laid low in my family also. My wife is a good mother, and I'm not scared of her for the way she acts, but I always feel so incompetent and worthless. When I consistently feel that way, I end up just slinking away into my own shell. I lay low for different reasons than my mother, but I still lay low.

Therapist: And how does that relate to your mother loving you?

Man: Because I love my kids. I don't show them because I'm so tied up with my own feelings, but I really do care for them.

Therapist: [*Long pause.*] So, if you lay low and really do love your kids, you believe that your mother also loved you even though she laid low.

Man: I think so. It had more to do with her stuff than it did with not loving me. [*Long pause.*] The same is true with my kids. They probably feel like they are not important to me. Actually, they are everything to me. I just don't show them.

Therapist: The reason you don't show them. …

Man: Too tied up in my own stuff—just like my mom.

This was essential identification that the man made in understanding how his mother's behavior did not make a commentary on his own worthiness and lovability and understanding his own feelings about his failure to show love toward his own children. This opening and connection gave a tremendous therapeutic opportunity as the therapist could now help the man make the transition and consolidation of his own worthiness and start changing the actions in his behavior with his children.

Therapist: So, if it is true that your mother just got too tied up with her own fear to take up for you and show you love, what does that mean about this feeling of unworthiness that you carry around?

Man: It means that I am no more unlovable and unworthy than my children.

Therapist: Can you say that you are lovable and worthy?

Man: I am lovable and worthy. Easy to say but hard to believe.

Therapist: Say it again.

Man: [*Slower and tears up.*] I am lovable and worthy.

Therapist: [*Long pause.*] If you were able to hold that for just a little, what difference would it make for you?

Man: [*Long pause.*] It would free me up some. I could be more loving to my wife and kids.

The man made tremendous connection with this session through the use of understanding. He stated later in the session, "I just feel like something shifted in me a bit, and I'm a little energized to go back to my family and act a little differently." When the therapist asked if he had any different feelings toward his mother, he said, "I don't think I am as angry with her, but mainly I feel like there is something good about me." These were sure signs that the intervention of understanding had a good effect on the man's sense of self and his reactivity of shaming self and escape behaviors.

Finding and Identifying the Truth About Self

There is little doubt that the intervention of understanding is a powerful step in helping the individual toward self-healing. Another power step in assisting the individual toward this self-healing is helping him or her identify the essential elements of truth about him- or herself and integrating those into a sense of self through the idea of self-parenting. As stated, individuals are usually taught the essential elements of identity and safety when they are young and have little choice or knowledge about how love and trustworthiness are communicated. They are largely passive participants as they are taught about love and trustworthiness through relationship and largely are shaped through the experience and self-reactivity that was not a cognitive choice. As a result, the individual is usually brought up in an environment in which the actions of caregivers set the stage for meaning made around identity and safety. Over time, these original actions are repeated, with the individual reinforced with certain status concerning this identity and safety. Soon, the individual, with no cognitive effort, has integrated automatic assumptions about his or her identity and safety just the same way as he or she learned to speak and communicate with language. It is so natural for the individual that the assumptions that he or she makes about identity and safety are treated as the truth for that individual. Unless this truth about identity or safety is challenged effectively, the individual often remains trapped in the primary feelings associated with lack of love and trustworthiness.

Some will challenge us here from a postmodern and constructivist viewpoint in our use of the word *truth*. As we have discussed, we believe that the meanings of identity and safety are constructed elements, but that the elements are constructed in ways consistent with meaning/actions, love and trustworthiness. Here, we go a step further in stating that we also believe that there are elements of intrinsic value for human beings that are more than just a social construction. We believe that there is intrinsic value in humans because there is evidence of innate values such as justice (Buber, 1958) and love (Rogers, 1961). Because we feel these values are innate and not socially constructed, we would hold firm to the idea that all humans *should* experience being lovable and safe consistent with their intrinsic value. While we acknowledge that the construction of identity and safety are dependent on experience, the value of humanity is essential in our therapeutic work.

We feel, therefore, that it makes sense that an individual should be able eventually to have a choice concerning identity and safety in line with his or her innate value. While this identity and sense of safety are constructed for him or her in early foundations, we believe it is possible for the individual to reorient or reconstruct his or her sense of self and safety as he or she approaches or is in adulthood. Therefore, when we say we want to help the individual reorient to the truth about him- or herself, we are making a case for this freedom and ability to choose the truth that is most consistent with his or her value. In essence, it is the confrontation of the "lie" that was taught to an individual concerning the sense of self and safety in which he or she can make personal choices concerning who he or she is and how the person wants to behave in relationships.

To find and identify this sense of truth about self and safety, we have identified three essential sources. The first is the absolute essential element in this reconstruction because without it, all other resources become meaningless. We identify the *self* as the essential element of this truth concerning identity and safety because if the individual chooses not to believe what others say or trust interactions, his or her brain is indeed powerful enough to reject all other possibilities. For instance, if a therapist were to sit in a room of therapists and tell them that he or she thinks that he or she is unlovable and unwanted, chances would be high that all the therapists would be willing to comment on the individual's lovability and how he or she was wanted. Even though the therapists might be sincere, the individual therapist could easily reject their efforts simply because they were not powerful enough to overcome what he or she decided to believe in his or her brain. Unless the individual chose first to make something powerful and to speak to his or her personal sense of self and safety, the individual therapist would likely continue to regard whatever he or she had decided the personal truth was about his or her sense of self and safety. However, if the therapist did choose to make decisions and choices regarding a personal status of love and trustworthiness, *others* could become a powerful tool for reinforcing those beliefs. Finally, some will find that they can effectively redress some of these issues through *spiritual sources* if they are willing to make the decision individually to redress the status of the meanings made in the past (Hargrave & Pfitzer, 2003).

Self

How does an individual become powerful enough to challenge the constructs of identity and safety that were taught through relationships and experiences when the individual had no choice? While we certainly acknowledge that this is a more difficult task, we have found that it is clinically effective to have the individual take a personal position that is intentionally one of *reparenting*. We do believe that original caregivers and parents maintain a powerful position in determining a child's sense of self and safety, and much of that power remains even as the child grows into adulthood. But we also have found that the adult has power to speak to him- or herself as if he or she were a parent and remake these decisions concerning identity and safety. The most powerful times we have seen this work were in the use of imagery, by which the adult gains an image of the self at a particular vulnerable age. This vulnerable age is many times associated with times when the individual identified harmful messages or actions given during childhood. When the client or patient is able to conceptualize him- or herself at this vulnerable age, the therapist directs the individual to talk to this child from his or her adult position with the expressed intent of reparenting the person's perspective on identity and safety. For instance, the following is from the case in this chapter; the client is walked through this process of speaking to his 7-year-old self:

Man: [*Eyes closed, imagining himself as a 7-year-old.*] All I can see is that little boy sitting in his room alone. He is afraid to go out because he will get in the way, get a negative message, or get abused. He hates being there in his room, though. He really wants something but is stuck.

Therapist: As you see this boy, can you make yourself be inside of him?

Man: [*Pause.*] Yes. I hate being there, but I'm scared to go anywhere else. I'm frozen.

Therapist: [*Long pause.*] As you sit in that room, I want you to see yourself as you are now as an adult come through the door and enter the room. [*Pause.*] And as you see yourself come in the room, I want you to make yourself be in your adult self looking now at the 7-year-old you. [*Long pause.*] Knowing what he feels and knowing that you are an adult who has the power to speak into him, what do you want to do or say?

Man: [*Long pause; voice is shaky.*] I want to say to him. …

Therapist: Say it to him directly.

Man: You are okay. You are a precious guy, and I know exactly how you feel. But, you are an individual who is wanted by me if no one else. You weren't safe when you were alone, but I have enough power now to make sure that you are safe. You don't have to sit here and be by yourself anymore. You can be with me. I care for you. You are loved.

Therapist: [*Pause.*] What is it you do?

Man: I take him in my arms and take him out of there. He doesn't have to hide anymore.

This kind of experience is so much past the old *Saturday Night Live* skits in which the therapist practices self-talk with a celebrity saying, "You are good enough. You are smart enough. And doggone it, people like you." This kind of experience helps the individual actually make an emotional connection of speaking to him- or herself. It gives the individual an opportunity to integrate a new truth about his or her identity and safety that is based on personal choice. As a result, the therapist can help the client or patient recall this action or practice new imagery often as the new truth about his or her identity is integrated. Frankly, we have been consistently amazed and pleased with the outcomes of this intervention in helping the individual who carries negative and recurring thoughts concerning identity and safety replace these thoughts with a firm construction. As a result, when the individual ties into or reconstructs new primary emotions, it enhances his or her ability to make choices that are based in human agency instead of self-reactivity.

But, there is also a corresponding effect if the individual is unwilling to make this effort at giving him- or herself the message of identity and safety. The result is often that the individual becomes stagnated in the belief that there is indeed nothing that can be done in his or her circumstances or a truth that will convince him or her differently. The individual, in essence, continues the lack of growth by which he or she depends on others or the situation to convince him- or herself of identity or safety. As mentioned, because others or even spiritual resources are unable to comment or make this key difference without the power and consent of the individual choosing to reparent him- or herself, even when others try to convince the person of worth or safety, it is rejected. The individual stays stuck in his or her "lie."

Others
If the individual is willing to take this step of having him- or herself accept new truths about identity and safety, then the words of others can become powerful in helping to address the same issues. It is as if the willingness of the individual to reparent him- or herself provides power to make the construction of others actually count. Who is powerful enough to speak to a person's life concerning identity or safety? Certainly, we would consider that original caregivers or parents have such power. This does not necessarily mean that all violations of love and trustworthiness can be addressed as sometimes the people who caused the original damage are still damaging. Other times, these original caregivers are dead and gone. But, if possible, we have found that when the people who are responsible for the original programming of love and trustworthiness can speak directly to those issues in a different way than they originally did, it can make a dramatic difference. It is much like adding an update to an old computer program. Even when the individual is an adult and the programming of love and trustworthiness took place decades ago, key family members and caregivers retain power to speak to identity and security

issues like few others. Therefore, it always is a good idea to make this redress effort if possible (Hargrave, 2001).

How does one know if the redress effort is possible? First, it is good to see if the family members or caregivers are more mature and wiser. As folks mature, they usually see where they fell short in the issues of love and trustworthiness and wish to make a difference. Although there is a variety of responses to this knowledge, many caregivers long for a way to communicate their missteps when they were younger. In these cases, they mostly need specificity and opportunity. The psychotherapist can assist both the patient/client and the caregiver by facilitating direct communication about the issues of love and trustworthiness and looking for opportunity to bring the two together. When these direct interchanges concerning love and trustworthiness can take place between an individual and his or her caregiver, there can be a dynamic effect on the meanings the individual places on identity and safety. In essence, the psychotherapist helps the client or patient and his or her caregivers make a map to rewrite the original program (Hargrave & Pfitzer, 2003).

Second, it is essential to see if the individual client or patient realizes the effects that the violations of love and trustworthiness had in contributing to personal destructive entitlement. As stated, violations of this love and trustworthiness often result in self-reactive efforts that mostly become damaging not only to the individual but also to his or her relationships. In other words, victims often also become victimizers. When an individual recognizes his or her contribution to damaging others in terms of love and trustworthiness, the individual often becomes more open to recognizing the need for redress of his or her identity and safety issues. If this is the case, the redress from family or caregivers will become much more effective for the client or patient.

Finally, it is necessary to look for the desire of the client and family member for this type of redress. Individuals and family members often desire the issues to be redressed but are sometimes locked into such deep reactivity—particularly blame and shame—that they will refuse the opportunities for love and trustworthiness for which they long in relationships. If this type of reactivity and coping is locked in, it is often better for the therapist to look at other means to address this issue, primarily through self-redress and reparenting.

It is also essential to realize that other individuals have the power to be able to speak this truth to someone else if the client or patient sees these individuals as powerful in speaking to identity and safety. Mentors, seniors, siblings, spouses, and sometimes even children can have a special sense of the client's identity and power in relationships and can speak directly to help reshape the meaning of those issues. Much of this power, of course, is dependent on the client or patient and whether the person will make the meaning powerful in reshaping identity and safety issues. But, some of the power lies with the psychotherapist's skill in moving the client along in the process of reshaping the beliefs about him- or herself and presenting opportunities for these types of important individuals to speak to the client.

Spiritual Sources

Not every client or patient who comes to therapy will have spiritual beliefs that are important personally, but many are devout in the importance that spirituality plays in their life. According to Doherty (1996), many in psychotherapy have treated spirituality in a morally neutral way to avoid the possibility of offense. We see this as problematic because any resource that is a possible strength for the client in helping him or her redress issues of identity and safety should be used. Also, neutrality or staying away from a person's spirituality most likely communicates disapproval or an attitude that may come across to a client as patronizing. If spirituality is an important resource to the client or patient, we believe that it simply must be a part of reshaping this love and trustworthiness (Hargrave & Pfitzer, 2003).

A psychotherapist need not become an expert on all spiritual realms or religions to use them as a resource. We simply believe that the psychotherapist must treat spirituality similarly to a gender or multicultural issue. In these issues, competent therapists are often curious, open, and willing to be taught by the client or patient on how the issues play into the client's or patient's view of the world, relationships, and sense of self. Spirituality, in our opinion, should be treated in the same way as gender or multicultural issues in that the psychotherapist takes the issue seriously and looks for ways that the spiritual beliefs of the client can be used therapeutically to address the sense of identity and safety. Most spiritual resources promote senses of love, peace, honor, tranquility, trustworthiness, power, justice, and community. Often, these ideals can be used effectively to help the client or patient gain a sense of being loved by God or a higher being and that there is a community around the individual that can function in a redemptive and trustworthy fashion (Hargrave & Pfitzer, 2003).

Working Up and Working Down

It is always beneficial for the psychotherapist to have in mind at least a three-generational complex when working with these issues of love, trustworthiness, and self-healing. Even when working with an individual, the psychotherapist has this multigenerational complex available because of the nature of the beliefs and meanings that the client or patient made from his or her family of origin, the way that he or she is acting and behaving in current relationships, and the identity and safety issues that the client or patient is shaping or will shape in the next generation. This three-generational complex is always present and gives the psychotherapist a unique ability to address issues of love and trustworthiness actively (Hargrave & Metcalf, 2000).

In the technique of working up one generation and working down one generation, the psychotherapist has the unique opportunity to identify violations of love and trustworthiness without provoking defensiveness and aggression (Hargrave & Pfitzer, 2003). In individuals who come from backgrounds in which there was damage to identity and safety, the opportunity for self-justifying, reactive, and destructive behavior is high. If the therapist simply focuses on these issues only with the individual and tries to drive certain points of identity or responsibility home, it likely will provoke the kind of defensiveness and aggression in the therapeutic relationship that is not helpful. In this technique, the psychotherapist is sensitive to being partial to all members' ledger issues and is still able to avoid the defensiveness or aggressiveness by switching the generational focus. For instance, a woman who came to therapy was referred by the courts for having abusive outbursts with her two children, ages 7 and 5. After four sessions exploring the woman's background and her history of abuse, the therapist pointed her toward her mother's history of pain, one of her children's pain, and then finally her own pain. This oscillating balance of working up and down from the various generations gave the woman a clear opportunity to identify those issues of love and trustworthiness that most needed addressing within herself and enabled her to address the issue using responsibility and self-parenting.

Woman: I know that I did some things wrong with my children, but I still have trouble with being required to be here. Not once have people been concerned about my history or what I have had to put up with in my past.

129

Therapist: [*Long pause.*] It seems like your mother should be the one to have to be here taking some of the responsibility for the damage she caused you.

Woman: Exactly.

Therapist: I do wonder about your mother. Because I know that you were victimized by her and made some mistakes with your children, I wonder if she was victimized since she did such damaging things to you?

Woman: [*Angry.*] I know she was. She was abused by her father and mother. She passed it right along to me.

Therapist: To be in that position … to know that you are being abused by the people that are supposed to love you … what does that do to the way you think about yourself?

Woman: [*Long pause. Much softer in tone.*] It makes you feel awful. It makes you feel defective. You wish that you could do something to make the situation different, but you can't.

Therapist: What did your mother feel when she was growing up?

Woman: I don't know what she felt.

Therapist: You know what it is like to be in that situation.

Woman: [*Long pause.*] She felt worthless. She wanted someone to make her feel like she was wanted and loved. [*Long pause.*] She sure didn't get that from her parents, and I suppose that is why she had me. She wanted me to make her feel like she mattered. She was way too young to have me.

Here is the first substantial connection in the working up one generation. Notice how the woman started the transaction in an angry and self-justifying stance. When the psychotherapist moved the connection up one generation, the psychotherapist was able to connect the woman with underlying emotion connected to primary feelings about lack of love and trustworthiness. If the psychotherapist would have asked the woman directly about how she felt, she would have likely focused on the secondary feelings connected with her reactivity and coping—mainly anger and blame. In working up, the psychotherapist was able to connect her with her primary feelings by focusing on the feelings that the mother must have felt. Because of the nature of the slate of injustices and violations that were passed from one generation to the next, the psychotherapist could be sure that these feelings that the woman was identifying about her mother were indeed feelings that she also felt. As the session continued, notice how the psychotherapist now used those feelings to work down one generation to the woman's 7-year-old daughter.

Therapist: [*Long pause.*] Your daughter. She longs also for those feelings that she is loved and wanted. How do you communicate those things to her?

Woman: I tell her that I love her. [*Long pause.*] But I also know she gets confusing messages from me. I lose it with her and expect way too much of her for her age. [*Starts to cry.*] I sometimes look at that child and just wonder what she is thinking about her situation.

Therapist: [*Long pause.*] What does your daughter think about herself and her situation?

Woman: [*Long pause.*] She must be confused. She hears me say that I love her but then gets this anger and abuse from me. I'm sure it makes her feel like she is worthless and unloved. She probably just doesn't know what to do.

The psychotherapist made the connection with the generation below the woman and found a substantial connection in terms of confusion and powerlessness. Not only did the woman identify with key identity issues but also she now connected safety issues. The psychotherapist can use this opportunity to move in several directions, ranging from partiality to each generation to the mother's responsibility. But, in our opinion, the technique of working up and working down is most effective in helping the client or patient connect these feelings to him- or herself and utilize the connection as an opportunity to self-parent. The psychotherapist in this case drew the woman into imagery of speaking to her daughter and then utilized the identified words to work back up to the generational complex eventually to speak to herself.

Therapist: If your daughter were here in the room with you now and you could look into her eyes and see that confusion and the sense that she is not loved, how would you respond?

Woman: [*Long pause; cries.*] I would like to say I would say something that would help her, but honestly I would feel like I would make an excuse.

Therapist: What would you say to her? Tell her now?

Woman: I'm doing the best I can do. I know that I don't do the things I should, but I have a lot of pressure on me.

Therapist: [*Long pause.*] How does your daughter feel when she hears this?

131

Woman: [*Long pause.*] She probably has the same confusion she did before. It does nothing for her.

Therapist: And how do you know it does nothing for her?

Woman: [*Pause.*] Because I have heard these excuses all my life. It does nothing to make you feel any differently about yourself or the situation. It is just an excuse.

Therapist: What did you need to hear?

Woman: I needed to hear that my mother was sorry for when she lost it and needed to hear that I was okay. I needed to hear that she was going to do better for me and treat me with love.

Therapist: Say it like a mother to yourself.

Woman: [*Pause.*] I am sorry for losing it with you. I am sorry for my mistake. I have these feelings that confuse me, and I get off track, but they are not your fault. You are okay. You are just fine. I will get it right.

Therapist: [*Long pause.*] When you hear yourself say those things, what would those things have meant to you?

Woman: [*Long pause.*] I think that it would have made all the difference. Maybe I wouldn't have had to carry so much confusion.

Therapist: I really don't want you to carry that confusion either. It seems like that it is being passed along from your mother, to you and to your daughter. It would be good if you could give that message of clarity to yourself.

Woman: To my daughter.

Therapist: Yes, but to give it to you daughter, you must first give it to yourself. [*Long pause.*] Just give it a try. Speak those words to yourself.

Woman: [*Pause.*] Your mother made a lot of mistakes with you. They are not your fault. You're okay. You don't have to make excuses. You can be loving.

The psychotherapist intentionally had the woman speak to herself first instead of speaking to the daughter. The technique of working up and working down not only helped the woman identify which feelings exist within her and other generations but also pointed toward the direction that she must go to heal herself and other generations. At the beginning of the next session, the woman reported that she not only gave this message to herself but also had given the message to both her mother and daughter, even though the therapist did not suggest it. Working up and working down often gives this kind of broad therapeutic intuition to the client or patient by which the client or patient can work on his or her self-healing and restorative efforts.

INTERVENTIONS DIRECTED AT RELATIONAL ACTIONS

We believe in the power of individuals to make a difference in life within the intergenerational complex we call family. We often think of the family as a long bridge that extends backward through seemingly infinite generations and moving to the other side of generations yet to be born. Each individual stands on that bridge. The condition of the structure—the love and trustworthiness that has been passed along to him or her—has been determined and has left the individual on either a firm and solid platform or a damaged, insecure, and unsure foundation. But, no matter what the condition of the bridge going backward, it is the individual's turn to do work on the bridge. How he or she does the work of love and trustworthiness in the present will largely determine the condition of the bridge as it moves forward for generations to come.

It is imperative, therefore, in the restoration therapy model to help the individual move from self-healing actually to practice these new behaviors in a context that can make a difference in current relationships and the future relationships that move across the bridge of family. We utilize two primary interventions designed to start an individual interacting differently in current relationships. These interventions are *right script but wrong players* and *balancing obligations and entitlements.* In both of these interventions, the primary focus is to help individuals behave differently in current relationships to produce an atmosphere of increased love and trustworthiness.

Right Script but Wrong Players

A good friend and colleague, Glen Jennings, used to say that often what we see in an individual in terms of behavior or feelings is an effort for working out their relational claims and turmoil. He would say, "They have the right relational script that they are trying to correct but [they are] trying to correct it with the wrong relational players." We often see this in therapy when it is helpful for an individual to recognize that he or she has a legitimate relational claim, but he or she is trying to redeem or play out that claim with the wrong people (Hargrave & Pfitzer, 2003).

133

In other words, an individual has been violated in terms of love and trustworthiness but the individual's reactivity and coping with the violation is most often directed toward innocent parties, who are further hurt by their irresponsibility. The innocent parties can do nothing to address the violations the individual feels, yet the individual feels driven and justified to seek love and trustworthiness. The key elements of the technique, then, are to help the individual clearly recognize his or her relational claim, make the inappropriateness of the demand of the relational claim on innocent parties, and then help the individual address their just entitlement to love and trustworthiness in a more appropriate way (Hargrave & Pfitzer, 2003).

Recognizing the Relational Claim

In the following case example, a middle-age woman was struggling with issues in her family and marriage. She stated that she consistently felt overwhelmed by the irresponsibility of her two sons in being truant from school and not doing their "fair share" at home and neglected and ignored by her husband of 14 years. She stated that her husband did not do a good job of taking care of her and was "never around when I really need him." At the time she came to therapy, she said that she was seriously considering divorce because there was a man whom she had become interested in at her work. Although she reported elements of having an emotional affair with this man at work through their interactions in person and online, she said the relationship did not have any physical aspects yet.

In the first three sessions, the woman reported that she had come from a background in which she was sexually abused by an older brother on three occasions. Her mother and father both worked and were largely absent from giving her care and appropriate supervision. She reported being afraid of her older brother but at the same time felt that he was the only person on whom she could depend. When asked about her feelings growing up, she reported that she did not want to focus on the past because "it never did her any good" but instead wanted some direction on how to make her current relationships different. The psychotherapist in the case wisely recognized that some of her reactions in current relationships came directly from her self-reactivity to the lack of love and trustworthiness that she felt growing up in a neglectful and abusive environment. The woman's dissatisfaction with her husband and sons, as well as the emotional connection with another man, was likely connected to her trying to work out old issues of love and trustworthiness in the context of current relationships. The therapist's first step in working the intervention of right script but wrong players was to help the woman identify her right relational claim from the past. Notice how the psychotherapist in the case moved the woman from the feeling that in her current relationships she had to the focus these feelings where they rightly belonged—in her family of origin:

Therapist: Think about your marriage for a few moments. When you think about how you feel in your marriage, what are the words that come to mind?

Woman: Unimportant. Ignored. [*Pause.*] Unloved. Angry. There are probably more, but those are the main ones.

Therapist: And tell me about the length of time that you felt these things in your marriage?

Woman: I probably felt them from almost the beginning of the 14 years.

Therapist: Okay. Now think about your boys for a couple of moments. When you think about how you feel about being a parent, what are the words that come to mind?

Woman: I feel powerless. Hopeless. [*Pause.*] Resentful.

Therapist: [*Pause.*] Those are powerful emotions.

Woman: I haven't always felt that way about them. It is just the last few years. I've given everything to my boys, and now they treat me like I don't matter. They don't mind me, and they don't give me the time of day. They are doing exactly as their father taught them and not how I taught them.

Therapist: [*Long pause.*] When you look back on your life with your parents and the feelings you felt back then, what words come to mind?

Woman: I don't know. [*Pause.*] I wasn't important enough to them for them to make time for me. They left me on my own way too much. I had to take care of myself, and it was scary at times. I wasn't protected by them.

Therapist: [*Long pause.*] And the feelings you feel when you think about your brother and the abuse?

Woman: [*Pause.*] I felt so disempowered. I was used.

Therapist: [*Long pause.*] When you hear yourself say those words of feelings from your husband, unimportant, ignored, unloved, and when you hear those words that you feel in relation to your boys, powerless, hopeless, resentful, they sound very close to the words that you use when you are talking about your parents and your brother.

Woman: Pretty much so. [*Long pause.*] I've probably felt those things all my life. I am so sick of feeling that way.

Therapist: I can imagine so. It makes sense to me, however, how you would feel these things for a long time.

Woman: How so?

Therapist: You come from a situation where you were largely ignored by your parents and left on your own and unprotected from your brother. You needed them to love you, pay attention to you, and protect you. You were abused by your brother, who should have looked out for you and given you respect. You have been looking for love, meaning, respect, protection, safety, and power all your life.

Woman: Are you saying that I married my husband because he is like my parents?

Therapist: Not so much, although there may be something in your unconscious that has something to do with that. What I am saying here is that you deserved something from your family that you did not receive. You deserved love, attention, and protection from them. You didn't get it, and you still feel the drive to get those things.

Woman: I do. Those are the things that are most important to me. That is why I am so upset when I don't get love, attention, and respect from my family now.

Therapist: I understand that clearly. But, I do want you to understand that this intense need that you have to be loved—to be important, powerful, and respected—comes first from the relationships you grew up with. Your original family was the one that set the tone for those feelings, and they were the ones that should have provided you with those things.

Woman: That is definitely true.

Therapist: Your family that you grew up in are the ones that owed you this love, respect, and safety. When you didn't receive those things, you felt pain and damage, and you have sought to cope with it in particular ways. This is where the original violation exists.

Woman: When I hear you say that. … [*Pause.*] It really does make sense to me. I've been carrying around this sense that I had to justify myself. In reality, I just didn't get what I deserved.

The psychotherapist helped the woman close in on the issue of relational imbalance and the specific source of the violation of love and trust. By staying with this focus, the therapist clearly set the stage to help her recognize her relational claim and separate it from her actions that made the claims on her innocent spouse and children.

Inappropriate Claims on Innocent Parties
The focus of the session for the woman in the preceding section now switched to make clear that the self-reactivity and coping that the woman manifested unintentionally victimized her husband and her boys. Here, the psychotherapist moved from recognizing her relational claim that it was justified to pointing out where she needed to shift from using that right script against the wrong players.

Therapist: It makes much sense to me that you have done what is necessary to protect yourself. You married a man that you wanted to take care of you the way that you were not taken care of in your family. When you didn't get what you wanted from him, you really focused on your boys.

Woman: I think I am a good mother.

Therapist: I think you are a good mother also. What are your strongest points as a mother?

Woman: I am totally dedicated to my boys. There is nothing that I would not do for them.

Therapist: I certainly believe that. What is it that you expect in return for your good mothering?

Woman: I expect them to respect me and appreciate what I do for them. It wouldn't hurt them to focus on me every now and then to let me know how much I mean to them.

Therapist: This is where it gets a little confusing to me. When you say that you are looking for respect and recognition from them, it sounds like that you want them to give you what you didn't get from your mom and dad. It sounds like you want them to love you.

Woman: Well, sure I want them to love me. They should!

Therapist: I believe you are a good mother because there is nothing that you would not do for your boys, but I think that when you expect them to love you the way that your parents never did, you make them responsible for what they are not responsible for.

Woman: What do you mean?

Therapist: Your parents owed you love, protection, and respect. You owe the same thing to your boys but not to your parents. Your boys owe it to their children but not to you.

Woman: [*Long pause.*] It never occurred to me that I was expecting them to love me in that way. My mother used to say to me that it was my job to take care of her. I used to think, "It is not my job to take care of you; you are supposed to take care of me." [*Pause.*] I've taken care of my boys, but you are right; I've expected them to love me like I want to be loved.

Therapist: It is understandable. You do deserve to be loved and paid attention to. It is just that the responsibility for that exists with your parents and not with your boys.

Woman: I am beginning to get it how I've asked them to do things that don't belong to them. It was my job to love them but not their job to love me back.

Therapist: Not their job to love you back as a parent. Just to love you as a mother.

The discussion between the therapist and woman then expanded into how she expected her husband to often love her as a parent instead of like a partner. It become clearer to the woman that she was requiring efforts to take care of her and love her that were more associated with what she did not receive from her parents. With this kind of acknowledgment from the woman, the psychotherapist could again reinforce the woman's right script by identifying the proper targets for the entitlement that she did not receive from her parents.

Getting Entitlement Appropriately Addressed
There are times where the redress from parents or family members is possible. In this case, however, the woman did not believe there was a possibility of significant change on the part of her parents or brother. In fact, she felt that her family of origin might use the opportunity to accuse her or to do further damage to her. In cases such as these, the psychotherapist must rely on the client's or patient's resources in terms of understanding and self-parenting while clarifying his or her appropriate expectations family. In the next three sessions, the psychotherapist worked with the woman to clarify her actions to make sure that she was appropriately getting her needs met.

Therapist: So tell me a bit about how you have thought about this just claim that you have in terms of being loved, protected, and respected.

Woman: I still long for those things, but I really think that I was putting myself in a position where my husband and sons were trying to fill a hole that could not be filled. They can love me, but not like a parent loves a child. They can give me some protection but more like a partner who would go through a difficult time with you instead of someone who would keep all difficulty away from you. I've found out that I have more power than I thought.

Therapist: In what ways do you have more power?

Woman: When I just take care of myself more and love myself instead of leaving my husband or boys to do it, I end up happier with them, and they are happier with me.

Therapist: For instance?

Woman: For instance, when I just ask my husband to do something with me instead of complaining about what he is not doing, he responds much better. He actually has been spending more time with me because I think we are moving closer to being a partnership instead of him feeling like he has to parent me.

Therapist: But, how are you getting those parenting needs met? You are still owed those things that you didn't receive from your parents.

Woman: I don't know. I am working on parenting myself like we talked about, but mainly I'm just clear now on the issue. My husband and kids should not have to pay for things that were caused by my parents. When I keep that clear, I actually do a better job of doing what I am supposed to be doing for them.

Here, the woman clearly identified the fact that her more functional behaviors of not mixing up her old entitlement with her husband and boys—in essence, her own agency—provide her with reinforcement for her own identity and safety. She indeed had become more powerful because she was responsible for her actions. When we use the intervention of right script but wrong players, we are seeking not only to identify the proper place for the entitlement of a client or patient but also to help the client identify areas in which he or she can become more responsible in not damaging innocent family members.

Balancing Obligations and Entitlements

The technique of balancing obligations and entitlements was first identified by Hargrave and Anderson (1992) in their work with intergenerational aging families. It was noticed that, in some of these older families, the oldest adult who was receiving care from the younger generations felt overbenefited from the care without much expectation or obligation to give to the relationship. It is essential to remember regarding trustworthiness that imbalance or injustice in the ledger of merits and obligations produces destructive entitlement associated with threat, manipulation, or withdrawal. When older adults experienced this overbenefit, many times they would lash out in anger toward their caregivers, become manipulative, or withdraw from all relationships. When these older adults were given obligations to fulfill in the family, such as sharing wisdom, helping with meals, and checking on family members, they often improved substantially.

Although we agree that the psychotherapist can never know the full extent of the merits and obligations in the intergenerational ledger (Boszormenyi-Nagy & Krasner, 1986), we do believe that the general imbalance in obligations and merits can be detected by the psychotherapist. When these imbalances continue over a longer period of time, there is a family mythology that creeps into the belief system that the imbalance cannot be changed or that the imbalance is impossible to address because of some member's personality (Hargrave & Pfitzer, 2003). When these issues become stagnant, imbalances harden in the family like concrete, and members stop trying to change. In balancing obligations and entitlements, the psychotherapist is not trying to perfectly balance an intergenerational ledger but rather is seeking to get members of the relationship moving again in interactions that are loving and trustworthy. If these interactions are balanced, then the love and trustworthiness experienced create the opportunity for increasingly balanced interactions. As family members give to one another and receive from one another in a balanced fashion, they usually take more steps to give to one another. Therefore, the likelihood of the outcome of balancing efforts is that there will be an ever-increasing spiral of giving between members (Boszormenyi-Nagy & Krasner, 1986).

In the case of the woman discussed above, the psychotherapist had surmised that she had created a tremendous imbalance in her current family relationships by being attentive to giving on some care issue like cooking, cleaning, and being present at functions but had been particularly withholding on issues of appropriate emotional connection. Her work on right script but wrong players had helped her situation, but she still felt disrespected because of the discrepancy in the amount of work done in the home. This imbalance created a tremendous amount of resentment on her part because she worked doing most of the physical chores at the house with little support or help from her husband or sons. Yet, on the other hand, she expected her sons and her husband to express emotional love and appreciation for her. When she did not receive this emotional expression, she would almost totally cut off making any emotional expression to her family members. The therapist also surmised that this was the reason that she sought out the emotional affair with another man. She continued to work hard to try to manipulate some emotional expression for her husband and sons. In response, they would not do much around the house and would not be forthcoming in response to her manipulation. She in turn would work harder and express less emotionally to them, instead complaining of their lack of emotional nurturing. This was a destructive cycle that was born from the imbalance of the relational ledger.

To address the imbalance, the psychotherapist asked the woman to bring her husband to a session. Notice in the following dialogue how the therapist moved the woman to balance expecting more physical labor from the husband and more emotional expression on her part. At the same time, the husband became more responsible to the balance by responding in a more trustworthy and loving fashion.

Therapist: So, what has transpired in your relationship is that you [*points toward the wife*] do almost everything in connection with the house and complain that he does not give you the respect and affection he should for doing so much. And you [*points toward the husband*] don't do much around the house and in fact avoid your wife because she complains. Am I getting this correct?

Husband: Yes, that is just about it.

Woman: Yes, that is right, but I have been much better in making complaints. I don't make the same statements that I used to.

Therapist: I am sure that is the case. I think you are really getting the idea clearly that you didn't get the love and respect from your parents that you deserved, and that it is not your husband's responsibility to make up for what your parents did not give you. But, I am still concerned with the imbalance in the relationship between you two.

Woman: I am, too. He does nothing around the house.

Husband: I don't do anything because I can never do anything that pleases you.

Therapist: That is not the imbalance that I would like to take on first. The first issue that I am concerned about is the amount of emotional connection and expression between the two of you.

Woman: [*Silence. Couple is clearly uncomfortable.*] I'm not sure that we have much emotional connection.

Therapist: [*To the husband.*] What has happened to the emotional connection between the two of you?

Husband: I suppose we have just drifted apart. We just have little to do with one another anymore. We don't touch and don't say much of anything to one another. Then, there is this thing she got involved with—this other guy.

[*Long pause.*] I just think that we have drifted apart and now there is too much hurt. It is just about raising the boys.

Therapist: I can appreciate that the emotional affair caused hurt. What is it that the hurt indicates? What is that pain that you feel telling you?

Husband: I suppose it means that I must care some. [*Long pause.*] I just don't know how we could ever get back on track.

Therapist: Tell me how you wish you could be connected to your wife, even if you don't think it is possible.

Husband: [*Long pause; stares at the ground.*] I just wish she would want me for something other than what I can do. I wish that she would find me a little desirable, and that she even liked me some.

Therapist: And have you [*to the husband*] ever expressed that need or want to her?

Husband: No.

Therapist: Have you ever expressed to her that you thought she was desirable, and that you liked her?

Husband: Not in a long time.

Therapist: How about you [*to the wife*]? Have you expressed any emotional connection to your husband?

Woman: Not in a long time.

Therapist: This is the imbalance that concerns me the most. You both know as a husband and wife that you have a need to be desirable; you need to physically touch one another, be sexual with one another, and move toward one another. Yet, you do not do what you know you should. It is hard.

Woman: It is hard to get something like that back especially when you don't feel it.

142

Therapist: I understand that. Yet, both of you have something that the other needs. To be desired. To be liked. It seems, however, that you don't express it to one another, preferring instead to stay away or do housework.

Husband: So, how do we get out of this situation?

Therapist: I'm not sure it will work magic, but I do know that your relationship will not be right until you both take some responsibility to do more emotionally connecting. Just starting out by expressing to one another that you desire and like one another would be a good start.

Husband: [*Long pause.*] I do love you despite all the problems. I still think of you as my wife and friend.

Woman: [*Starts to cry; long pause.*] I am so sorry for the things I've done and getting involved with this other guy.

Therapist: [*Interrupts.*] While you may want to apologize for the affair at some point, right now I am asking you if you want to address what you feel toward him emotionally.

Woman: [*Continues to cry; long pause.*] I love you, too. I do think that you know me better than anyone. I still would like us to work.

Just this simple interaction had a significant effect on the couple. The couple became much more emotionally connected and certainly more open to one another. The psychotherapist assigned the couple for the next week to find one new thing each day that was desirable in the spouse and report it to the spouse. When the couple returned the following week, they reported that they had a much better week and perhaps the best week in their marriage since their children were born. As the therapist surmised, when the woman became more emotionally expressive, she became less manipulative in her efforts to get the husband to express care. As the husband became more balanced in his expression of emotion, he became less distant and destructive in his criticism. Surprisingly, during the week the couple also had sexual relations for the first time in over a year. In addition, the woman reported that the husband had actually been more active concerning housework and parenting the boys.

Although few cases show such dramatic effect in one week, it is not unusual for balancing efforts to produce clear and solid results toward change. The simple fact is that when individuals responsibly give to one another in a trustworthy and loving manner, they earn entitlement for themselves, and the other in the relationship is likely to respond in a similar way. Balance and justice in the give-and-take of a relationship produce mutual giving (Boszormenyi-Nagy & Krasner, 1986). The intervention of balancing obligations and entitlements often calls for the psychotherapist to be clear on the imbalances that are present and be specific in the requests to address the imbalances.

INTERVENTIONS DIRECTED AT LOVE AND TRUSTWORTHINESS IN THE INTERGENERATIONAL FAMILY

Forgiveness, Salvage, and Restoration

Although Chapter 8 is dedicated to the ideas and process of forgiveness in the restoration therapy model, it is good to put the process in the context of the other therapeutic interventions. When interventions that are directed at relational actions have a dynamic effect on *current* relationships with regard to love and trustworthiness, these sets of interventions are more directed at addressing not only current relationships, but the *future* relationships that are essential to the growth and nurturing of the intergenerational family. We have previously seen how issues of reactivity, coping, and lack of love and distrust create a spiral of damage in the intergenerational family. In other words, trauma and victimization that are left unaddressed by individuals or the family tend to create more trauma and victimization in the next generation. When one steps into the interventions that deal with forgiveness, the psychotherapist and the client or patient alike decide to do the loving and trustworthy thing for this intergenerational group. Of course, this decision has a dynamic effect on the individual as he or she makes these loving and trustworthy actions; it not only secures different and constructive agency in the current relationships but also positively reinforces that he or she has an identity and is a safe individual. But, the decision to broach forgiveness in the intergenerational group also changes the course for the family. Just as the destination of a spacecraft is changed dramatically by adjusting course a few degrees as it speeds into space, each generation that potentially lives differently in the future finds itself increasingly removed from old destructive and reactive entitlement and more on the right course of love and trustworthiness. Interventions that deal with the issue of forgiveness can be directed into relationships that have simple violations of love

144

and trustworthiness or have heinous insults to those same constructs. It is not that we believe that some abuse and violations are not worse than others because we certainly do believe that to be the case. But also, within the human framework that we have observed clinically, it always surprises us that sometimes seemingly simple violations can produce the same types of reactivity that are present in more heinous forms of abuse (Hargrave, 2001). While it may be true that we think of the work of forgiveness for these more serious violations of identity and safety, it is still true that the intervention may be applicable to a variety of cases. In whatever case it is used, the clear intent is to improve the status of identity not only for the individual but also for his or her current relationships and the intergenerational relationships to come.

Much of the literature on forgiveness focuses on the ideas of letting go of past injustices or hurt and anger associated with the injustices (Hargrave, Froeschle, & Castillo, 2009). While we feel that this is certainly a good idea, we feel it may come up short of what a good model of forgiveness should entail. As we have stated many times, forgiveness is not so much about letting go as it is about putting back. In other words, forgiveness is primarily about putting back as much love and trust in relationships is as feasible and possible (Hargrave, 2001).

Here, we detail the model of forgiveness that we have used for many years (Hargrave, 1994a, 2001; Hargrave & Anderson, 1992; Hargrave & Pfitzer, 2003) and then illustrate the clinical use of the model in Chapter 8. This model is illustrated in Figure 5.1. In this model, we conceptualize the work of forgiveness as having the broad categories of *salvage* and *restoration*. These distinctions are important in that the work of salvage in forgiveness by the victim does not necessarily seek to restore or reestablish the relationship with the victimizer or the person who violated love and trustworthiness. Instead, the victim seeks to prevent the victimizer from continuing to hurt him or her, seeks ways to prevent his or her own destructive tendencies for the sake of future relationships, and seeks

The Work of Forgiveness			
Salvage		Restoration	
Insight	Understanding	Giving Opportunity for Compensation	Overt Forgiving

FIGURE 5.1   Hargrave's model of forgiveness.

constructive ways to understand and address the emotional pain of the past (Hargrave, 2001).

The division of restoration, on the other hand, has a different relational implication in that the victim tries to restore love and trustworthiness in the relationship with the very relationship that caused the violation of love and trustworthiness (Hargrave, 1994a). In restoration, the individual who has been damaged or hurt may seek to restore this love and trust-worthiness by slowly reengaging the violator to see if he or she is not as destructive as before and more loving and trustworthy. In addition, the victim may engage the victimizer directly by confronting and addressing the old relationship overtly. Using this option, the two individuals or vic-tim and victimizer confront the violations of the past together and decide to move in a more loving, trustworthy, and fulfilling relationship.

Under these two categories of salvage and restoration, we define dif-ferent stations of forgiveness (Hargrave & Pfitzer, 2003): insight, under-standing, giving opportunity for compensation, and overt forgiving. We make a distinction that these stations are not *stages* in which a victim will proceed from insight to eventual overt forgiving. Instead, the stations represent the different ways that victims find in going about the work of forgiveness and being loving and trustworthy in relationships. One indi-vidual may find that the only work of forgiveness to be done with a past harmful relationship is the work of insight, while another may eventually use not only insight but also understanding and giving the opportunity for compensation. The point is that this model is not a prescribed pathway or map of how individuals must proceed to get to the issue of forgiveness. Instead, the model represents a process in which most individuals find a method or methods to continue to refine and recover from the violations of the past (Hargrave, 2001).

Insight

The first station of the work of forgiveness under salvage is called *insight*. Insight enables the individual who has experienced damaging violations of love and trustworthiness to explore the mechanisms and interactions by which he or she was harmed. In using insight, the psychotherapist seeks to help the client or patient develop a clear understanding of the sequences and interactions that caused the violations and damage. Once this sequence is identified, the client or patient is encouraged and prac-ticed in the process necessary to set boundaries or take different actions to make the damaging outcome different (Hargrave, 2001). Even though many of these actions and behaviors are done through imagery, there are some instances for which insight is useful in actual interactions with people who have violated the individual in terms of identity and safety. As stated in Chapter 4, the individual client most often was violated when he or she did not have a substantial choice. Using insight, the psychotherapist can help the client draw these boundaries and make different behavioral decisions for the sake of present relationships (Hargrave, 1994a).

Many would wonder why insight is part of the work of forgiveness. How does it "put back" love and trustworthiness in relationships? We believe that it is the work of forgiveness first because no love or trustworthiness can be restored to any relationship if violations continue to occur. Insight offers the client of patient the possibility of stopping the damage to his or her identity and safety. It is also the work of forgiveness in that when an individual clearly identifies and is able to stop violations of love and trustworthiness that have happened to him or her, the person is also empowered to stop him- or herself from the destructive self-reactivity that results in the victimization of others. In short, the victim is able to have more loving and trustworthy future relationships (Hargrave & Pfitzer, 2003). In these two ways, the client or patient who has past violations is able to salvage through insight an ability to protect him- or herself from future violations of love and trustworthiness and keeps him- or herself in a position of resisting destructive tendencies in current relationships.

Understanding

Although we have discussed the issue of understanding in the context of interventions that produce self-healing, we do want to point out that it is a powerful resource in the work of forgiveness under salvage category. Understanding, as the victim remembers enables the victim to make human identification with the violator of love and trustworthiness who caused the victim so much pain. As the individual makes this human identification, he or she has the ability to be relieved of much of the pain, anger, or self-condemnation that can often result from violations and victimization. As discussed, the violator of love and trustworthiness is not inherently evil but rather is destructive because he or she also was the victim of violations. When the victim realizes that his or her victimizer had these limitations with regard to love or trustworthiness, development, or past abuse, it gives the opportunity to realize that the victimizer is not evil. This is significant in the work of forgiveness because when an individual feels victimized by another, the pain often manifests itself in the form of contempt, hate, or disgust for the wrongdoers. In turn, this contempt, disgust, or hate fuels the very kind of reactivity that becomes damaging or hurtful in other relationships. In addition, the person who has been victimized often believes that he or she deserved the mistreatment and abuse. The victim often feels that being treated in unloving or untrustworthy ways was deserved because he or she reacts or copes through shaming self. Without understanding, the victim of this blame or shame is often left frozen in the emotional violations of hate for the victimizer, hate for him- or herself, or both (Hargrave, in press). With understanding, the victim makes compassionate identification with not only the victimizer but also him- or herself. This opens up the redress of the primary emotions with respect to love and trustworthiness and helps the victim live in future relationships more constructively.

It is important to remember that this kind of understanding does not remove responsibility from the victimizer or remove his or her victimizing behaviors. It does not excuse or let the victimizer "off the hook." Instead, it makes the victimizer responsible for the wrong actions, abuse, or neglect because it assigns the quality of humanness to him or her. Instead of being regarded as a monster who hurts, he or she is a person who must be held accountable for his or her actions. These actions may be understandable given the legacy of abuse, but it does not excuse the perpetuation of the abuse (Hargrave, 1994a).

Giving Opportunity for Compensation

It is essential to remember that when one crosses over into the category of *restoration*, there is real and palatable relational risk as the victim of lack of love and trustworthiness is taking a step into the relationship that caused the violation. The work of forgiveness in this broad division usually goes in the direction of correction and transformation of the victimizer from destructive patterns toward loving and trustworthy action (Hargrave et al., 2009). The intents of these interventions are to rehabilitate the damaged relationship and have the victim and victimizer interact directly. It is always wise for the victim and psychotherapist to be thoughtful about the work of forgiveness in this category to ensure that there is reason to believe that the relationship actually can become loving and trustworthy (Hargrave, 2001). The third station in the work of forgiveness and the first in the category of restoration is *giving the opportunity for compensation*.

In this station, the victim of violation allows the victimizer to engage in a relationship in small interactions to test whether he or she is able to be more loving and trustworthy in current interactions. For instance, the victim may engage the victimizer in a small interaction, such as an e-mail or a short phone call, to see if the victimizer can handle the interaction in a responsible and constructive manner. If so, then the victim may enter the exchange at a little deeper level, such as a more lengthy phone call or even a visit in a public place. If the victimizer proves to have some form of trustworthiness, the victim may be able to take more involved steps, like doing something with the victimizer or even having dinner at a neutral place. The point is that in this station of forgiveness, the victim is able to take increasingly interactive steps with the victimizer as the victimizer proves to be loving and trustworthy. In this way, love and trustworthiness would be restored to the relationship a little at a time over a long period of time (Hargrave, 2001). If the victimizer is not loving and trustworthy, the victim can more easily extricate him- or herself from the relationship with minimal damage because there was minimal risk built into the interaction (Hargrave, 1994a).

There are concerns and therapeutic issues with this station in the work of forgiveness. First, it is rare that the victimizer will do everything right, and that he or she will be absolutely loving and trustworthy. Change is slow, and the victim who wants to pursue this area of forgiveness has to have patience counseled as the victimizer learns how to become increasingly loving and trustworthy. The victimizer is not and cannot be perfect but can make progress in this station of forgiveness and should be held accountable by the victim to continue to improve and get better (Hargrave, 2001). The second issue that is apparent in this station of forgiveness is that the violation and the roots of the victimizer's behavior may never be discussed between the victim and victimizer. In this station in the work of forgiveness, the concentration is not on understanding, talking things out, or even discussing correction but rather on changed behavior. In giving the opportunity for compensation, the former victimizer may learn to behave in loving and trustworthy ways, and the victim may learn to heal from the current relationship even if a discussion about the previous violation never takes place. This is often acceptable to the victim but is often more difficult for the psychotherapist. We simply remind the psychotherapist that it is our experience that this station does help recover love and trustworthiness and thereby contributes to the intergenerational health of the family. The psychotherapist must put his or her conceptions of "talking issues out" as secondary to the pragmatic fact that people are recovering. Forgiveness, in this station, is achieved because love and trustworthiness have been reestablished, and the memory of the violation fades in light of the current behavior (Hargrave, 1994a). It works for the family, and that fact must be good enough for psychotherapist. The final issue in giving the opportunity for compensation is that this station does not ever give the victim what he or she missed out on from the victimizer. Love and trustworthiness can be present, and this can be some compensation for the victim to enable him or her to have a healthy relationship with the victimizer. But, the victim does have to reckon with the reality that nothing the victimizer can do will erase past pain or distress (Hargrave, in press). Engaging in a current relationship to try to erase past memory is a doomed effort in this station, and the psychotherapist must help the victim who wants this to be the case to appreciate what can be captured in the present and not get trapped in the grief and sadness of the expectation of rewriting the past (Hargrave, 2001).

Overt Forgiving

The last station in the work of forgiveness is *overt forgiving*. This process is many times what most people think of in the work of forgiveness because victim and victimizer come together to talk overtly about the relational transgression with the intent of correcting the relationship to become loving and trustworthy in the future (Hargrave, 2001). Although there are many ways to go about this process, it can be a meeting that produces extreme emotion and thereby can be volatile and produce a destructive interaction between victim and victimizer. For this reason, we most often suggest that the process involve a skilled psychotherapist to keep the process and intent on track (Hargrave, 1994a).

In overt forgiveness, the victim and victimizer are helped by the psychotherapist first to come to some *agreement* about the crux of the violation. This agreement basically confirms the facts and behaviors that resulted in lack of love or lack of trustworthiness because of the victimizer. Often, both the victim and victimizer have different recollections of the relationship and the violations that surround the relationship. It is important, therefore, that the psychotherapist assist the pair in keeping on track and focusing not so much on the specifics of the violation but instead on the broad perspectives on the violation. For instance, instead of focusing on the specific occurrences of times and places of sexual abuse, it is often much more successful for the psychotherapist to help the victim and victimizer to reach the agreement that indeed there was sexual abuse in the relationship. This type of broad agreement keeps the therapeutic work on task and often makes progress in the session possible (Hargrave, 2001).

The second issue therapeutically is to help the victim and victimizer *acknowledge* responsibility for the damaging or destructive behavior that harmed love and trustworthiness. This acknowledgment is key because essentially it holds the key to responsibility for the relational injury. When a violation occurs, the victim must hold a victimizer responsible for his or her violation to make sense of emotional pain. When the victimizer acknowledges responsibility for his or her damaging behavior and holds him- or herself responsible for the past violation, the victim is no longer required to carry the responsibility (Hargrave, 1994a). This transfer of responsibility from the victim to the victimizer is the key therapeutic moment in the work of forgiveness (Hargrave, 2001).

Finally, the therapeutic process of overt forgiving is capped with *apology*. In this step, the victimizer essentially is consolidating the work done in the session by asking overtly for forgiveness or apologizing for the violation. In essence, the work done in apology is a promise or intent for the victimizer to live in a loving and trustworthy way in the future with the victim. Such promises of intent give the victim the opportunity to accept the apology or consolidate the work by saying the words, "I forgive you" (Hargrave, 2001).

Many psychotherapists are surprised that one conversation can have such a dramatic effect on a relationship that has possibly been violating and damaging in the past. We can confess that we have been surprised at times ourselves. In reality, we know that when these types of sessions occur, there is much work to be done by victim and victimizer in actually living out the forgiveness process; often, they need to go back and do work in other stations. But, the reality that something significantly has changed in the therapeutic momentum of the family cannot be denied. Victim and victimizer, who often came into therapy cross and with great enmity between them, often leave these sessions arm and arm or hand and hand. We think of it as testimony to the fact that individuals really do long for the hopefulness that relationships can be healed for the sake of themselves and the intergenerational family that follows. But, whether the work of forgiveness is achieved in this overt way or through the other three stations, there is little doubt that the effort is trustworthy and can make a qualitative difference in the individuals, relationships, and lineage to come (Hargrave, 1994a).

6

Consolidating Change in the Brain

INTRODUCTION

Old ideas die hard. There is something that is deep in the heart of our clients and patients that keeps them holding on to the very thoughts, ideas, and behaviors that end up destroying them and their relationships. We see this every day when we see a depressed person cycle down into negative, weak, and shaming behavior repeatedly. We see it in an angry, violent, and abusive person as he or she is "triggered" physiologically, and the person once again flies into a rage or a fit of blaming. We see it in an anxious controlling person who seems to be convinced that if he or she simply expresses his or her logic and reasoning again, others will see the sense it makes and change their behaviors to match what the controlling person wants. We see it when individuals who are unhappy and stuck in their own isolation and lack of involvement of relationship once again shy away from any type of intimacy or vulnerability with others. Somehow, even though we know that certain thoughts and behaviors are bad for us and are rooted in our own self-reactivity, we return to those behaviors and usually find that these actions further assault our identities as human beings and our sense of closeness and safety in relationships. Old ideas die hard.

Old ideas also die hard with psychotherapists. Most of us love the therapeutic moments when clients or patients finally "get it" and realize in a flash of insight what they have been doing that has been counterproductive or destructive in their lives. When we are present at these moments, we know that something significant and important has happened, and we want to believe that it will make all the difference in the world to the people we help. As psychotherapists, we often live for these moments and look passionately for the opportunity for them to occur. But, as we have seen, these clients and patients may report that these insights are life changing, but they often do not change their lives. As much as we as psychotherapists want to believe that insight alone is powerful enough to produce lifelong change, we must acknowledge that it often does not, and our clients slip into the thoughts and behaviors that are so destructive.

What we know through the field of neuroscience is that old ideas die hard because the brain holds on to those functions in an automatic fashion. Once the brain has learned certain thoughts and behaviors, it is tenacious in holding on to them and, indeed, actually prefers the old behaviors to new learning. Why does the brain do this, and how do we as psychotherapists work with the brain in such a way that consolidates behavioral and thought change that connect the motivating influence of insight? Although we have learned our craft of therapeutic insight well through the years and believe that it is clearly illustrated in Chapter 5 through our techniques, we have also learned that we must be attuned to how to make this insight turn toward productive and long-lasting change.

UNDERSTANDING THE BASICS OF NEURAL CHANGE

A substantial amount of brain research shows that most of our thoughts, reactions, and behaviors are a result of automatic, or at least semiautomatic, executive operating systems that help us live in everyday circumstances (Siegel, 2007). These executive operating systems are powerful, keep our attention on essential items, and motivate us toward certain behaviors. Because we use the executive systems so much for everyday living, the neurons in these systems are almost preprogrammed to react (Atkinson, 2005). When the brain runs across information or a stimulus that calls for interpretation and reaction, it does so in this preprogrammed and automatic fashion. As a result, the neural states that we have learned well are the states that we return to repeatedly, even when we do not particularly like the thoughts or behaviors. As we have stated, we find this particularly true when we deal with neural states locked into primary beliefs about self and safety and the learned behavior around self-reactive behavior of blaming others, shaming self, controlling behaviors, or escape/chaos behaviors.

The reality is that most therapeutic insight simply is not integrated sufficiently into the brain to have an effect on changing these executive operating systems. While it is true that some of the most powerful executive operating systems deal with the reactions of fight and flight, there are additional systems that prompt curiosity and various aspects of bonding, including emotional closeness, care for others, spontaneity, and sexual intimacy (Atkinson, 2005). It is our belief that while the executive operating systems of fight and flight function most actively around threats to identity and safety, the other, more positive, executive operating systems that are more focused on learning and bonding are underutilized and underdeveloped. There is sound evidence for this belief in that neural states that involve emotion seem particularly influential in controlling thoughts and behaviors (LeDoux, 1996). When we run across information or interactions that are particularly vulnerable to emotions—as we would postulate in the case of identity and safety—we actually lose our freedom to chose thoughts and behaviors, and our emotions activate thoughts and actions we have previously learned and perfected.

Emotion in general is powerful in the brain, and it can be heavy handed, forcing the individual to do these learned patterns in the executive operating systems (LeDoux, 1996). This emotion and reaction can in turn create a physiological response that further complicates the neural state. In a matter of seconds, we can literally be put into a neural state of exploding with aggression, crumpling under shame and guilt, shutting down, and withdrawing or moving with power to fight the situation. In spite of the power of our cognitions, the emotional trigger to the executive operating systems out of self-reactivity proves to be much quicker and much more powerful (Atkinson et al., 2005). Simply stated, before you realize what you have done, you have moved from the emotion into self-reactivity, for which damage to yourself, others, and the relationships is already done. After the damage is done, you then are left with your cognitive components analyzing the fallout and the resulting attacks on self in terms of lovability, worthiness, and safety. It is a vicious cycle that is driven by emotion and the brain.

So, where is the hope of having clients or patients actually integrate and consolidate change into their thoughts, emotions, and behaviors if these executive operating systems are so powerful and humans are so vulnerable to emotion? We find encouragement in the story of Flight

155

1549. In January 2009, Flight 1549 was taking off from LaGuardia Airport in New York City; shortly after takeoff, geese were sucked into both jet engines, rendering them nonfunctional. The pilot of the plane, Chesley "Sully" Sullenberger, took the controls from the copilot, and both started working to deal with the situation. As the copilot worked to restart the engine, Sullenberger quickly radioed to the control tower to get clearance to land after declaring an emergency. As seconds went by, Sully made the call that getting back to LaGuardia would not be possible. The ground controller gave him clearance to land in New Jersey. After a few more seconds, Sullenberger made the decision that he would make a water landing on the Hudson River.

As Sully reported this to the ground controller, you can almost hear the dread in the ground controller's voice because he knew that this type of landing would be difficult and dangerous, and the chance of fatalities was high. All the while, Sully and his copilot continued to work through the checklist for a water landing, and the crew prepared for a crash. Seconds later, Sullenberger skillfully guided the plan down, keeping the nose slightly up and reducing the speed to a survivable rate while keeping it fast enough to keep the plane flying. Although the plane hit the water hard, the 155 passengers and crew all survived the landing. The plane sank, but all the human beings were alive.

Now, the truth is that if we would have been the in pilot's seat during that awful moment when the engines were taken out, we would have flown into a panic. We would have made moves and decisions that would not be based on reason but based on our executive operating systems being overwhelmed and flooded with emotion. Sullenberger had the same type of executive operating system in his brain, yet he was able not to panic and to overcome his emotion. Was this a miracle? If you heard Sullenberger speak about the landing afterward, you know that he consistently repeated that he did not panic, and he simply did what he was trained to do. He had the training and repetition of doing the right things over and over until those new actions became an operating system within themselves. He practiced until he knew what to do in the face of emotion. If someone can learn how to keep cognition engaged in such a dire situation, then it is indeed a sure bet that clients and patients can learn how to keep cognition engaged in terms of thoughts and behaviors and not just be subject to automatic responses and self-reactivity.

Like any skill that is learned, emotional learning and reacting are learned by practice. In spite of psychotherapists believing that insight alone is enough to produce change, the brain is only able to integrate and make likely new behavior when it is practiced. Those in neuroscience agree that the main mechanism that allows the brain to acquire new habits and skills is based on repetition (Atkinson et al., 2005). The brain processes that occur repeatedly are the ones that tend to create new neural connections and make new neural states possible. But, most of the time in psychotherapy, we neglect to practice these new thoughts and behaviors with clients and fail to give them sufficient homework that will ensure practice. In the restoration therapy model, we absolutely have become convinced that changing these old fundamental states that exist in the executive operating systems of individuals requires us to give clients and patients clear insight about their processes, give them clear and identifiable cognitive and emotional maps that make sense, and practice with them until thoughts and behaviors are affectively changed. To our knowledge, this process is a sure way of moving clients and patients into new neural states in which their executive operating systems dealing with learning and emotional bonding are brought more into play. As we have learned, we have to teach the client or patient the skill necessary not only to combat the existing pattern but also to teach him or her an effective way of moving to a new and more effective neural state.

THE FOUR STEPS

There are many ways and versions of intervening cognitively and emotionally on this executive operating system that causes so much self-reactivity. Much of the work has focused on the practice of mindfulness (Siegel, 2007), which is a great example of training the mind in alternative practices to avoid emotional flooding. Others (Atkinson et al., 2005) focus on moving the therapeutic messages into practice steps and homework when the client is on his or her own. In the restoration therapy model, we utilize a process known as the four steps to interrupt the old pattern of behavior that the client or patient is used to performing and to move the client to a new emotional state in which he or she can chose behaviors more in line with agency. Although these four steps seem simple and are said aloud, they can have a profound effect on the neural state of the client and give the client a tremendous opportunity to change old identity and safety thoughts and feelings as well as explore resourceful and connecting behaviors in relationships.

Step 1: Say What You Feel

In Chapters 2 and 3, we clearly explored the dynamics of feeling that occur when individuals feel stress because of lack of love or trustworthiness. These assaults to identity and safety produce a variety of primary emotions that relate mostly to identity issues of feeling alone, unworthy, and not special or safety issues concerning feeling insecure, unjust, and unknown. It is essential that the psychotherapist help identify those primary feelings most associated with the client's identity and sense of safety so that he or she can say what is felt. As we have seen, these primary emotions that the client feels are usually the same emotions presented repeatedly in the executive operating system. Once the client or patient learns what these emotions are, he or she finds that these emotions are most likely felt an overwhelming majority of the time when they are emotionally activated into self-reactivity.

Many individuals will be tempted to say things like, "I feel angry," "I feel frustrated," or "I feel ashamed." It is important for the therapist to point out that these types of secondary feelings are actually more associated with reactivity and action in response to the primary emotions most often related to feeling unloved or unsafe. The client may indeed feel angry, but it is secondary to the larger emotion of how he or she is reacting (Hargrave & Stoever, 2010).

To interrupt the old pattern of behavior and start working on a new neural state, we have the client or patient actually say out loud which primary emotion he or she is feeling. This saying the feeling out loud does several positive things: First, the fact that the client says the feeling out loud requires that the client identify the feeling from past information (using cognition) and move that information to the left hemisphere of the brain, where the language is actually processed, formulated, and activated. Further, when the client hears him- or herself speak the words of the primary emotions, it brings into play new brain activity and focuses the client's attention differently. These actions of speaking and hearing actually call the attention of the brain away from the emotional heavy-handedness we mentioned regarding the executive operating system taking the client down the same old patterned pathway and giving him or her the attention needed to make change possible (Arden & Linford, 2009). Second, we would argue that the process of naming the feelings helps the client *actualize* the feeling. We have seen in previous discussion how, once triggered, emotional flooding in the brain results in automatic reactions from the executive operating system. When clients and patients react in this manner, they usually have no idea how they feel and have great difficulty calming themselves. If the client names the feeling, he or she is not shortcutting the feeling or stuffing the feeling, but rather the client is actually discovering a new accuracy of finding the way he or she currently feels. These two actions give the cognitive elements of the brain a fighting chance when taking on emotion.

We are often asked by clients and patients if saying the feeling out loud is all that necessary and whether it would be just as effective simply to identify the feeling through thinking. The fact is that when a threatening neural state is triggered around identity or safety, part of the brain actually shuts down (Atkinson et al., 2005), and all neural attention is governed by the emotion. In our normal neural state, our brains are capable of handling vast arrays of information and stimuli in a matter of milliseconds. It is as if the brain is able to deal with a whole stack of cards, looking at every card at once and making some kind of sense of it. But, when we are flooded emotionally, the brain stops listening to all other input and focuses almost exclusively on the thoughts, emotions, and actions that belong to the activation. All attention is drawn to reactivity. Frankly, just thinking about what I actually feel just is not powerful enough to direct the emotion to a different place. As a result, it becomes necessary to give the cognitive part of the brain a fighting chance. Saying the feeling out loud and focusing attention on the feeling gives the cognitive part of the brain a fighting chance to deal with the charge of the emotional trigger.

Step 2: Say What You Normally Do

If you refer to the material in Chapter 3, you will see that people are remarkably consistent not only in the primary emotions that they feel with regard to identity and safety but also in the behavior with which they react and cope. If the psychotherapist works with the client or patient to identify the process and patterns of these emotions and behaviors, a clear picture of what the client does when he or she is emotionally activated will begin to emerge. It is essential, however, that the psychotherapist get this pattern and process identified correctly so that the client or patient knows the reactivity by heart. Only with this knowledge will the client have the motivation and clarity needed to be able to name the reactions when the emotional activation has taken place.

After the client or patient has named what he or she feels in Step 1, it is then necessary to say out loud what he or she normally does when he or she feels that way. We have the client or patient say the actions out loud for the same reasons as we did in Step 1; it greatly assists the cognition of the brain in the ability to stand up to the overwhelming emotion. But, it also offers a paradoxical deterrent to the behavior. When the client or patient actually names his or her normal pattern of self-reactivity, it makes it less likely that the client will repeat those same behaviors (Haley, 1987). A 50-year-old female explained her reaction to the second step:

> When I first said what I felt out loud, it felt very familiar to me because I am used to saying what I feel in almost every situation. But when I said what I normally do when I felt that way, there was this moment of truth for me. It was like I was identifying exactly how I normally become destructive and justify the behavior with the feelings. I can do that justification when I just keep it hidden, but when I named what I intended to do, it was different. It was like I was going to have to take responsibility for my destructive behavior if I continued my cycle. The issue of responsibility kept me going with the steps because I certainly knew that I couldn't continue with the old behavior after I said it out loud.

Self-reactivity, as we have seen, is so programmed into our being from our past experiences that behaviors come automatically or at least with little effort. Actualizing and calling attention to the behavior works not only because the attention that is called to action interrupts the emotional flooding but also because it raises the client's or patient's consciousness of reactivity. Steps 1 and 2 combined, therefore, give the client or patient a special privilege of the ability to choose cognition in the face of the emotional turmoil he or she feels. It is a powerful intervention that can produce an interruption of automatic brain processes and sets the stage for changes in emotions and behaviors.

Step 3: Say the Truth

Changing neural patterns is not easy. We often remind ourselves that water will flow down the path of least resistance automatically when going downhill. So it is with the brain. If the brain is to be able to do something differently, it needs to be thoughtful and intentional. If there is not a clear and practiced alternative, it will revert to the old patterns that are most familiar and most practiced. We know that to get to new feelings and behaviors, new neural pathways must be made and developed in the brain. Like any new pathway that is made in the wilderness with the effort of intentionally clearing obstacles and wearing a place that marks direction, neural pathways must be disrupted by change. The more the new neural pathway is used, the greater the possibility of the pathway being easily accessed in the future.

In Steps 3 and 4, the formation of these new neural pathways is absolutely essential. In Steps 1 and 2, the psychotherapist is simply helping the client or patient call attention to the old pattern of primary emotions and reactivity. While this is good and necessary work and gives the client power of choice, it does not necessarily mean that the client will do something different over the long haul. We must, as psychotherapists, take the responsibility for helping the client create new neural pathways when the emotional activation takes place.

We believe that the therapeutic interventions outlined in Chapter 5 create clear possibilities for prompting different feelings and behavioral actions. But, we also have learned through our therapy that unless the client or patient integrates these insights into new cognitive truths, it is unlikely that he or she will behave differently when the emotional trigger occurs in his or her life. For instance, if a client does the work of understanding and clearly comes to the conclusion that his or her caregiver was not a monster and he or she was not a bad or worthless person, the knowledge only makes a difference if the client integrates the information as a new truth about him- or herself: "Just because I was treated in an unloving or untrustworthy fashion does not mean that someone deserves punishment or that I am a worthless person." This would be a clear example of a truth that should come from the intervention of understanding. Another would possibly be as follows: "People make mistakes because they are human. Because people make mistakes with me, it does not mean that they should be blamed, and when I make mistakes, it does not mean that I am bad or useless." An extension of this truth for an individual would be, "People are good, and I am good, no matter if they or I make mistakes." The more this truth gets into the cognition of the individual, the greater the possibilities that arise to have an impact on the brain and the old reactive patterns.

This is never truer than in the intervention of finding and identifying the truth about self. We made the point in the explanation of the intervention that the individual client or patient must come to the realization that he or she must give him- or herself reparenting messages concerning love and trustworthiness. When he or she is willing to give the self these messages, then the client can also become more open to the messages and redress of love and trustworthiness from others as well as spiritual sources if applicable. But, the key remains that if the individual is to get these key messages of primary emotions into his or her brain where they can be effective weapons against old pattern behaviors, then it is necessary for the truth to be familiar, repeated, and at the ready.

We suggest that these messages of reparenting and truth must be repeated and made clear repeatedly within the course of therapy. In our experiences, we have found that clients and patients will be resistant to the idea of naming themselves lovable, powerful, worthy, capable, unique, trustworthy, and not alone. It is not that the idea is undesirable as much as it is that the client or patient is unfamiliar with the language and brain connection that would make such a self-nurturing statement. Even when a client can do Steps 1 and 2 with ease, it is not unusual for the client to become hung up on the ability to say the truth to him- or herself. This was the case with a 38-year-old female who was trying to work through the four steps when she had been hit with feelings of inadequacy and worthlessness at her job. Notice how the woman works through the first two steps easily but finds it hard to deal with the truth about herself. Notice also how the therapist in the case reworked the issue of the truth with her and then repeated the process of the steps to offer more practice.

Therapist: So, identify how you feel when you think about your work and the problems of the day.

Woman: I feel inadequate, worthless, and like a failure.

Therapist: And what is it that you normally do when you feel that way?

Woman: What I normally do when I feel that way is I start shaming myself, feeling hopeless, and withdrawing from all interactions.

Therapist: Very good. And, what is the truth about you?

Woman: [*Long pause; starts to cry.*] The truth is that I am inadequate and a failure. I can't do anything right.

Therapist: [*Pause.*] Is that the message that you want to give yourself?

Woman: It isn't the message that I want to give myself, but it is the only message that I believe right now.

Therapist: That is understandable. [*Pause.*] It is a message that you have received from others and given yourself for a very long time. [*Pause.*] Close your eyes. [*Woman closes her eyes.*] If you can, just for a moment, see yourself as that little girl that was rejected by your mother. [*Long pause.*] Can you see her?

Woman: [*Nods her head while crying.*] I can see her. She looks so dejected and alone.

Therapist: What is the message that you want to give to her?

Woman: [*Long pause.*] I want to say that she is loved, acceptable, and capable.

Therapist: Say it to her.

Woman: You are. You are loved, acceptable, and capable.

Therapist: Do you really feel that toward that little girl?

Woman: Yes, I do. I don't have any trouble saying it to her.

Therapist: Then say it again.

Woman: You are loved, acceptable, and capable.

Therapist: [*Long pause.*] Okay, you can open your eyes. [*Pause.*] If you can give that message to a little girl who was you, then you have to learn to give that message to yourself. You are no less lovable, acceptable, and capable than you were then. [*Long pause.*] Say it to yourself.

Woman: I am loved, acceptable, and capable.

Therapist: Say it again.

Woman: [*Takes a deep breath and relaxes.*] I am loved, acceptable, and capable.

Therapist: So, what is it you feel when you think about your problems at work today?

Woman: I feel inadequate and like a failure.

Therapist: What do you normally do when you feel that way?

Woman: When I feel inadequate and like a failure, I tend to shame myself and withdraw.

Therapist: But, what is the truth about you?

Woman: [*Pause.*] I am loved, acceptable, and capable.

Here, we see how the therapist reworks the issue of truth by reviewing and utilizing imagery techniques to help the woman imagine reparenting herself. When she sufficiently recontacts that message about her truth that she would want to give herself, the therapist then draws the situation into the present. The woman then is able to use the strength of the insight from speaking to herself as a child to be able to speak the truth to herself as an adult. Notice also that when the woman speaks this truth, she does so with a physiological reaction of a deep breath and relaxation. We often find that when people really are speaking to the primary emotions that they feel, it results in a feeling of peace, as we saw in Chapter 2. This peace brings with it an emotional calmness that we see reflected in the physiology of relaxing.

It is essential that the psychotherapist assist clients and patients in getting to the truth that they want to claim about themselves. It can be truth about identity that can come through understanding or identifying the truth about oneself, or it can be the truth that relates to safety and trustworthiness as the individual identifies responsible and powerful actions in the interventions of right script but wrong players, balancing obligations or entitlements, or even the work of forgiveness through salvage and restoration. But, no matter the truth identified, the psychotherapist must move that truth from simply an insight or one-time meaningful contact to a repetitious experience that creates new neural pathways. Going through the four steps and working and reworking the steps as illustrated provide a firm methodology to make this repetition and practice happen.

Step 4: Make a Different Behavioral Choice

When an individual is able to make emotional contact with the truth that he or she wants to give to him- or herself that is rooted in the self-parenting, it has the opportunity to replace the emotion of violation with regard to love and trustworthiness. Instead of feeling unloved, unwanted, unworthy, alone, unsafe, insecure, unbalanced, and unknown, the client or patient has the opportunity to contact feelings of safety, uniqueness, worthiness, desirability, security, balance, and intimacy. These feelings go far in stimulating those executive operating systems that are associated with new learning and emotional bonding. In short, the emotion of peace creates opportunity to move the feeling into a position of human agency.

Figures 6.1 and 6.2 are illustrations of the possible strengths that can come from primary emotions of love and trustworthiness that are rooted in peace. These words give clients or patients clear ideas of what a map of action looks like to start building neural pathways that are positive and directed toward agency instead of negative and based on reactivity. It is important for the psychotherapist to remember that when explaining and giving these new behavioral options to clients, the focus should be on doing something that is the opposite of the old behavior.

For instance, for someone who chronically blames others, a good behavioral choice of agency would be to nurture others. For one who engages in self-reactivity to be controlling, a good choice would be to work to be more balanced in relationships of give-and-take and more vulnerable. In this way, the therapist helps the client or patient identify constructive behaviors that they can return to repeatedly that will always be

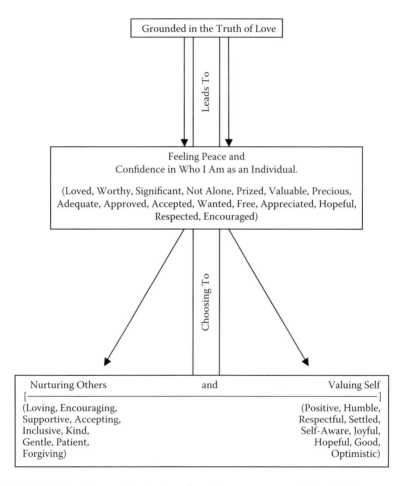

FIGURE 6.1   Feelings and behaviors from the peace connected with love.

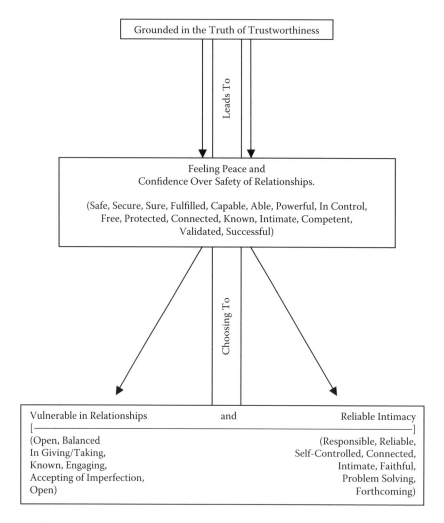

FIGURE 6.2 Feelings and behaviors from the peace connected with trustworthiness.

in direct response to combat the old pattern and a positive for the client or patient and the relationships of that client or patient.

The psychotherapist, in working with this type of framework, needs to make the cognitive map of the new behavior clear to the client or patient. It is always best in terms of identifying the truths that the client wants to speak to him- or herself to narrow the truths down to the essential three or four items that speak most directly to the volatile messages that he or she received concerning identity and safety. Likewise, when identifying new actions that the client wishes to integrate as a behavioral choice, the psychotherapist wants to help narrow the choices down to the three or four that make the most sense in creating the new neural pathway. These new maps or patterns of process are easily drawn for the client or patient in the same fashion as illustrated in Chapter 2. Essentially, the therapist helps the client identify the truth and the actions that he or she will choose.

When the client or patient does make this different behavioral choice, does he or she actually follow through? We have found remarkable results when the client actually makes emotional contact with the truth about him- or herself in Step 3; he or she becomes successful in making a different behavioral choice that is constructive. To illustrate this, in the following case of a marital couple, the husband chronically felt unloved and unimportant to his wife. He reacted or coped with this pain by shaming himself, becoming needy, and being negative. Notice how he reacted differently with his wife when utilizing the four steps and how it changed the framework of the couple's interaction.

Woman: [*Speaking to the husband.*] I just really don't know if you will ever really want to be involved with the same types of things that I enjoy. It is a real difference between us.

Therapist: [*Noticing the emotion from the husband.*] I can tell that the last statement your wife said did something to you. These are the critical times that you must use the four steps. What is that you feel?

Husband: [*Stares at the floor a moment and then looks at his wife.*] I am feeling unloved and unimportant right now.

Woman: I wasn't trying to comment about you.

Therapist: [*To the woman.*] I appreciate your clarification, but it doesn't matter. He is in the feeling, and it is his responsibility to work to move himself from this difficult place. [*Looking back at the husband.*] Continue.

Husband: I am feeling unloved and unimportant. Normally, what I do when I feel this way is to start pouting, feeling bad about myself, and start reacting negatively and hopeless.

Therapist: [*Pause.*] And what is the truth?

Husband: [*Pause.*] The truth is that I am loved, and I am important. I love myself, and I know you love me. I am important. [*Pause.*] So, what I will do differently is not pouting and stay hopeful about what we are doing.

Therapist: Great. But, it is important not to just say what you will do differently, it is important to actually do it here.

Husband: [*Looks at the wife.*] I am not taking what you say personally. What you are saying is actually true, but I am hopeful that we can learn more about what we do well together and get closer.

Woman: [*Pauses.*] Wow. That is a big difference.

Therapist: Tell me him what you mean.

Woman: [*Looking at her husband.*] Just that small little change just fills me with hope. It makes me want to think of the things that we can do together.

Obviously, the psychotherapist in this case had been over the four steps with this couple many times, and there was a familiarity with the process. But, when the woman related what she did, the husband was triggered with the same emotions that he had felt many times. If the psychotherapist let him stay with those emotions, he would follow the same pathway that he always followed of shaming himself and becoming negative. The psychotherapist needed to be attuned to these types of opportunities, which Atkinson et al. (2005) called "game conditions." These are the conditions by which the individuals actually receive the emotional triggers that force them into reactive and counterproductive behaviors. These critical moments are the most important for individuals to learn how to take on the thoughts and behaviors that are producing negative outcomes. When the husband in this case actually worked himself through the four steps, he emotionally put himself in a different place because he was able to believe the truth about himself. As a result, he made connecting statements that offered the opportunity to move the relationship forward. This was good for his wife but was most beneficial for him. Instead of wallowing in shame, he reinforced himself about how positive, competent, and powerful he can be in the relationship. These actions assured him that he was lovable to himself.

This illustration was of a marital couple, and it is important to notice that we did not make the spouse responsible for understanding the man's feelings, and we did not ask the spouse to try to make the husband feel loved. While there are many aspects of the emotionally focused therapy approach (Johnson, 2004) that we appreciate and like, we would feel that the individual is responsible for his or her own neural states. It is a much more reliable form of regulation of the brain to be responsible for oneself than to be dependent on another to make a healing moment happen for an attachment injury. However, we would also point out that when the husband took this responsibility for his own neural state and his own truth, the result became connecting in the relationship. We feel that this aspect of individual responsibility prompts the possibility of more positive attachment rather than attachment dependent on neediness. Also, these four steps give the individual a clear map of how to get out of emotionally activated states on his or her own. As a result, the individual can use these four steps in a variety of relationships, even when another individual who can provide secure attachment is not available. We are not so much making a case here against emotionally focused therapy as we are pointing out some differences and why we prefer to address emotional regulation through the four steps instead of addressing the attachment injury through another.

PRACTICE, PRACTICE, PRACTICE

It should be noted that clients and patients might have difficulty learning the four steps. We usually find that clients and patients have most difficulty in identifying the truth when they are emotionally triggered. This does make sense, and it happens often that when a psychotherapist is working the four steps a client will say something like, "I feel unappreciated and alone. What I normally do when I feel that way is to get angry and aggressive. The truth is—I am unappreciated and alone!" This reaction simply indicates that the client is unwilling at this particular point to incorporate the truth. What he or she is saying is what he or she feels again. The psychotherapist need not panic at this point but simply recycle to the first step by saying, "That is how you feel; now tell me what you normally do when you feel that way." The psychotherapist may have to utilize this process several times in going through Steps 1 and 2 before the client can actually say the truth, but if the psychotherapist is patient, the client will eventually make the movement and calm him- or herself. It is always important to remember that these new neural pathways are hard to form. In some instances, if the client is unable to move to the truth, it may be an indication that the therapist needs to "chase the pain" so that the client feels understood. This again is simply part of the balance of using the four steps wisely and therapeutically.

Another reality with the four steps that we have discovered in our clinical work is that sometimes it is difficult initially for some individuals to identify how they feel. We have particularly noticed this with males more often than females. In these cases, it is sometimes easier for the client who struggles with identification of primary emotions first to identify what he or she does when emotionally activated with pain. In this case, the psychotherapist starts with Step 2 ("Say what you normally do") and then tracks backward to Step 1 ("Say what you feel"). Normally, as the psychotherapist helps the client become increasingly familiar with his or her cycle that produces pain, the identification of primary emotions and corresponding reactivity becomes easier.

We have found that the four steps are effective in helping address and correct the executive operating system of the brain with regard to primary emotional violations and fight-and-flight responses. But, we hope that it is obvious that this technique takes much therapeutic work. First, the psychotherapist must help the client clearly identify the violations and feelings associated with lack of love and trustworthiness. Second, the psychotherapist must help the client make identification not only of the key feelings but also of the process patterns that come from those feelings and the resulting patterns of self-reactivity. Third, the work of addressing those wounds and violations must take place to help the client or patient identify key truths that are essential in his or her life. Finally, the psychotherapist must be helpful in giving the client a map of the emotional truths and the agency actions that will result in more positive outcomes.

This list represents significant therapeutic work. Still, it is not enough simply to feel the client's pain, identify key clinical insights through therapeutic moments, and plan new strategies. The psychotherapist must *practice* these new thoughts and behaviors with the client repeatedly. This practice must take place within the context of the therapy session, during which the psychotherapist looks for the game conditions in which to address the emotional self-reactivity. It also must take place when helping the client or patient learn the patterns of reactivity as well as the maps of peace and agency. The client or patient must become skilled not only at

170

knowing the four steps by heart but also at utilizing the steps at the critical times he or she is emotionally activated. When the client or patient fails in a key situation, the psychotherapist helps the client walk through the situation again using imagery to repeat the four steps and imagine different outcomes. When the client is successful in interrupting the cycle that produces pain and his or her old emotional reactivity, the psychotherapist helps the client recognize the strengths and gives encouragement. The four steps can offer a tremendous advantage in helping the individual make changes, but it takes significant work and practice to make these four steps a part of the client's everyday life.

But, the hopefulness of this approach is this: The four steps can work. In even the toughest cases for which emotional regulation seems impossible, we have seen clients calm themselves from their self-reactivity to be extraordinarily resourceful, nurturing, positive, connecting, and balanced. They will not be able to do this every time and will fall back into the old cycle that produces pain and the accompanying behavior many times. The good news is that the more that they practice the four steps, the more they find themselves able to work from a position of peace and make action choices that are based on human agency. We believe that once an individual practices this process around 90 times, the individual become familiar with all the components of the old reactive cycle as well as the process involved in the new cognitive map. The individual also has some history of successes of fighting off the old triggers and has experienced the reinforcement and reciprocation that results from the agency behavior. Ninety times is a lot of practice, but we believe that it can be done efficiently and effectively through the combination of therapy sessions and homework.

Section III

Utilizing the Restoration Therapy Model

7

Restoration Therapy and Couples

INTRODUCTION

Couples present some of the most challenging work in relational therapy because, in many ways, they are so confusing. Here are two people who usually come together, and many married because they were intoxicated with love for one another. Yet, within a matter of months or years, they are coming to therapy because they simply cannot stand one another any more. Many are absolutely convinced that the partner is his or her enemy, and he or she cannot ever conceive how the thought of having a permanent relationship with this person ever could have worked. How did this couple who was once so in love lose one another along the way and become estranged, distant, and emotionally disillusioned?

Many of these couples from the start of their relationship lose one another because of differences in their relationship focus. We mean that many couples come into a relationship expecting the partner to give emotional fulfillment and happiness. They want a partner who will share joys and intimacy and provide comfort and protection in time of need. What they often find is a person who triggers the emotional executive operating system discussed in Chapter 6, a person who does not fulfill them but creates many questions in terms of identity and safety. Instead of safe, they feel insecure. Instead of love, they feel unloved, unwanted, and alone.

Many who go into relationships looking for this type of fulfillment and happiness are actually missing the point of what relationships in general do. Relationships—especially deep mating and family relationships—force us toward growth and maturity (Hargrave, 2000). In essence, relationships force us to deal with the deepest part of ourselves that needs to grow in terms of learning who we are and how we can become capable and powerful in a world that is not always safe. As much as we would like it to be so, a partner is not built to give us our identity as a person or protect us in an unsafe world. There is but one time in our lives when that is programmed into us, and it is in the vertical relationship between caregiver and child. What we have in a horizontal relationship of coupling is an opportunity to walk together and share, struggle together and grow. As individuals, we must be responsible for our own sense of self and our own power, or we cannot partner. Instead, we become dependent on the partner and force him or her into a position of trying to provide us with the parenting that we may never have received. Since partners cannot supply this type of parenting competently to one another and certainly cannot make up for what was not given in childhood, the relationship is bound to be filled with conflict, strife, and difficulty, and one or both of the partners is constantly trying to get the other to behave, feel, or act differently. Relationships are intended to make us grow instead of making us happy (Hargrave, 2000).

INTIMACY, "US-NESS," AND COUPLE THERAPY

Some will ask, however, if partners cannot supply this kind of identity and safety for one another, what is the source of intimacy? If the relationship is all about growing as an individual, why bother with coupling? Intimacy is a wonderful thing, but the primary thing that makes it good is that it is generative by nature. By this, we mean that intimacy brings forth a new relationship and new creativity. Partnering through marriage is not just two people who commit to experience life together and stand by one another. They actually create something new because of their relationship.

This became clear to me (T.D.H.) a few years ago when the family therapist Carl Whitaker was still alive. One time, when we were having breakfast, he looked at me and spoke about his wife, Muriel, to whom he had been married for over 50 years. He said, "You know, as much as I would miss Muriel if she were to die, I would miss much more what we are together." Carl used to call this experience of what we are together "we-ness" and what we have now begun to call "us-ness" (Hargrave, 2000). The wonderful quality of this us-ness is that it is neither you nor me. The relationship contains both individuals and is more than just the sum of their individual parts. Even though this relationship is invisible, it does have identifiable parts that are dynamic and visible. For instance, us-ness has its own personality, likes, and dislikes. For instance, my wife likes ballet, and I do not. However, our us-ness likes ballet. When I say this, I do not mean that since my wife likes ballet, I simply acquiesce to her wishes and go to the ballet. I mean that when we go to the ballet together, the experience of dressing, interacting concerning the performance, and spending time together is a part of who we are. Our us-ness likes ballet, although I would never chose to go on my own. Us-ness is also predictable. As family therapists, we can look at a marital system or a family system and tell when tension is increasing and its power alignments and belief patterns. Most times, for instance, we not only can predict when a couple or an us-ness is going to have a conflict but also can predict what the us-ness will say next in the conflict (Hargrave, 2000).

And, even though this us-ness is invisible, there is a metaphorical element that is indeed visible. In coupling between a man and a woman, there are sexual relations that usually involve the deepest kind of physical intimacy that two can share as they give to each other and eventually lose control of their voluntary reactions during orgasm. It may be the only time in our conscious experiences when we actually lose control of ourselves under the influence of another. But, this loss of control is usually not one that produces fear; rather, most people find it fulfilling and peaceful. This kind of giving of self—when we know who we are and give ourselves freely—can actually be calming and peaceful when we have a partner who is able to do the same. Even past this sexual intimacy, there is the possible result of the intimacy in terms of conception. Conception involves exactly half of one person's genetic material and half of the partner's genetic material. When these two halves combine in their magical and mysterious way, the resulting fetus is not a replica of either parent. The new life is a whole new human being. In the same ways that children have similarities to their parents but are human beings all their own, us-ness between a couple is similar to the partners but is representative of an identity itself (Hargrave, 2000).

How do parents keep a child alive? With few exceptions, parents feel an overwhelming drive to provide the love and trustworthiness that the child needs. They see the child as unique, valuable, and worthy of sacrifice. They desire to be around the child and make the child's environment safe, predictable, and secure. In other words, they feel a drive to provide the child with love and trustworthiness. Although parents make many mistakes, we find it characteristic that they take into account the interest of the child first rather their own well-being. They do not enter into a competition with the child to get their interests met before those of the child or negotiate with the child about whose interests are most important. Parents take care of themselves individually but usually put the best interest of the child first.

This concept is extremely applicable to coupling between partners. Taking care of a couple relationship is much like caring for a child. It does not mean that the individuals are totally inattentive to their own needs and wants, but it does mean that they recognize that they also are responsible for the care and nurturing of the relationship. Us-ness, just like a child, must be kept alive by love and trustworthiness given by the partners. They nurture the relationship. And, just as parents grow as individuals as they learn how to raise a child, individuals inevitably grow when they give love and trustworthiness to their us-ness. Coupling is not a competition between two individuals to see if one can get more happiness from the other. Intimacy is not one partner meeting the need of another. Coupling and intimacy are about sharing love and trustworthiness for the sake of the relational us-ness, thereby prompting growth, fulfillment, and intimacy in the individuals (Hargrave, 2000).

This idea has much to teach psychotherapists about couple therapy. Many times, psychotherapists approach couple therapy as a competitive framework in which one individual is making a case against the other. Many psychotherapists would believe that individual happiness is the driving force behind whether a couple should stay together. As a result, it is not surprising to find that many couples find marital therapy actually damaging to their relationship, and many are forced by a psychotherapist to look for relational answers through individual therapy (Doherty, 2000). In the restoration therapy model, we believe that multidirected partiality extends not only to the individuals in a coupling relationship but also to the relationship itself. We are committed to the individuals in the relationship, but we also feel strongly that the relationship needs therapeutic advocacy. We see couple therapy as primarily an effort to help the couple work *cooperatively* in moving their relational us-ness to a place at which it is characterized by love and trustworthiness. Only then, we believe, will

178

the couple's relationship be helped and the individuals in the relationship grow. Although we can imagine cases when a couple would be split up in individual therapy, the overwhelming majority of the time we believe that the couple should be kept together because together the individual issues of growth that need to come out will be most evident and there the opportunity for the couple to connect to one another through their us-ness will be available

RESTORATION THERAPY WITH COUPLES

There is a variety of therapeutic approaches that focus on couples; these range from cognitive-behavioral couple therapy (Baucom, Epstein, LaTaillade, & Kirby, 2008), to integrative behavioral couple therapy (Dimidjian, Martell, & Christensen, 2008), to emotionally focused couple therapy (Johnson, 2004). Most of these models recognize the cyclical patterns of couple relationships but have different solutions for seeking healing in the couple, ranging from making behavioral interventions, to acceptance and avoiding polarization, to seeking to heal old attachment wounds. These outcome-based models are certainly effective in helping couples.

In applying the restoration therapy model to couples, however, we believe that we have found an efficient and manageable way for couples to deal with their issues and learn skills that assist them to keep on track. The overwhelming majority of couples come to therapy because of instability and conflict in their relationship (Hargrave, 2000). Of these, most have concerns regarding unresolved issues from their family of origin that get in the way of the couple's ability to solve the conflicts that come between the partners in their relationship (Hargrave, 2000). It only makes sense that for therapy to be effective we need to help couples quickly come to the heart of their conflicts and difficulties and then give them skills to manage this conflict. In other words, if the couple can learn to manage the heart of their conflicts, then they will have a much better chance of looking out for the best interests of their us-ness and achieve intimacy and closeness. We believe that the restoration therapy model excels in helping couples manage this conflict successfully and arriving at intimacy. In the restoration model of couple therapy, we proceed through four phases: identifying the pain cycle, identifying the peace cycle, moving to transition, and creating intimacy.

Identifying the Pain Cycle

We start the therapeutic process with a couple by listening carefully to their individual stories not only of the relationship but also of their past experience with their family of origin. We do feel that the psychotherapist must exercise wisdom and patience in pursuing each story while he or she listens for pain associated with identity and safety. A genogram is often helpful in acquiring much of this information (Hargrave, 2000). If the therapist does not take the time to get this essential information at the beginning of the therapeutic process and instead opts to try to manage conflict or stabilize couple interactions, precious time will be lost. It is not that we are against managing such conflict or stabilizing the situation, but we have found through years of practice that the psychotherapist must clearly understand the emotional components that *drive* the instability in the relationship to be able to intervene effectively. We believe that a couple does not come in with 10, 20, or even 30 issues of conflict, even though they may fight over various things like finances, parenting, friends, and so on. We instead believe that there is a central pattern of primary emotions that relate to self-reactivity that creates a systemic dynamic that locks in conflict and makes solutions impossible, no matter what the current subject involves. In other words, couples do not have 20 fights a month but rather have one fight 20 different times.

In the restoration therapy model, we are first concerned with finding out what is driving this cyclical pattern. In Chapter 3, we discussed how these individual patterns of process occur related to issues of love and trustworthiness and how these cyclical patterns occur in relationships of with a common pattern (pursuer/distancer, overfunctioner/underfunctioner, etc.). In couple therapy, we specifically listen to a couple's story to start developing a clear idea of the pain associated with each partner's identity and safety issues and obtain a clear understanding of how each copes through self-reactivity. What we almost always find is that the couple interacts on individual issues of pain concerning identity and safety in such a way that creates more pain related to those same identity and safety issues. We call this cyclical pattern in the restoration model the *pain cycle*. This pain cycle has all the elements of emotional activation of the executive operating system concerning threat, stress, and fight-or-flight responses. In the following case example, a 42-year-old male and 41-year-old female had been married for 13 years. They had two children together, and this was a first marriage for both. The couple explained that they were ready to give up on the marriage, and that this was a last-ditch effort to see if they could possibly resolve some of their issues. They reported that they had fought with one another for years, but the conflicts now were more volatile, yet less frequent. The dialogue is from the first session, in which the psychotherapist used the opportunity to obtain a clearer picture of their individual processes. She then used the information to draw some conclusions and draw the couple's pain cycle.

Therapist: [*Speaking to the husband.*] So, tell me a bit about the family you grew up in?

Husband: I always knew that there was something off in my family. There wasn't any abuse or anything, but the nature of my family was about absence. My father died when I was about 3 years old, so I knew nothing about him, and my mother never spoke of him. My mother remarried, and I have a vague memory of the wedding when I was about 5. From as far back as I could remember, I was on my own. I remember thinking that I should be close to my mother, but she had two more daughters with my stepdad. It wasn't that they abused me or anything, but it was clear to me that they spent much more time with my sisters than with me. My stepdad had very little to do with me, and my mother spent time with me as a special event. It never really seemed that I was a part of the family. I always felt like I was on the outside looking in.

Therapist: How did you know that you did not belong?

Husband: Oh, they would do family activities without me. From the time I turned 11, I remember being largely on my own. They functioned as a family and did things together, but I was rarely asked along. I was on my own.

Therapist: [*Pause.*] And so when you remember those times growing up, what were the emotions you felt?

Husband: I felt alone. I felt unwanted. I always felt like I didn't measure up.

We see how the psychotherapist utilized the story the husband told about his growing up to zero in on his primary emotions concerning his experiences. Sometimes when people are forthcoming with their stories, as is the case in this example, they have little trouble in identifying the primary emotions that they felt in connection with their family experiences. In other circumstances, the psychotherapist must be patient in exploring the intricacies of the client's story and help the client identify primary emotions. Sometimes, it is helpful to ask the client such questions as, "What is it that you really wanted from your parent?" or "What would have made your situation better?" These types of questions allow the client to identify feelings associated with primary emotions without asking about emotion directly. This particular husband relayed many stories to the therapist about his growing up that continued to confirm that he was a person who basically was left to raise himself emotionally. Although he was provided shelter, food, and education, the definite message that he was raised with was that he did not belong to the "real" family, and that he should be thankful. His mother consistently stressed this message of "being thankful" for the stepfather and the provision that he provided for the mother and the son. He reported never feeling comfortable asking for anything emotionally. In the next section of dialogue, the therapist turned his attention to the wife.

Wife: My family was actually pretty stable in terms of love, but things got turned around so much by circumstances.

Therapist: Tell me what you mean.

Wife: I mean that my mom and dad and my brother got along great, but my father lost his job during a recession and was out of work for about 24 months.

Therapist: That is a long time.

Wife: That is not the worst of it. I grew up in Southern California, and our house was severely damaged by a quake. The house was condemned, and we had no money to get it fixed. I'm not sure of all the details because it is still very painful for my mother and father, but we ended up losing our house.

Therapist: [*Pause.*] I can see how painful that memory must be.

Wife: [*Cries a bit.*] It was painful. We ended up just being shifted around from one relative's house to another or one friend's house to another. We lived almost a full year and a half like that.

Therapist: And what was that like for a young girl being shifted around?

Wife: Scary. I mean my parents were doing the best they could do, but the not knowing and not having a place made you feel like you were totally at the mercy of someone or something else. My parents loved me, and it was not their fault, but it was a really scary time that shaped me a lot.

The woman identified a common experience. Her untrustworthy or unsafe situation did not come from her caregivers but instead from an unstable situation of unemployment and a disaster. As a result, she still had primary emotions that were damaged by the instability. She reported feeling fearful, unsafe, and out of control. These emotions are sure signs that things were not predictable and were unfair. Also, it is important to see that these issues were not talked about openly. Even though the woman's parents likely did this to try to protect the children or perhaps themselves emotionally, it resulted in a lack of openness that affected the woman deeply and added to the lack of safety.

With the primary emotions identified, the psychotherapist worked to identify the primary self-reactivity used by both. The wife in the case reported that her coping and reactivity developed into controlling behavior, and that she always sought to be perfect to make sure that her parents had nothing to worry about with her. Typical to controllers, she was a high performer and hypervigilant to any potential threat. When she was small, she reported that she often would seek to manage control over the something to comfort herself. For instance, when her family moved so much, she kept an orderly backpack with all that she would need if they had to leave at a moment's notice. The psychotherapist continued the exploration with the husband:

Therapist: Growing up where you were on the outside looking in and feeling unwanted and alone, how did you learn to survive?

Husband: I just learned to survive. I stayed on my own. That is really it. I kept to myself so very few people could get close to me. I just put my head down and depended on no one. I didn't want to be hurt, and so I just didn't have relationships.

Therapist: You survived by working hard and staying by yourself. Minding your own business.

Husband: Exactly. Not risking anything emotionally.

The man talked about his own behaviors and secondary emotions. He obviously felt hurt by the lack of love he received, and the psychotherapist suspected that he shamed himself in response to the situation because he had no apparent anger or blame toward his mother. To compensate, he likely worked hard to manage his identity by making himself invulnerable to other relationships and performing well.

The psychotherapist now felt that she had a preliminary idea about the couple's pain cycle but wanted to confirm this information by talking about a painful sequence in their relationship. Remember that it is most common for these patterns and sequences surrounding primary emotion and self-reactivity to be first learned in early experiences. When the psychotherapist asked about the couple's last argument, they reported that the sequence was similar. The wife had high expectations of the husband and was in a constant state of checking on him or correcting him on issues—in this case finances. The husband felt that she was never satisfied with anything that he tried to do; therefore, he would give up, withdraw, and shut down. When he did withdraw, the wife would become angry and accuse and blame the husband until he would leave. The therapist asked if this were a "typical" type of argument, and the couple acknowledged that it was typical.

The psychotherapist felt secure enough from the information gathered that she could draw the couple's pain cycle. It is important to remember that this drawing is to be shown to and learned by the couple. While it is important that it relate closely with the stories told to the psychotherapist, there will often be elements that have to be corrected and changed as therapy progresses. The pain cycle does not have to be perfect but simply an accurate representation of what actually occurs in the relationship. Figure 7.1 shows the couple's pain cycle.

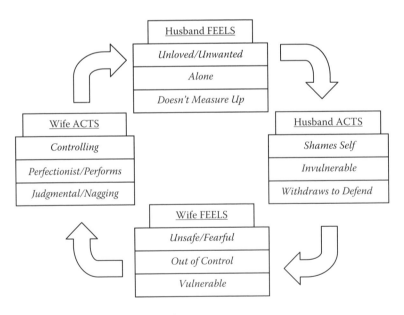

FIGURE 7.1   The couple's pain cycle.

When the psychotherapist went through the couple's pain cycle, the couple indeed confirmed that it was on target. It is important to remember that with these cycles, what the individual spouse is doing to try to cope or react to his or her own feelings of violation of primary emotions is usually the thing that further stimulates the violating emotion in the spouse. For instance, with this case, when the wife was managing her fear, lack of safety, and vulnerability with her reactivity of controlling behaviors that included being perfectionistic and judgmental, it would further complicate the husband's feeling like he was unloved, unwanted, alone, and a failure. When he would cope with these feelings out of self-reactivity by shaming himself, becoming invulnerable, and withdrawing, it would complicate the wife's feelings that she was indeed unsafe, out of control, and vulnerable. In short, she did not feel that she had a partner who would help her make life work and give her protection, and he felt that he had a partner who had little regard for him as a person and was only interested in what he could do for her. When the psychotherapist played out this cycle in the financial argument that the couple reported, he drew attention to the fact that she believed that this might be the "argument behind every argument," and that the couple likely felt this way regarding every conflict. When asked about being on target, the husband and wife agreed. The husband stated:

> This is exactly what we do. This is exactly nailed in terms of the way I feel and the actions I take when I feel that way. I don't think we've ever come this close to getting such a clear picture about what drives us in our conflict. This is very helpful.

Identifying the Peace Cycle

The fact that the couple was so confirming of the pain cycle is not unusual. Most often, when the psychotherapist gets the pain cycle correct for the couple, they become highly interested, insightful, and motivated in therapy. In the next several sessions, the psychotherapist moved the couple to identify the alternate primary emotions and agency behaviors that would make the cognitive map for where the couple needs to aim. We call this map the *peace cycle*.

Like the pain cycle, the peace cycle is somewhat reciprocating for the couple. When they practice human agency behaviors like nurturing, self-valuing, balanced give-and-take, and reliable connecting, it tends to stimulate primary emotions in each spouse that helps them feel that they are loved and that the relationship is trustworthy. In this way, the peace cycle tends to spiral the couple upward in a more loving and trustworthy relationship as each interaction begets a greater likelihood of a positive interaction taking place.

The psychotherapist will typically need to spend several sessions helping the couple identify the old wounds from their pasts in detail and chase the pain of how these wounds occur. The psychotherapist is then going to use these emotional opportunities to do the powerful work and interventions that provide insight to the individuals, such as understanding, identifying truths about self, balancing obligations and entitlements, right script but wrong players, and the work of forgiveness. In each of these techniques, the aim is to help the individuals redress their primary emotions and injuries not only with insight but also with the thought of new behaviors. In a few instances, the psychotherapist will find that this work can go quickly and efficiently. But most often, the process of the clients feeling this type of pain and working through the redress is hard and time consuming.

Using the technique of identifying truths about self, the psychotherapist worked with the husband to identify several key areas in which he was left on his own. Through this process, it became apparent that the man had always longed for someone to make him feel loved and wanted. When he found that his wife was attracted to him a few years after college, he was ecstatic, believing that he finally had met someone who could make him feel loved and feel like he belonged. Later, when she identified that she was attracted to him because of his stability and seemingly emotional steadiness, he was crushed. Through the use of imagery, the psychotherapist guided the husband through several instances of growing up when he was left to manage on his own and had the man talk to himself as a child from his position as a parent, as illustrated in previous chapters. The work was successful in helping the husband take control of giving himself positive messages of love and belonging and making situations in which his wife and children did express love to him count.

In terms of the wife, the psychotherapist primarily used the technique of right script but wrong players. Using the process of helping the woman recognize her relational claim, the psychotherapist spent significant time helping her understand how the unpredictable circumstances of her life had led to such feelings of being unsafe, fearful, and out of control. This partiality allowed the woman to relate, "I know that it is understandable, but I also know that I have been way too controlling for my husband and my kids. My anxiety gets the best of me way too often and causes many of our conflicts." This kind of insight is invaluable and was a clear indication of the woman's willingness to redress her inappropriate attempts to get her entitlement met. The next therapeutic move was to help the woman identify appropriate ways in which she could get her safety needs met without being overcontrolling. The psychotherapist would ask her, "When that fear kicks in and reminds you of all those things that were out of control as a girl, is there anything that can soothe the fear?" The woman thought for several minutes and replied as follows:

> You know, what was so scary was the not knowing. If someone would have just told me what we were facing, I think it would have been so much better. My parents were great in terms of being there, but they weren't very good at making me informed. I know he [the husband] is steady like a rock. If I could just remind myself that he will walk through this with me and that he will be open to talk about the issues with me, I think that I could be much more balanced.

The psychotherapist used the strengths identified by each partner to draw the elements of truth that could be used during a four-step process. In addition, she asked the couple if they were able to contact this type of truth, how would they behave differently in the relationship? Both partners identified positive elements of human agency. The husband identified that if he were able to hold to the emotional truth of being loved, wanted, and more than enough, he would not only nurture himself but also be much more engaging and involved in the relationship. Then she identified that if she were able to hold on to the truth that she was powerful and capable and that she had a partner who would stand by her, she would likely be much more balanced in the give-and-take in the relationship as well as more nurturing and accepting. With these elements, the psychotherapist constructed the peace cycle map for the couple and confirmed the elements with each of the partners. Again, the partners confirmed that if they could successfully act this way with each other, it would make a tremendous difference in their relationship. The peace cycle for the couple is found in Figure 7.2.

Moving to Transition

As is often said, "The Devil is in the details." This couple had experienced tremendous hopefulness and insight during the first five therapy sessions in which they had clearly identified their pain cycle, learned how

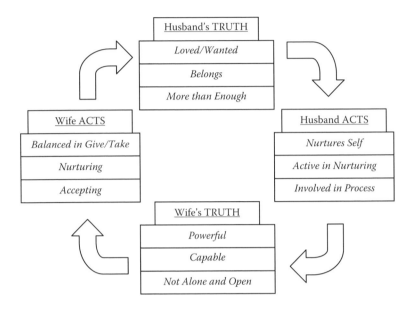

FIGURE 7.2 The couple's peace cycle.

to integrate truths about themselves, and then learned about how that process could work in the peace cycle. However, the process of making the transition from the pain cycle to the peace cycle is a significant challenge not only for the couple but also for the psychotherapist. Many times in couple therapy, the psychotherapist so badly wants the couple to get better that the psychotherapist tends to avoid issues that are potential problems. But, as discussed in Chapter 6, practicing the new thoughts and behaviors that run counter to the old executive operating system is absolutely essential if individuals are to learn new habits. The brain simply needs this repetition to form these new neural connections that generate new responses to emotionally charged situations. Again, the therapist must be reminded that the couple must confront the very issues that are problematic to be able to get to "game conditions" and make sure that the transition and work are successful.

The psychotherapist then works with the couple utilizing the four steps outlined in the Chapter 6 of interrupting the pain cycle and switching the interaction to the peace cycle. Again, these four steps are (a) say what you feel; (b) say what you normally do; (c) say the truth; and (d) make a different behavioral choice. We emphasize again that it is necessary for the individuals to verbalize these four steps to help the brain integrate, actualize, and gain cognitive leverage against the old automatic pain cycle that operates because of the executive operating system.

In the case in this chapter, the psychotherapist worked two sessions with the couple to help them learn the words associated with their pain and peace cycles, as well as to become proficient at the process of the four steps. Like any learned process, the couple had to be walked through the four steps slowly during sessions when they first were exposed to the process. At the beginning of one of the sessions, the couple came in obviously upset with one another:

Therapist: Well, I can clearly see that something is going on that has caused a lot of upset. What has happened?

Wife: [*Very angry.*] Well, I think we are right back where we started from. I've lost it again, and he is withdrawing and pouting.

Therapist: What has happened?

Wife: I was feeling nervous about my son's doctor appointment. I was not able to take him, so I wanted him [*points toward the husband*] to take him and be sure to ask the questions that we need to know. I started trying to tell him what I wanted him to do, and he just started withdrawing. [*Very agitated.*] I know I was pressing, but this issue with my son is very important, and it is important that we get it right. He just stopped listening and went into the other room.

Therapist: [*To the husband.*] And what happened next?

Husband: [*Very quietly; acting hurt.*] She just blew up at me saying that this is the same old story, and that I would never be her partner in helping her work through issues. It was all up to her to make the family work, and that she couldn't count on me.

Therapist: What did you do?

Husband: What could I do? There is nothing that you can do when she is like that. I just left. We came here in separate cars.

Therapist: I see. [*Pause.*] I think this is very good that this happened and is still going on. It is a good opportunity to put what we have been working on to the test. [*To the husband.*] It makes perfect sense to me how you got locked down in your pain when your wife was telling you what you needed to do with your son like you were not capable and that you were not an adult. Tell me how you feel.

Husband: [*Hesitant at first but then looks at the pain cycle.*] The same thing that I always feel. I feel like I don't measure up, and that I'm unwanted. I feel totally incompetent and alone.

Therapist: And when you feel that way, what do you normally do?

Husband: [*Again hesitant, but then looks at the pain cycle.*] Like always, I felt bad about myself and withdrew. I just didn't want to feel bad any more.

Therapist: I do understand that. But what is the truth about you?

Husband: [*Pauses and tears up.*] I don't know.

Therapist: Your brain at this point wants to tell you that you cannot find your way out of this, but you can. What is the truth about you?

Husband: [*Looks at the peace cycle.*] I am loved, wanted—I belong and am good enough.

Therapist: Close your eyes and say it again.

Husband: I am loved, I belong, and I am more than enough. [*Sighs heavily.*]

Therapist: And if that is true, what would you like to do differently?

Husband: [*Long pause.*] I'm not going to shame myself. I am okay and capable. I am also concerned about our son, and I can hear what you have to say without withdrawing from you.

Therapist: Good. Very good work. [*Pause.*] Are you okay with where you are?

Husband: Yes, I know this is true, and I can stay connected.

Therapist: [*To the wife.*] So, when you think about this situation with your son and what happened today, what do you feel?

Wife: I felt fearful, unsafe, and out of control. Totally vulnerable.

Therapist: And what do you do when you feel that way?

Wife: [*Looks at the pain cycle.*] I totally fell right into the cycle.

Therapist: I know, but your brain needs to hear it from you. What do you normally do when you feel unsafe, out of control, and vulnerable?

Wife: I switch into control mode, and I get judgmental about the ways that I think it should be done.

Therapist: And what is the truth about you?

Wife: The truth is that I deserve to be alone. I am so locked in and unreasonable at times.

Therapist: This is not the truth about you. You will want to beat yourself up with guilt now that you are coming out of your pain cycle, but it will do no good. You can only turn this situation around if you are willing to confront the old pain. What is the truth about you?

Wife: The truth about me is that I am powerful and capable and good at what I do. But I also have a partner that is dependable.

Therapist: So, if you hang with that truth, what is it that you want to do differently?

Wife: [*Pauses and looks at the peace cycle.*] I want to engage him about my concerns and ask him about his concerns. I want us to share the load—I want to be willing to share the load. I want to tell him that I can trust him and depend on him.

Notice that during this process of working through the four steps, the emotional tenor of both partners shifted dramatically. This is sound evidence that the couple has made the transition from the pain cycle to the peace cycle using the four steps. Also, notice that the couple used the charts that the psychotherapist has put out to remind them of the feelings and actions associated with each step. This is a necessary part of helping the couple learn the material and become increasingly proficient at the skill. Finally, notice that the psychotherapist had to keep each individual on task at moving through the four steps. This is not unusual as the old habits of wanting to hold on to familiar pain and actions are deeply engrained.

Creating Intimacy

The psychotherapist must be committed to working this four-step process with the couple repeatedly. He or she must help the couple analyze conflicts that they have had during the week to help them overlay the four steps to see how they could have changed the conflict. The psychotherapist must be willing to bring up conflict that exists with the couple in sessions to help the individuals become activated into a game condition in which they can walk through the four steps actively. And, the therapist must be trained to look for the emotional activation that happens with the individuals over the slightest issue, big or small. All of these help the couple learn the process of transition from the old pain cycle to the new peace cycle so that they become proficient at being able to do it themselves during a conflict or to avoid a conflict.

When they do start becoming proficient, it is wise for the psychotherapist to use the fourth step—make a different behavioral choice—to create an opportunity for intimacy. This is most often done by the psychotherapist simply making a suggestion to the individual not just to talk about what he or she wants to do that is different but actually to do it with his or her spouse. This almost always provokes deep intimacy, which produces bonding. In the tenth session with the couple in this case, one of these

191

opportunities presented itself. The man had reported that he was feeling stressed over the couple's financial situation and was not sure how things were going to work out. Although the man was speaking to the therapist, the man's wife immediately became emotionally triggered.

Therapist: I notice that something is going on with you.

Wife: [*Pauses and looks at the ceiling. Takes a deep breath.*] Okay, I'm going to give this a try. [*Turns toward the husband.*] When I heard you talking about our financial situation, I felt overwhelmed, scared, vulnerable, and out of control. What I normally do when I feel that way is I usually get very controlling and start barking orders of what you should do. I get hard on you and expect everything to be done my way. But the truth is that I know that you are a reliable man that I can count on. I am capable, and together I know that we can solve this. So, what I want to do differently is not control the situation and express confidence in you.

Therapist: That was very good. Notice how you have taken your emotions that would normally send you into the pain cycle and done something different. How are you feeling now?

Wife: I'm feeling surprisingly calm. I feel empowered—like I can do this.

Therapist: You can do this. And since you have gone this far, maybe you can go a little further. Instead of just telling him what you would like to do differently, do it here right now.

Wife: [*Long pause. Turns and faces her husband and takes his hand.*] You are a good man that is rock solid. I know I can count on you, and I appreciate you being honest about our finances. I want to know what you think we ought to do about our situation. I want to know how you think we can work better together.

Husband: [*Deeply touched. Pauses.*] I just want you to know that you are great, and I appreciate your work. We can sit down together and work out a plan. I know that we can when we stay in this frame. We just need to work together on this situation, and we are going to be fine. [*Pause. Couple embraces.*]

This presents one of the hallmarks of the restoration therapy model. We do not use intimacy for the emotional regulation itself, but instead use the therapeutic insight and four steps to create the emotional regulation. With this executive operating system under control as it relates to fight or flight, the individual is now free to explore new options with other operating systems in the brain to create intimacy. In other words, we use emotional regulation in the restoration model to create moments of intimacy that are not only reciprocated but that also pattern new pathways in the brain. This couple, who had not had intimacy for years in the marriage because of their pain cycle, clearly experienced an intimate moment that really did make a difference in the course and history of their relational conflict.

It is important to remember that working with this couple was not an easy process, and they were at the end of their energy in working on the marriage. What is amazing is that they were so different in the span of 10 weeks. This is what is possible when couples are able to utilize the restoration process and learn how to regulate their emotions so that they can be successful in applying the insight they gain from therapy. Certainly, this couple has had many more times when they found their way into the pain cycle. But, what is different from the skills that they learn through the peace cycle and the four steps is that they have the tools to be able to work themselves out of this difficult place. They must continue to work and practice, but they definitely had found a way to restore hope, regulation, and emotional intimacy to their relationship. The couple terminated therapy after 12 weeks and were able to continue the process of using the four steps and the peace cycle on their own.

8

Using Forgiveness in Restoration

INTRODUCTION

In talking about the therapeutic work of forgiveness, we find that there is nothing more foundational to the restoration therapy model. We believe the heart of the work of forgiveness is to restore as much love and trustworthiness to the individual, relationship, and intergenerational family as possible and feasible. When an individual or family takes on this work of forgiveness, in essence the individual or family is taking not only the needs of the individual into account but also the needs of the lineage to come in terms of the love and trustworthiness that it will need to survive. Like any generative work, it is essentially work that will change the lives of generations that the individual who is doing the work in the present will never see. In this way, it is always an effort of transcendence (Hargrave & Pfitzer, 2003). It is something that the individuals do in restoring love and trustworthiness in the present that potentially lives long past the lives of the individuals.

In Chapter 5, we outlined the therapeutic process that we have used with individuals and families to achieve this work of forgiveness. As psychotherapists, we are always concerned that the work we do in this area has integrity for all concerned in the process. For instance, we do not find it necessarily true that when one chooses not to forgive that he or she only does him- or herself harm through harboring resentment and anger. Most individuals who have been violated in ways that call for forgiveness have been harmed in real and profound ways, ranging from murder, sexual abuse, prostitution, and abandonment to manipulation, isolation, and neglect. When an individual is harmed by such heinous violations, the damage and potential damage are real. As psychotherapists, we find little good in someone forgiving someone who will turn around and do the same types of heinous violations again. Forgiveness, as we conceptualize the process, is always relational and has tremendous implications for healing. But, such potential for healing comes at a risk in that there is always potential that the individuals who we forgive may also violate us again with lack of love and trustworthiness (Hargrave, 2001).

Because of these concerns, we always are interested that the process of forgiveness has integrity. We believe that the four stations of forgiveness represented through insight, understanding, giving the opportunity for compensation, and overt forgiving are relational elements of forgiveness that are good for the individual victim, the relationships with victimizers, and the relationships represented in the intergenerational lineage not yet born. It is good for the individual in that the model is first concerned with making sure that violations of love and trustworthiness cease. Therapy focuses on insight in drawing boundaries that are significant in protecting the individual. Further, understanding provides a methodology to help the individual heal from the damage that violations have done to his or her identity. In addition, the model provides the individual with a sense of responsibility that he or she must account for his or her victimization to make sure that his or her own destructive entitlement does not victimize future relationships and innocent parties.

The model has integrity in helping the victimizer also. It does not accuse the victimizer unjustly or assume that he or she is a monster or beyond the reach of love and trustworthiness. Instead, the model sees the victimizer most often as a human being who has also been a victim of violations of love and trustworthiness. In this way, the model humanizes the victimizer and moves him or her to a position of responsibility from which he or she can choose to become responsible in love and trustworthiness in the future. Giving the opportunity for compensation and overt forgiving provides the victimizer an opportunity to rewrite the past with current expressions and actions of love and trustworthiness. Such actions not only go about the healing work of identity and safety in the victim but also do much good in healing the victimizer as he or she forms a new identity and proves that he or she is safe in relationship to him- or herself. Finally, the process of forgiveness is good for the intergenerational lineage yet unborn. We have seen how human agency is used for constructive purposes, and that however love and trustworthiness are passed along in a relationship, it makes better the future relationships of those who have experienced this identity and safety (Hargrave, 1994a). Forgiveness is no guarantee that healing will continue for generations to come, but unforgiveness and continued violations of love and trustworthiness are a guarantee that future generations have little chance for healthy identity or relational safety.

ANOTHER LOOK AT LOVE, JUSTICE, AND POWER

It is also important to remember that forgiveness with integrity always involves this balance of love, justice, and power (Tillich, 1954). We believe that if there is true stability and human agency, power, justice (or trustworthiness), and love become stabilized forces that work in balance and harmony with one another. When in such balance, essentially they make each other meaningful. If one only has power, then he or she can use his or her power only for gratification of self without any concern whatsoever for other human beings or even family members. If one is only concerned with power and justice, then actions would likely be based on retribution or revenge as individuals who performed violating acts would be subject to similar or even worse violating acts in retaliation. Although generations have seen love as the "answer" to all the evils of the world, if it is in isolation by itself, it also produces outcomes that are suspect. If one only loves and accepts in response to violation, then it means that the one will accept anything and everything in the relationship whether or not it builds identity or safety. In essence, love becomes paltry and weak to protect the one who loves, and he or she likely will become a victim of others' misuse of power or violations of justice.

This idea represents our most essential concern in stepping into the work of forgiveness and where, frankly, we find other models of forgiveness lacking. Any model of forgiveness that purports to adhere to integrity must have at its heart this balance for love, power, and justice. In our opinion, any time these three issues are separated in a relationship you have an opportunity that is ripe for exploitation and manipulation. We believe that we can point to much of the dysfunction that exists in relationships in the world at any local, regional, national, or global level and clearly demonstrate that when these three qualities are separated, relationships tend to fly apart, and individuals and relationships suffer. How do we then recover some sense of sanity, stability, and function?

197

We believe that this is why forgiveness with integrity is so necessary. The model of forgiveness that we put forth has at the heart of its intention an attempt to stabilize these three forces where the forces have been misused in the past. In the restoration therapy model, we seek to make interventions that not only stabilize power, justice, and love but also bring them closer in harmony. For instance, in insight, we are concerned not only about giving the victim the power to be able to stop victimizers from violating love and trustworthiness in the future but also about helping the victim see and stop his or her own potential violations of love and trustworthiness in other relationships. Again, in understanding, we focus on the work of love to make human connection between victim and victimizer. We do not do this, however, to excuse the irresponsibility of the past but instead to humanize both victim and victimizer so that they can be held accountable and responsible for loving and trustworthy actions. Further, giving the opportunity for compensation and providing overt forgiveness are designed therapeutically to give stabilization of trustworthiness, leading to opportunities to express love and power constructively.

As stabilization and consideration are given to all three factors, we believe that individuals can start to use their power for loving and trustworthy actions. As loving and trustworthy actions are taken, the individuals gain much more power in their identities and abilities to make relationships safe. In other words, as forgiveness proceeds and the stabilization of love, justice, and power takes place, these three factors increasingly become one. At their apex of damage, these three factors are isolated from one another and produce increased distress. As they are put together, they combine for a powerful force of healing through human agency.

THERAPEUTIC WORK IN THE STATION OF INSIGHT

The primary point in the restoration model of forgiveness is the fact that any work in the four stations that is directed toward love and trustworthiness is worthy work in that it improves the function of the individual as well as the relationship. No station is better than another, but rather it is important to look to a particular station of forgiveness as appropriate to a relationship at a particular time. For instance, a person with a history of sexual abuse with a victimizer who has no indication of change may find the work of insight as all the work that is possible and feasible. Another may find the work of overt forgiveness the only work that makes sense to him or her and the only work that will bring relationship satisfaction. Some situations indicate only one of these stations be used, while others demand that two, three, or perhaps all four stations be used in no particular order. The point is that the work of forgiveness is often messy and imprecise as individuals and families go about the hard work of putting their relationships back together (Hargrave, 2001).

In the following case example, a 46-year-old woman was seeking to put her relationship back together with her husband after he had a second infidelity. As is the case when there is repeated infidelity, the woman had thought that she had recovered and forgave the first instance only to find out that her husband had gone back to the affair 2 years later. The woman had found that it was much more difficult to consider forgiving him after this second offense. The woman was convinced that she and her husband could be good together because "deep down, I know he loves me." The woman was also motivated to stay in the relationship for the stability and well-being of her two early adolescent children. She was deeply hurt by the affair and confused at how to proceed with her husband or if she even should. As with many issues, insight is often a good place to begin in the work of forgiveness as it allows the psychotherapist to work with the victim in such a way to empower the victim to stop the violations of love and trustworthiness. Again, no forgiveness is ever possible when love and trustworthiness continue to be violated (Hargrave, 1994a). In the first session, the woman expressed her confusion and quandary over wanting the affair to stop or the marriage to end. At the same time, she was deeply hurt by the affair, and while wanting her marriage to work, was fearful that if she took a "stand" with her husband, he would leave her for the other woman. Notice how the psychotherapist worked with her in this initial session to clarify not only her feelings but also the sequences of events surrounding the interactions with her husband.

Woman: I just feel at times that I am half-way present—almost like an out-of-body experience. I think that this can't be happening to me again—then I am furious, and I am so done with him—then I am so weak and hurt that I can't go on with life. I don't know what I feel most of the time. Half the time, I just click into things that need to be done and act like my life is not falling apart. I don't want my kids' lives to be torn apart.

Therapist: It is a very confusing situation, and it sounds as if you are still dealing with a lot of the shock over the affair. It really is a traumatizing thing.

Woman: It is traumatizing. I never thought about that word before, but it is something that comes out of the blue and injures you deeply.

Therapist: Have you and your husband made any decisions concerning how to deal with the affair?

Woman: I really am unsure. [*Starts to cry.*] He is really unsure, too. He says he still has feelings about this woman but at the same time does not want to lose me or his family. [*Pause.*] I hate him for that. [*Pause.*] It leaves me hanging with all these terrible feelings.

Therapist: At those times, you say you hate him. I know you feel other things, but what is the hate about?

Woman: I hate that he is the one that has betrayed me, but he then puts me in the position of having to wait and see what he is going to do.

Therapist: [*Pause.*] It is like he has the power when you should have more power.

Woman: Exactly. I should be the one deciding, but instead he has the power to decide what is going to happen with the relationship.

Therapist: So, you know you really feel anger when he takes or keeps power that you believe you should have—it makes you feel like you hate him.

Woman: Yes. [*Pause.*] There are times when I hate the situation for how much hurt it has caused me and potentially the kids, but I don't hate him at those times. At those times, I am hurt. It is when he maintains the power over the relationship and this affair that it really pisses me off.

Therapist: That makes a lot of sense to me and is really a very helpful differentiation. You feel hurt because of the betrayal. You hurt for yourself and the potential of what this may mean for your family. But, you really get angry and hate him when you feel like he has unjustly taken your power away in the relationship to be able to respond to the affair.

Woman: Yes, that's right. That is good for me to clarify just those two feelings because there are times where I feel like I should be angrier and am not and times where I think I should feel hurt and do not. It really helps me clarify.

Therapist: I am glad it is helpful. [*Pause.*] Tell me, how do you usually respond to your husband when you are really angry because he has the power in the relationship because he has not decided between you and this woman?

Woman: [*Pause.*] I think I just usually become immobilized and don't do anything.

Therapist: You don't know what to do.

Woman: Some of it is that I don't know what to do, but some of it is that I am fearful that I will drive him further into the arms of this woman.

Therapist: So, when it comes to how you behave when you are angry about being without power in this situation, you get frozen with fear and don't know what to do.

Woman: That's right.

Therapist: These are powerful emotions that are really very specific. You are sad and deeply hurt by the affair and the thought of losing your family. You are angry and pissed off when your husband still has the power about deciding between you and this other woman, and you feel fearful about making a move toward power for fear that you will lose your husband. [*Pause.*] What is it that you do when you feel really sad about the affair?

Woman: Again, I get frozen. I don't want to show any sadness to the kids for fear that it will upset them and don't want to show sadness to my husband for fear that it will drive him away.

The psychotherapist in this interchange skillfully helped the woman clarify her feelings, which is appropriate for the first session, but also started the process of helping her get the idea that her behavior is fearful and frozen. At this point, the psychotherapist does not know if she "gets frozen" as an effort to control by withdrawing to defend, or the fearful reaction was a withdrawal to escape the situation. But either way, the psychotherapist had to move in the work of insight to help the woman recognize the circular process that left her in so much pain, sadness, anger, or fear. In making this connection, the therapist was not blaming the woman for the husband's irresponsibility but instead empowering her to take actions that would protect her from unfettered violations from the husband's behavior. The psychotherapist further helped the woman stabilize feelings associated with the betrayal in Sessions 2 and 3 and then started moving to consolidate this sequencing in Session 4:

Therapist: We have discussed several times in the last few weeks that your responses to the deep hurt and anger you feel are more often than not getting frozen with fear. Let's just concentrate on this anger that you feel for a few minutes. When your husband says

201

something like, "I have feelings for this woman, and I can't really decide what to do," what is it that you feel?

Woman: That is when I really feel the anger. I feel it now. [*Pause.*] I think that I am the one who has been exploited here, and he is the one that is telling me whether or not he is going to be in the relationship or not.

Therapist: And what is it that you do when you feel that way?

Woman: I just get stuck. I don't know what to do because if I tell him that I will make the decision, I am afraid that I will drive him away or give him an excuse to leave me. I just clam up.

Therapist: And so you are stuck. What does he do after you clam up?

Woman: He just goes on his way. I really think that he has no idea that it makes me so angry. He probably thinks from my actions that I'm being understanding of his problems.

Therapist: So, your reaction leaves you weak and perhaps even invites him to violate you again by saying the same type of thing.

Woman: [*Long pause.*] I think you may be right. I may be inviting him to say this thing that infuriates me. He says a lot that he is thankful for me being patient with him.

Therapist: [*Long pause.*] That would be concerning. My main concern here is that you do what you can do to stop the violations of trustworthiness from your husband. It has an effect on your sense of identity and self and certainly has an effect on whether you feel safe in the relationship. You do not have control over whether he eventually decides to leave the marriage or even if he decides to have this affair, but I would like you to consider that you do have some power and control over whether or not he victimizes you by assuming that he has the power to either have the relationship or not.

Woman: [*Long pause.*] My weakness just sets me up for more hurt. [*Pause.*] I know that, I just have let my fear take over.

Therapist: We can talk about this fear in depth, and you are free to make your own decisions, but I do want you to be powerful enough to make your own decisions concerning whether you let your husband say these things to you that make you so angry and leave you with the feeling of powerlessness.

The therapist helped the woman identify the sequence of behavior that left her exploited by the husband's comments. The woman saw this and agreed that her fearful nonresponse left her open to more and more exploitation. With insight, identifying these key sequences and then asking the client or patient to change his or her behavior so that systemically the victimizer will have to change is key in stopping the violation.

In this instance, the psychotherapist and woman talked about and identified much about her fear and how she could not control her husband's decisions about the affair or the marriage. In identifying the possibilities of further actions that would protect her from the husband believing that he had the sole power to decide whether he would stay in the marriage, the woman decided that what was appropriate was to have the husband move out of the house for a period of time while he made up his mind, and that she would be specific and honest with her feelings and expectation concerning times when the husband acted as though he had the power to make exclusive decisions concerning the relationship. In the sixth session, the woman came back with a report of an interaction she had with her husband.

Woman: I told my husband that I wanted to make some decisions concerning the future of our relationship. You know, it was shocking how immediately he went to taking the power explaining to me that he knew it wasn't fair to me, but he just couldn't still make a decision about how he felt about this woman and whether or not he wanted to stay in the marriage.

Therapist: And how did that feel?

Woman: Oh, I saw exactly what was going on this time, and I was furious. But, I did exactly as we practiced the whole process. I told him that when he acts as if he has control of whether our relationship will continue that it makes me angry, and that I am actually the one who has just as much power in deciding about the relationship. I told him that I have an expectation of fidelity from him, and that I won't be victimized or disempowered by waiting for him to make a decision.

Therapist: And how did he respond?

Woman: He all the sudden became a little frozen himself. He said that was not his intention, and then he asked me what I wanted to do. I told him that I wanted our marriage to work, but he would need to decide whether he was going to stay in or go with this woman. In the meantime, it would be best if he moved out until we both could decide our next moves, but him staying in the

203

house and still seeing this woman was revictimizing me over
and over again.

Therapist: And what went on with you during this discussion? What were
you feeling?

Woman: You know, I had envisioned myself saying this to him angrily sort
of like we practiced it here. But, when it actually came down to
it, I was feeling absolutely empowered and not fearful at all. I
was calm, clear, and reasonable.

Therapist: And his response?

Woman: He just couldn't quite believe it. He certainly could not believe
that I was so clear. He did move out because I stuck to my guns,
and he is staying with a friend. It does make me a little scared,
but I know that I am ready to find out what life has for me either
way and ready to not be victimized by this affair anymore.

Some of this woman's reaction was simply from the clarification of
her feelings and the amount of time that had elapsed from finding out
about the affair again. But clearly, the woman was also empowered by the
possibilities of taking charge of what she could take charge of—namely,
the decision concerning having her husband be in the marriage and faith-
ful to her or not. In the next session, the therapist furthered this work of
insight by helping the woman be emotionally clear and direct with her
emotions in explaining the situation to her children honestly. One of the
primary issues related to insight is not only helping the victim stop violations of love and trustworthiness from the victimizer but also learning
how to stop him- or herself from the ways he or she may victimize innocent parties. Although this mother was a loving and caring woman, she
was not emotionally honest with her children and checked out at key emotional points. When she took steps in the next session to be honest and tell
her children what was actually going on between her and her husband,
the children reported that they had already figured out what was going
on but did not know what to do. The woman's daughter was especially
responsive. The daughter reported that she had felt responsible for taking
care of the mother because she knew that she was so hurt. This was particularly helpful to the mother in seeing that her behavior was contributing to the victimization of the children and causing her daughter to care
for her inappropriately and in a confusing manner. As the woman became
empowered to stop her own victimization, she also became powerful in
stopping her victimization of innocent relational parties. This is classic

work of forgiveness in the station of insight because it helps love and trust-worthiness in the victim's relationships while stopping the exploitation.

In this case, there was an added benefit. When the husband realized that the wife also had the power to end the relationship, he became much more invested in protecting and investing in the marriage. He made moves to ensure that the affair was over and was willing to pursue psychotherapy with the wife. Although the woman was not ready to pursue couple therapy, she was open to having the husband move back into the house after 3 weeks as long as he could provide evidence that the affair had ended. This involved the woman having complete access to her husband's financial and cell phone records as well as the freedom to check on the husband when he was out of her presence. In this work of forgiveness, the victim had been protected from further violations, and it opened up the possibility for future hope of rebuilding love and trustworthiness between her and her husband.

THERAPEUTIC WORK IN THE STATION OF UNDERSTANDING

It is important that we remind psychotherapists that the stations of forgiveness are not stages. Some clients and patients will do work in only one station because that is what is appropriate for the possibilities of love and trustworthiness being restored in those particular relationships. However, it is possible that in some instances further work in the other stations of forgiveness is not only possible but also preferable. In the case discussed, the woman had gained dramatic power in her relationship with her husband in deciding whether they would continue in the marriage. She also gained dramatic power in her clarity of thoughts and feelings, which further enabled her to make sure that she did not use her own hurt, fear, confusion, and anger to inflict violations on her children. While her husband had moved back into the house to another room and she was committed to the idea that they would eventually pursue couple therapy, she wanted to come for a few individual sessions with the psychotherapist to help her work through some of her anger and "other feelings."

It is not unusual at all for victims of affairs when they become empowered to realize that they have put up with much and have anger and blame regarding the victimizing spouse that is close to being out of control. At the same time, it is also not unusual for the victimized spouse to feel as if he or she deserved the infidelity, and that the affair was "all his or her fault." These types of responses of course are directly related to the sense the victim has of his or her identity being violated. The victim tends to see the victimizer as an evil monster or see him- or herself as a pitiful person deserving of such abuse. This, as we have discussed, is a common reaction to violations of love and trustworthiness. Therapeutically, it is helpful to conceptualize the blaming of the victimizer or the shaming of self as a loss of identity that is extremely painful.

These are the types of situations for which the work of forgiveness in the station of understanding can be particularly helpful. In the station of understanding, the focus of the work is to help the victim make human identification with the limitations, development, thoughts, and reactions of the victimizer. When the violated makes this human identification with the violator, it essentially humanizes both and lets the victim realize that the victimizer is not some evil monster but a human who has made relational mistakes with profound consequences. Likewise, the victim is also humanized as he or she realizes that he or she did not deserve the abuse or poor treatment, but that the victimizer made relational mistakes. In this work of forgiveness, if properly achieved, the victimizer is left with the responsibility for the actions he or she has taken, and the victim is left with a sense of worthiness and value. Both, however, are human beings. When the victim makes this compassionate connection, he or she often feels like there is great reduction of the pain related to identity, and blame and shame are reduced.

In the case presented, the woman gained power but found that she was angry at her husband not only for the affair and his use of power in determining the outcome of the relationship but also for the ways that he had manipulated her over the course of their marriage. She was angry at him for the type of father he was, as well as how he provided for the family and was consistently absent. Rightly so, she recognized that if she did not get these aspects of her anger under control, there would be little good that came from couple therapy. In the ninth session overall and the first session after her husband moved back into a room in the couple's house, the psychotherapist listened to the woman's feelings but started moving her slowly toward this point of human identification.

Woman: I have got to get some handle on my anger toward him, or it is going to destroy me. Now that I have learned how to take some power in the relationship, I am literally mad about everything.

Therapist: Sometimes when you have been fearful a long time and have been used to reacting that way, power has a way of making you feel angry about being made to feel afraid.

Woman: Exactly. I am mad for all the neglectful things he did through the years and how he pushed his agenda at me. But, I'm also angry most about the way he has made me feel.

Therapist: And how is it you feel about yourself?

Woman: [*Long pause; shakes her head for a long time.*] I feel so stupid. I feel so weak. [*Starts to cry.*] I feel so upset with myself that I allowed him to do this. At times, I feel like I somehow brought this on myself.

Therapist: [*Long pause.*] You are never responsible for someone else's irresponsibility. You have a part in the marriage not being what it should have been, but you did not go out and have an affair twice. That responsibility lies with him.

Woman: I know. I know that he has been irresponsible. Before, I was just angry with him for the way he bullied me into thinking that he had all the power. Now, I'm angry at him for everything that he has ever done.

Therapist: When you think about your husband when you married him, what were the things that attracted you to him?

Woman: He was a good-looking man, but mainly it was just the way he handled himself. He seemed to be so sure.

Therapist: Where did he learn how to be so sure of himself?

Woman: You know, my husband has always been a man that had to prove himself. He was always trying to talk himself to the next level to impress someone. He came from a really hard background where his father drank too much. Even though he drank, he was one smooth talker. He [the father] still is. He could get people to believe anything and keep them on his side. Because he drank too much, he never delivered. I think that hurt my husband deeply.

Therapists: The fact that his father drank or the fact that he did not deliver?

Woman: [*Anger clearly gone at this point.*] A little of both, but mainly that his father had such a gift of being able to engage people and get them to believe in him and then not deliver. My husband has that same type of gift that I'm sure he learned from his father, but the real difference is that he is able to deliver. [*Long pause.*] Except on the promises that he made to me. [*Cries.*]

Therapist: When you think about that very human side of your husband—
the part that learned how to persuade people with his talk just
like his father and had to live with the disappointment of the
father not delivering—what do you feel for him?

Woman: [*Long pause.*] I think that he is just a guy—a guy that is still trying
to prove himself. A guy who just longs to have someone love
him for who he is and not how smooth he is. A guy that doesn't
feel the pressure to always deliver. He always has been the guy
that has to be the best and prove he is the best. I think that is to
himself.

Therapist: [*Long pause.*] Do you ever have feelings that you wish you could just
have someone love you for who you are without performing?

Woman: All the time. I always feel that I am loved for what I can do as a
friend or a mother. Sometimes, I'm not even sure that people
know me for who I am—they only know me for what I can do.

Therapist: And do you ever find yourself fitting into that expectation so people will continue to like you the way that you like to be liked?

Woman: [*Long pause.*] All the time. I feel like I've got to keep up the work and
the persona so people will not be disappointed in me. I feel like if I
let anyone down, I will cease to have anyone love me at all.

Therapist: Even though they don't love you for who you are, you have trouble being real with them and ask them those questions. Instead,
you just keep on performing?

Woman: Yeah. It is a vicious cycle.

Therapist: Ever feel like you can't take it anymore, and you just want to
escape the persona?

Woman: Yes. But I would beat myself up pretty badly if I ever gave in and
just let myself not perform. I guess I would find out who my
friends are, however.

Therapist: [*Long pause.*] I want you to hear me on this very carefully. I am
not saying that you are your husband, and you could have
had the affair. I am saying, however, that it sounds like you
do understand part of your husband's humanness very well. It
sounds like that you know he has this pressure always going on
inside of him to be the best and to perform at the highest level.
If he doesn't, who knows what he will have to face in himself.
You seem to understand that performance and fear that you are
not appreciated for who you are and are only okay if you keep
on performing.

208

Woman: Yes?

Therapist: So, if it becomes too much for you at times, what do you think your husband does when it becomes too much for him?

Woman: Have an affair?

Therapist: I'm not suggesting that or think that is a reason. I am wondering what you believe he does when it becomes too much for him to handle. You know him better than anyone else.

Woman: [*Long pause.*] I believe my husband is the kind of guy who would not speak about his fear. He would drink too much, or he would just suppress his feelings. [*Long pause.*] Or, he would be the type of guy who would go and have an affair.

Therapist: [*Long pause.*] Because he is a bad guy.

Woman: No—because he was scared.

The psychotherapist was careful here and later in the session not to excuse the affair of the husband, but it is also clear by the way the woman is making identification with him that she now suspects a new possibility. She suspects that the husband may have some of the feelings that she has about fear of performance, and that this might be an explanation for him acting out in the infidelity. Whether this is an actual cause or not, the psychotherapist has no way of knowing. But, the fact that the psychotherapist is able to join with the woman in her human condition about the possibility that her husband also has these same types of feelings humanizes both the woman and her husband. Her anger toward her husband after this session was greatly reduced; in fact, she talked to her husband specifically about his relationship with his father and if indeed he felt pressure to perform as the woman presumed. Although the husband could not pinpoint any feelings concerning performance as a reason he had the affair, he did confirm that he always felt a pressure to perform and was fearful that he would feel pressure a larger percentage of the time. He also confirmed that at times he drank to calm his fears. The woman did not understand the affair, but she clearly did understand fear and the drive to perform. As the psychotherapist tied these two facts together in the humanity of both the husband and the wife, you see that some of the work of forgiveness in the station of understanding was accomplished. The woman had understanding and compassion for her husband again, not out of fear that he will desert her but out of an understanding of his humanity. At the same time, she no longer saw him as an unfeeling monster or power monger; he was a scared human being like she was: sometimes scared. The fact that these human beings would make mistakes became apparent, and the woman no longer had to hate him for his personhood or hate herself.

The station of understanding can be used for a variety of intervention strategies, as seen in Chapter 5. Essentially, however, there is power when victim and victimizer make human connection. The psychotherapist who is practicing the process does not use it to excuse responsibility but rather uses the station in the work of forgiveness to remove as much of the victim's pain as possible. When the woman in this case began to have the pain about her identity subside, her anger and shame decreased. Not only was this better for her, but she was far less likely in this state to move toward self-reactivity and her own destructiveness in relationships. Thus, the station of understanding fit with the overall work of salvage: to help the individual stop his or her own victimization while dealing with the pain of the violations of love and trustworthiness in such a way that his or her own behavior becomes more loving and trustworthy instead of reactive.

THERAPEUTIC WORK IN THE STATION OF GIVING THE OPPORTUNITY FOR COMPENSATION

The woman in the case in this chapter had moved a significant distance along the road of forgiveness within 3 months. She had done much work to stabilize herself and clarify her feelings. In the work of salvage, she had made significant progress in the ability to claim her own power in the relationship and maintain expectations for the relationship. She had also made keen insight with regard to her own feelings and being open with those feelings with herself, her husband, and her children in appropriate ways. In addition, she had oscillated her own feelings of shame and anger through the work of understanding. She was convinced and the psychotherapist was supportive that the couple was ready to proceed with the work of forgiveness through restoration. This did require the couple to seek a new psychotherapist who was familiar with this kind of work of forgiveness using the restoration therapy model. Although the new psychotherapist had a release to examine the records of the work the woman had accomplished with the previous psychotherapist, the following discussion is of her first time seeing either the man or the woman in therapy.

In the station of giving the opportunity for compensation, recall that the primary focus of the work is to help the victim and victimizer start to rebuild trustworthiness a little at a time over a longer period of time.

The idea here is that the relationship has produced a violation of some kind, and to rebuild a history of trustworthiness, exposure to sequentially more risky interactions allows the victim to enter the relationship at little initial risk when trustworthiness is at its lowest. As the victimizer proves trustworthy, increasingly complex and riskier interactions are called for and tried (Hargrave, 2001).

One of the first negotiations with this station that takes place overtly with both victim and victimizer in the room is the ability of the victimizer to voluntarily take a *one-down* position (Haley, 1987). In essence, the victim becomes the more powerful person in the relationship for a temporary frame because he or she is basically deciding what he or she needs to be able to count the interactions for trustworthiness. If the victimizer is particularly hesitant to take this one-down position, it may be a clear indication that he or she is unwilling to proceed with the work of forgiveness through this station and unable to resign power for the sake of the relationship. The therapist skillfully negotiated this one-down position during the first session in this case:

Therapist: Although this will only be temporary, it is essential that you [the wife] be able to have the power to say what you need your husband to do to rebuild trustworthiness.

Husband: [*Nervous.*] I think that is fine, but I don't really understand why we can't get to the point where we just work on parts of our relationship where we had problems.

Therapist: That is a great question. Maybe you can explain it to me instead. For example, let us consider two business partners struggling to make their business work. Both partners were working hard, but things were still not being successful. One of the partners decided to steal part of the money from the business and then later thought better of it even though the money was gone. The question is where the two partners begin. Do they begin with the issue of trust and the partner who stole the money, or do they begin with their problems on how they ran the business? I don't necessarily like the answer that I have come up with, but if you can explain it to me in a different way, I really would like to listen.

Husband: I guess I was just hoping that she could just trust me again.

Therapist: Would you trust the partner who stole the money? Would you trust him if he had done it twice?

211

Husband: I can see what you mean.

Therapist: Of course, your husband is right. At some point, both of you will have to look at the problems in the relationship. But for a short period of time, between 1 and 3 months, I would suggest that both of you work on a sequential method of rebuilding trustworthiness into the relationship. After that time, if you are able to build some trustworthiness, you will have to make the decision of whether or not to trust one another, forgive, and restore your relationship to be able to work on long-standing problems.

Notice how the psychotherapist did not argue the husband down, but instead invited him to give an explanation for an alternative to rebuilding trustworthiness. During this session, the man clearly saw the logic and need to build trustworthiness. The woman was again asked the types of things that she needed from her husband to start the process of rebuilding trustworthiness. Some of the things that she requested focused on the husband's willingness to continue to be held accountable through his financial and cell phone records. She also desired for the husband to start engaging her and the children on an increasingly personal level that required him to be more open with his business and relationships during the day. This was an excellent place to begin, so the psychotherapist put in place some scenarios and homework that would require the couple to meet daily on issues of finances and the cell phone as well as a daily "download" of the day by which the husband shared his dealings during the day. It is important to note that the woman was not asked to do anything during these times but rather simply be the recipient of the husband's reporting.

After 2 weeks, the psychotherapist began to ask the wife for more complex interactions that would require a greater degree of trustworthiness. The woman stated that what she wanted next was complete honesty concerning the affair both times that it happened. Although the woman had some of the specifics about the affair, the husband had avoided much of the information because it would be painful for his wife and would be harder for her to forgive. This indeed is a salient point when one is dealing with infidelity. Many times, victims do not know the whole story of an affair, and the whole story would be retraumatizing. In light of this, the victim must be informed that what he or she finds out through the honesty and transparency of the victimizer may stick with the victim and may continue to disturb him or her to the point at which he or she cannot forgive.

The psychotherapist in the case gave this information to the woman, who still believed that she must know. "What I have to have from you is the knowledge that you can be open and honest with me. You are able to talk me into anything, but I've always known if you are leveling with me. If we are going to be married, I have to know if you can stand to be totally open with me." The husband reluctantly agreed to answer the woman's questions despite the painful consequences. The psychotherapist framed this openness not in terms of the pain that it caused in the relationship, but in terms of the potential trustworthiness that it would build between the couple in terms of honesty. The couple did this work over two sessions, and there were many painful revelations concerning sex, spending money on the affair, and times when the man was involved with this woman instead of being with the family. Although this did cause some distress and certainly did test the relationship, the woman felt satisfied after the two sessions that he was totally honest with her. As a result, she was able to count the work as representing a repair effort in rebuilding trustworthiness. The woman reported the following:

> I cannot say that the last several weeks have been easy, but at least I feel like I know this part of my husband's life, and there is not more to discover. The fact that he told me was painful, but it was more like the pain you feel when a wound is getting cleaned out. At least you know that the pain is doing some good.

The couple continued with the work of giving the opportunity for compensation for six more sessions. The work in the therapy mainly tracked homework and the issues that surfaced from increasingly deeper levels of transactions between the husband and wife in being open and honest with one another, going out socially together, and going out with one another for longer periods of time. Although there were predictable ups and downs in this process of rebuilding trust as the woman struggled with her feelings of anxiety and the man struggled with openness, the couple generally did a good job of staying on track. The psychotherapist in this station of forgiveness must be willing to tolerate this type of back-and-forth struggle in the give-and-take with a victim and victimizer. As stated, people will not be perfect in reshaping this love and trustworthiness, and mistakes will be made. The psychotherapist must always be measured in his or her responses of judging whether problems are indications that damage is about to occur in the relationship or whether it is indeed a relational mistake.

The woman and the husband had made clear progress after 8 weeks and were successful in restoring the relationship to the point at which they were ready to start addressing some of the long-standing issues in their relationship through marital therapy. As the psychotherapist started the transition toward realigning the power between the two, the woman said, "I believe that I am ready, and I think it would be good if we were able to speak the words of forgiveness toward one another." The husband was also in agreement. With the help of the psychotherapist, the couple planned one more session of overt forgiving before they started the couple therapy work outlined in Chapter 7.

THERAPEUTIC WORK IN THE STATION OF OVERT FORGIVING

Doing the work of forgiveness through overt forgiving when the victim and victimizer are present is much like preparing two people who have little experience for a difficult mountain climb. The psychotherapist must have the knowledge and experience of what to look for in the process and be able to help victim and victimizer when they start getting off the trail or doing something that will ultimately lead to their harm or damaging love and trustworthiness further. When two people engage in the process of overt forgiveness, they are doing so with the intent of making the relationship better and trying to heal from past wounds. Although this is not always feasible or possible when emotions are running high, the session at the minimum should not further endanger love and trustworthiness. For this reason, the psychotherapist must be well prepared for the session by knowing the markers that he or she needs to achieve, prepare both victim and victimizer for the process that will be expected, and finally be willing to stop the session and go back to the other stations of forgiveness if the overt forgiving session starts to go badly (Hargrave, 1994a).

The psychotherapist in the case discussed in this chapter used the week before the session to make sure that the woman and her husband knew what she was going to give them the opportunity to do through the process of agreement, acknowledgment, and apology outlined in Chapter 5. In addition, the psychotherapist asked both the woman and her husband to bring something to the session that would be representative of this hurt that had been caused by the affair.

In the first part of the session, the psychotherapist asked both the woman and her husband about their understandings of the crux of the violation that was represented in the affair. In this particular case, since the couple had worked with each other through the station of giving the opportunity for compensation, they reached agreement fairly easily that the element of the violation was the breaking of fidelity on the husband's part and continued damage to trustworthiness by the continued lack of openness with regard to the affair. Agreement, however, for many victims and victimizers is difficult, especially when the overt forgiveness session is the first time that the victim and victimizer might get together after years. The psychotherapist in these instances must be patient to hear each side and version of the history of violations, particularly remembering the skill and value of multidirected partiality (Hargrave, 1994a). In a typical 90-minute session, which is standard for these overt forgiving sessions, agreement will often take up to 80 minutes of the session (Hargrave, 2001). The psychotherapist must be willing to keep the victim and victimizer on track and be willing to rework difficult places in emotional intensity. It is also wise for the psychotherapist to remember that the agreement should shy away from numerous specifics concerning the violation. Broad consensus and agreement, as mentioned, are the kind of agreement that is possible in these types of sessions.

In the case here, the psychotherapist was able to move the couple to the point of acknowledgment. Notice in the following dialogue how the psychotherapist helped the man take specific responsibility when acknowledging the affair and the difference it made in the woman's reactions:

Therapist: If there is agreement then on the crux of the violation—the damage of the infidelity itself and the lack of openness that was maintained—who was responsible for this damage?

Husband: I think in many ways, we both were. We let our marriage get into a difficult place that was not good for either of us. [*Wife heaves a sigh.*]

Therapist: There is not a specific set of words that you need to say, but the point that you are making is important. If you believe that you both are responsible for the marriage not being as good as it should have been, then you should clarify. If you believe that the both of you are therefore responsible for the affair, then you should clarify.

Husband: [*Very surprised.*] That is not what I am trying to say at all! I guess I was getting ahead of myself. [*Takes his wife's hand.*] I am trying to say that I am excited now to work with you in confronting the issues in our marriage. I was in no way trying to say that you were responsible for my affair. You had the same marriage that I had, and you did not have an affair on me. We had difficulty, but when I stole the money from the business, you kept working. [*Woman sighs and looks much more hopeful.*]

Therapist: I appreciate your clarification. If you could just clarify and go back to my question so there is no question—who was responsible for the damage of the infidelity and the lack of openness?

Husband: [*Still holding his wife's hand.*] I was the one who stole from our marriage by having the affair and hiding it from you. You have every right to leave me, and I have no call on you to still be my wife, but I am asking you again to be my wife.

The final step in the station of overt forgiveness is apology. Remember that apology may come out as an apology like "I am sorry" or "I am asking for your forgiveness." In essence, however, apology is a promise to live differently in the future (Hargrave, 1994a). Many times, because these are such crucial therapeutic moments, many psychotherapists chose to combine this apology with a ritual to produce a heightened meaning around the emotional exchange. Many times, rituals are chosen by the victim and victimizer, and many times they are suggested by the psychotherapist. These rituals range from burying objects that represent the hurt, burning old issues in the session, or even asking forgiveness on one's knees (Hargrave, 2001). No matter the ritual used in the case, the intent is to help both victim and victimizer remember the event of overt forgiveness as an important new beginning in the legacy of love and trustworthiness in the relationship.

Therapist: So, the reason you came to this moment today.

Husband: [*Holding his wife's hand.*] I do not deserve a second chance, but I would ask that you forgive me for the affair and covering it up. I am not asking you to never remember, but to never forget. I would like to ask you for the chance to be a better husband.

Woman: [*Takes his other hand.*] I do forgive this. I don't know that I can do it perfectly, but I am committed to you to do my best to give us a new start. [*Couple embraces.*]

Therapist: [*Long pause.*] If you can, at this moment take out the thing that you brought that represents this hurt in the affair. [*The woman brings out a handkerchief, and the man brings out a cell phone.*] What do these things represent?

Woman: The handkerchief represents all the times that I was crying alone in fear instead of talking to my husband about my fears and suspicions. I don't want to cry alone or be afraid alone again.

Husband: This old cell phone is the one I was using when I started the affair. To me it represents my old ways of separating and hiding from my wife, and I want to be through with that forever.

Therapist: Great. [*Pause.*] What I would like you to do with these things is to place those things in this metal box. I would like you to bury the box out in your backyard together. At any point that either of you starts having the feelings that you are crying or are fearful alone or that you are hiding and being secret, I want you to go dig up the box and put it in your bed. I then want you to talk about the issue and the feelings until you can remind yourselves of the work and progress that you made here and get your forgiveness work back on track.

The couple finished the session with the psychotherapist clarifying the ritual and did indeed bury the box in the backyard after the session. The husband reported that, "Burying the box was like putting the past where it belonged, but it was helpful to know that the past can come back to haunt us unless we do the things that we have learned here." The couple took 1 week off from therapy and then began the work of restoration and rebuilding their relationship by addressing issues that had existed in the marriage apart from the affair. Much of this work entailed learning the pain and peace cycles and learning how to emotionally regulate away from self-reactivity. The couple continued in therapy another eight sessions and terminated therapy successful in their relationship and satisfied with the work restoration had played in re-forming their identities and relational safety through love and trustworthiness.

217

REFERENCES

Aggleton, J. P. (Ed.). (1992). *The amygdala: Neurobiological aspects of emotion, memory, and mental dysfunction.* New York: Wiley.

Ainsworth, M. D. S., & Bowlby, J. (1991). An ethological approach to personality development. *American Psychologist, 46,* 331–341.

Arden, J. B., & Linford, L. (2009). *Brain-based therapy with adults: Evidence-based treatments for everyday practice.* Hoboken, NJ: Wiley.

Atkinson, B. J. (2005). *Emotional intelligence in couples therapy: Advances from neurobiology and the science of intimate relationships.* New York: Norton.

Atkinson, B. J., Atkinson, L., Kutz, P., Lata, J., Lata, K. W., Szekely, J., et al. (2005). Rewiring neural states in couples therapy: Advances from affective neuroscience. *Journal of Systemic Therapies, 24,* 3–16.

Balswick, J. O., King, P., & Reimer, K. (2005). *The reciprocating self: Human development in theological perspective.* Downers Grove, IL: InterVarsity Press.

Bandura, A. (1989). Human agency in social cognitive theory. *American Psychologist, 44,* 1175–1184.

Bandura, A. (1997). *Self-efficacy: The exercise of control.* New York: Freeman.

Baucom, D. H., Epstein, N. B., LaTaillade, J. J., & Kirby, J. S. (2008). Cognitive-behavioral couple therapy. In A. S. Gurman (Ed.), *Clinical handbook of couple therapy* (4th ed., pp. 31–72). New York: Guilford.

Beck, A. T., & Weishaar, M. (2008). Cognitive therapy. In R. J. Corsini & D. Wedding (Eds.), *Current psychotherapies* (8th ed., pp. 263–294). Belmont, CA: Thomson Brooks/Cole.

Boszormenyi-Nagy, I., Grunebaum, J., & Ulrich, D. (1991). Contextual therapy. In A. S. Gurman & D. P. Kniskern (Eds.), *Handbook of family therapy* (Vol. 2, pp. 200–238). New York: Brunner/Mazel.

Boszormenyi-Nagy, I., & Krasner, B. (1986). *Between give and take: A clinical guide to contextual therapy.* New York: Brunner/Mazel.

Boszormenyi-Nagy, I., & Spark, G. (1984). *Invisible loyalties.* New York: Brunner/Mazel.

Boszormenyi-Nagy, I., & Ulrich, D. N. (1981). Contextual family therapy. In A. S. Gurman & D. P. Kniskern (Eds.), *Handbook of family therapy* (pp. 159–186). New York: Brunner/Mazel.

Bowen, M. (1978). *Family therapy in clinical practice.* New York: Aronson.

Bowlby, J. (1988). *A secure base.* New York: Basic Books.

Bradbury, T. N., & Karney, B. R. (2010). *Intimate relationships.* New York: Norton.

Broderick, P. C., & Blewitt, P. (2006). *The life span: Human development for helping professionals* (2nd ed.). Columbus, OH: Pearson Prentice Hall.

Buber, M. (1958). *I and thou.* New York: Charles Scribner and Sons.

Chomsky, N. (1972). *Language and mind*. New York: Harcourt Brace Jovanovich.

Corey, G. (2008). *Theory and practice of group counseling* (7th ed.). Belmont, CA: Brooks/Cole.

Crowell, J. A., Treboux, D., & Waters, E. (2002). Stability of attachment representations: The transition to marriage. *Developmental Psychology, 38,* 467–479.

Davies, C. T., & Cummings, E. M. (1998). Exploring children's emotional security as a mediator of the link between marital relations and child adjustment. *Child Development, 69,* 124–139.

DeMaria, R., & Hannah, M. T. (2003). *Building intimate relationships: Bridging treatment, education, and enrichment through the PAIRS program*. New York: Routledge.

de Shazer, S. (1985). *Keys to solutions in brief therapy*. New York: Norton.

de Shazer, S. (1988). *Clues: Investigating solutions in brief therapy*. New York: Norton.

Dimidjian, S., Martell, C. R., & Christensen, A. (2008). Integrative behavioral couple therapy. In A. S. Gurman (Ed.), *Clinical handbook of couple therapy* (4th ed., pp. 73–103). New York: Guilford.

Doherty, W. J. (1996). *Soul searching: Why psychotherapy must promote moral responsibility*. New York: Basic Books.

Doherty, W. J. (2000). How therapists threaten marriages. *The Responsive Community, 7, 31–42.*

Ellis, A. (2008). Rational-emotive behavior therapy. In R. J. Corsini & D. Wedding (Eds.), *Current psychotherapies* (8th ed., pp. 187–222). Belmont, CA: Thomson Brooks/Cole.

Erikson, E. H. (1963). *Childhood and society* (2nd ed.). New York: Norton.

Fairbairn, W. D. (1952). *An object-relations theory of the personality*. New York: Basic Books.

Freud, S. (1905). *Fragment of an analysis of a case of hysteria. Collected papers*. New York: Basic Books.

Friedman, E. H. (2007). *A failure of nerve: Leadership in the age of quick fix*. New York: Seabury Books.

Goldenthal, P. (1996). *Doing contextual therapy: An integrated model for working with individuals, couples, and families*. New York: Norton.

Guerin, P. J., Fay, L. F., Borden, S. L., & Kautto, J. G. (1987). *The evaluation and treatment of marital conflict*. New York: Basic Books.

Gurman, A. S., & Kniskern, D. P. (1981). Editor's note. In A. S. Gurman & D. P. Kniskern (Eds.), *Handbook of family therapy* (p. 185). New York: Brunner/Mazel.

Haley, J. (1984). *Ordeal therapy*. San Francisco: Jossey-Bass.

Haley, J. (1987). *Problem solving therapy* (2nd ed.). San Francisco: Jossey-Bass.

Hargrave, T. D. (1994a). *Families and forgiveness: Healing wounds in the intergenerational family*. New York: Brunner/Mazel.

Hargrave, T. D. (1994b). Therapeutic utilization of video life review. *Journal of Family Therapy, 16, 3,* 259–267.

Hargrave, T. D. (2000). *The essential humility of marriage: Honoring the third identity in couple therapy*. Phoenix, AZ: Zeig, Tucker & Theisen.

220

Hargrave, T. D. (2001). *Forgiving the devil: Coming to terms with damaged relationships.* Phoenix, AZ: Zeig, Tucker and Theisen.

Hargrave, T. D. (2005). *Loving your parents when they can no longer love you.* Grand Rapids, MI: Zondervan.

Hargrave, T. D. (2010). Restoration therapy: A couple therapy case study. *Journal of Psychology and Christianity, 29,* 3, 272–277.

Hargrave, T. D. (in press). Saving oneself: Forgiving the poisonous parents as an act of kindness to oneself and future generations. In S. Dunham, S. Dermer, & J. Carlson (Eds.), *Poisonous parenting: Toxic relationships between parents and their adult children.* New York: Routledge.

Hargrave, T. D., & Anderson, W. T. (1992). *Finishing well: Aging and reparation in the intergenerational family.* New York: Brunner/Mazel.

Hargrave, T. D., Froeschle, J., & Castillo, Y. (2009). Forgiveness and spirituality: Elements of healing in relationships. In F. Walsh (Ed.), *Spiritual resources in family therapy* (2nd ed., pp. 301–322). New York: Guilford.

Hargrave, T. D., & Metcalf, L. (2000). Solution focused family of origin therapy. In L. VandeCreek & T. L. Jackson (Eds.), *Innovations in clinical practice: A source book* (Vol. 18, pp. 47–56). Sarasota, FL: Professional Resource Press.

Hargrave, T. D., & Pfitzer, F. (2003). *The new contextual therapy: Guiding the power of give and take.* New York: Brunner/Routledge.

Hargrave, T. D., & Sells, J. N. (1997). The development of a forgiveness scale. *Journal of Marital and Family Therapy, 23,* 1, 41–62.

Hargrave, T., & Stoever, S. (2010). *Five days to a new marriage.* Amarillo, TX: Hideaway Foundation.

Hockenbury, D. H., & Hockenbury, S. E. (2000). *Psychology* (2nd ed.). New York: Worth.

Hoffman, L. (2002). *Family therapy: An intimate history.* New York: Norton.

Jacobson, N. S., & Christensen, A. (1998). *Acceptance and change in couple therapy: A therapist's guide to transforming relationships.* New York: Norton.

Johnson, S. M. (2004). *The practice of emotionally focused marital therapy: Creating connection* (2nd ed.). New York: Brunner/Routledge.

Johnson, S. M. (2008). *Hold me tight: Seven conversations for a lifetime of love.* New York: Little, Brown.

Johnson, S. M., Makinen, M., & Millikin, J. (2001). Attachment injuries in couple relationships: A new perspective on impasses in couple therapy. *Journal of Marital and Family Therapy, 27,* 145–155.

Karney, B. R., & Bradbury, T. N. (1995). The longitudinal course of marital quality and stability: A review of theory, method, and research. *Psychological Bulletin, 118,* 3–34. doi: 10.1037/0033–2909.118.1.3.

Keeney, B. P., & Ross, J. M. (1985). *Mind in therapy: Constructing systemic family therapies.* New York: Basic Books.

Kernberg, O. F. (1966). Structural derivatives of object relationships. *International Journal of Psychoanalysis, 47,* 236–253.

221

Kieffer, C. (1977). New depths in intimacy. In R. W. Libby & R. N. Whitehurst (Eds.), *Marriage and alternatives: Exploring intimate relationships* (pp. 267–293). Glenview, IL: Scott, Foresman.

Kilmann, R., & Thomas, K. (1975). Interpersonal conflict: Handling behavior as reflections of Jungian personality dimensions. *Psychological Reports, 37,* 971–980.

Kosslyn, S. M. (2005). Reflective thinking and mental imagery: A perspective on the development of posttraumatic stress disorder. *Development and Psychopathology, 17,* 851–863.

Krumboltz, J. D., & Thoresen, C. E. (Eds.). (1969). *Behavioral counseling: Cases and techniques.* New York: Holt, Rhinehart, and Winston.

Lazarus, A. A. (2008). Multimodal therapy. In R. J. Corsini & D. Wedding (Eds.), *Current psychotherapies* (8th ed., pp. 368–401). Belmont, CA: Thomson Brooks/Cole.

LeDoux, J. E. (1996). *The emotional brain: The mysterious underpinnings of emotional life.* New York: Touchstone.

LeDoux, J. E. (2002). *Synaptic self. How our brains become who we are.* New York: Viking.

Lieberman, A. F., Weston, D. R., & Pawl, J. H. (1991). Preventive intervention and outcome with anxiously attached dyads. *Child Development, 62,* 199–209.

Luborsky, E. B., O'Reilly-Landry, M., & Arlow, J. A. (2008). Psychoanalysis. In R. J. Corsinni & D. Wedding (Eds.), *Current psychotherapies* (8th ed., pp. 15–62). Belmont, CA: Thomson Brooks/Cole.

Madanes, C. (1981). *Strategic family therapy.* San Francisco: Jossey-Bass.

Madanes, C. (1984). *Behind the one way mirror.* San Francisco: Jossey-Bass.

May, R., & Yalom, I. (2000). Existential psychotherapy. In R. J. Corsini & D. Wedding (Eds.), *Current psychotherapies* (6th ed., pp. 273–302). Itasca, IL: Peacock.

Meidonis, G. G., & Bry, B. H. (1995). Effects of therapist exceptions questions on blaming and positive statements in families with adolescent behavior problems. *Journal of Family Psychology, 9,* 451–457.

Minuchin, S. (1974). *Families and family therapy.* Cambridge, MA: Harvard University Press.

Minuchin, S., & Fishman, H. C. (1981). *Family therapy techniques.* Cambridge, MA: Harvard University Press.

O'Hanlon, W. H., & Weiner-Davis, M. (1989). *In search of solutions: A new direction in psychotherapy.* New York: Norton.

Olds, J. (1958). Self-stimulation of the brain. *Science, 127,* 315–324.

Olson, D. H., & DeFrain, J. (1997). *Marriage and the family: Diversity and strengths* (2nd ed.). Mountain View, CA: Mayfield.

Pelaez-Nogueras, M., Gerwirtz, J. L., Field, T., Cigales, M., Malthurs, J., Clasky, S., et al. (1996). Infants' preference for touch stimulations in face-to-face interactions. *Journal of Applied Developmental Psychology, 67,* 1780–1792.

Perls, F. S. (1969). *Gestalt therapy verbation.* Lafayette, CA: Real People Press.

Pipp, S., Easterbrooks, M. A., & Harmon, R. J. (1992). The relation between attachment and knowledge of self and mother in one- to three-year-old infants. *Child Development, 63,* 738–750.

Pipp, S., & Harmon, R. J. (1987). Attachment as regulation: A commentary. *Child Development, 58,* 648–652.

Rogers, C. (1951). *Client-centered therapy.* Boston: Houghton Mifflin.

Rogers, C. (1961). *On becoming a person.* Boston: Houghton Mifflin.

Satir, V., Banmen, J., Gerber, J., & Gomori, M. (1991). *The Satir model: Family therapy and beyond.* Palo Alto, CA: Science and Behavior Books.

Saxton, L. (1993). *The individual, marriage, and the family* (8th ed.). Belmont, CA: Wadsworth.

Scharff, D., & Scharff, J. (1987). *Object relations family therapy.* New York: Aronson.

Siegel, D. J. (2007). *The mindful brain: Reflection and attunement in the cultivation of well-being.* New York: Norton.

Smalley, G., & Paul, R. S. (2006). *The DNA of relationships for couples.* Carol Stream, IL: Tyndale House.

Stanley, S. M., Whitton, S. W., Low, S. M., Clements, M. L., & Markman, H. J. (2006). Sacrifice as a predictor of marital outcomes. *Family Process, 45,* 289–303.

Stierlin, H. (1977). *Psychoanalysis and family therapy.* New York: Aronson.

Tillich, P. (1954). *Love, power and justice.* London: Oxford University Press.

Valenzuela, M. (1990). Attachment in chronically underweight young children. *Child Development, 61,* 1984–1996.

Van Heusden, A., & Van Den Eerenbeemt, E. (1987). *Balance in motion.* New York: Brunner/Mazel.

van Lange, P. A. M., Rusbult, C. E., Drigotas, S. M., Arriaga, X. B., Witcher, B. S., & Cox, C. L. (1997). Willingness to sacrifice in close relationships. *Journal of Personality and Social Psychology, 72,* 1373–1395.

Watzlawick, P., Bavelas, J. B., & Jackson, D. D. (1967). *Pragmatics of human communication: A study of interactional patterns, pathologies, and paradoxes.* New York: Norton.

White, M. (1997). *Narrative of therapist's lives.* Adelaide, Australia: Dulwich Centre.

White, M., & Epston, D. (1990). *Narrative means to therapeutic ends.* New York: Norton.

223

INDEX